USING PRIMING METHODS IN SECOND LANGUAGE RESEARCH

Kim McDonough, Northern Arizona University
Pavel Trofimovich, Concordia University, Montréal

Routledge
Taylor & Francis Group

NEW YORK AND LONDON

First published 2009
by Routledge
270 Madison Ave, New York, NY 10016

Simultaneously published in the UK
by Routledge
2 Park Square, Milton Park, Abingdon, Oxon OX14 4RN

Routledge is an imprint of the Taylor & Francis Group, an informa business

© 2009 Taylor & Francis

Typeset in Goudy by
RefineCatch Limited, Bungay, Suffolk
Printed and bound in the United States of America on acid-free paper by
Sheridan Books, Inc.

Library of Congress Cataloging-in-Publication Data
McDonough, Kim.
Using priming methods in second language research / Kim
McDonough, Pavel Trofimovich.
p. cm.
Includes bibliographical references.
1. Second language acquisition–Methodology.
2. Priming (Psychology) I. Trofimovich, Pavel. II. Title.
P118.2.M337 2008
401′.93–dc22
2008017143

ISBN10: 0-415-99983-9 (hbk)
ISBN10: 0-8058-6255-2 (pbk)
ISBN10: 0-203-88094-3 (ebk)

ISBN13: 978-0-415-99983-0 (hbk)
ISBN13: 978-0-8058-6255-3 (pbk)
ISBN13: 978-0-203-88094-4 (ebk)

CONTENTS

3   Semantic Priming   58

CONTENTS

CONTENTS

BOXES

FIGURES

TABLES

PREFACE

Since it was observed over 100 years ago that people can identify a word more quickly if they have recently heard a word with a related meaning (Cattell, 1888, cited in Harley, 2001), priming methods have become one of the predominant experimental paradigms used in psycholinguistic research. The term *priming* refers to the phenomenon in which prior exposure to specific language forms or meanings either facilitates or interferes with a speaker's subsequent language processing. Priming methods originated in first language (L1) perception and production research, and began to be adopted in bilingual and second language (L2) studies beginning in the early 1980s. With rising interest in psycholinguistic approaches to L2 acquisition, there has been an increase in the number of L2 studies that have adopted priming methods. However, the L1 priming studies may be somewhat inaccessible for L2 researchers who are unfamiliar with the theories, terminology, and experimental procedures commonly reported in psycholinguistic research.

Our purpose in writing this text, therefore, was to help bridge the gap between psycholinguistic studies that use experimental priming methods and L2 processing and acquisition research. The text provides a guide to the use, design, and implementation of priming methods, and an overview of how to analyze and report priming research. Through reference to the numerous L1 studies that have used priming methods, this text summarizes key principles about auditory, semantic, and syntactic priming and outlines issues for L2 researchers to consider when designing priming studies. This text also features L2 studies that have adopted these priming methods, illustrating how to apply experimental techniques from psychology to L2 processing and acquisition research.

The text was designed for use by researchers who would like a comprehensive introduction to priming methods as well as by instructors who teach courses in research methods, psycholinguistics, second language acquisition or related subjects. Although priming methods are frequently used in neuropsychological research to explore the neurobiological processes associated with language tasks, in this text we do not specifically target neuropsychology researchers as part of our intended audience. We have, however, included in chapter 1 an overview of the use of priming research in neuropsychological studies that investigate language learning and use. While other experimental procedures used in psycholinguistic research, such as sound discrimination and identification tasks, semantic categorization, eye-tracking, and sentence-matching, can also play an important role in L2 research, these techniques are beyond the scope of the current text.

Our primary goal is to introduce three types of priming research: auditory, semantic and syntactic priming, which are introduced in chapters 2, 3, and 4, respectively. Each of these chapters gives an overview of the topics that have been investigated through priming and provides details about the specific tasks used for each type of priming research. Chapter 5 provides an explanation about analyzing priming data and reporting priming research in applied linguistics and psycholinguistics journals. Each chapter concludes with follow-up questions and activities that provide additional reinforcement of the chapter content. Chapter 5 also includes complete data sets that can be used to practice the statistical tests commonly used with priming data. Instructors may choose to cover the auditory, semantic, and syntactic priming chapters before working more closely with the data analysis and interpretation presented in chapter 5. Alternatively, they may integrate the analysis and statistical information from chapter 5 into the earlier chapters. Each chapter was designed as a stand-alone introduction to the topic so instructors can reorder the chapters to suit their syllabi.

There are many people whose assistance we would like to acknowledge. We would like to thank the series editors, Susan Gass and Alison Mackey, for their valuable suggestions and support throughout the process of writing the proposal, drafting and revising the manuscript. We also appreciate the comments of Bill Grabe, Norman Segalowitz, and Randall Halter, and those of the reviewers who read the proposal and the manuscript and offered helpful suggestions that we were able to incorporate into the final version. Hyojin Song provided invaluable help with locating and cataloguing priming studies, and Randall Halter graciously read the entire manuscript suggesting many helpful improvements. We are grateful to everyone at Taylor & Francis for their support throughout all phases of the project. We would like to thank the publishers of SPSS for granting us permission to use screen shots of their software. We especially appreciate the support of our spouses, Ron Crawford and Sarita Kennedy, for their assistance with the manuscript and for putting up with us while we were writing this book.

Kim McDonough   *Pavel Trofimovich*

1

INTRODUCTION TO PRIMING METHODS

In this chapter, we explain what priming is and introduce the three types of priming covered in this textbook: auditory, semantic, and syntactic priming. We describe some of the topics that have been explored using priming methods and provide a sampling of experimental studies that used priming tasks to investigate L2 processing and acquisition.

What is Priming?

In the context of language use, priming refers to the phenomenon in which prior exposure to language somehow influences subsequent language processing, which may occur in the form of recognition or production. In most scenarios, the initial language form or aspects of its meaning,

1

referred to as the *prime*, facilitate the recognition or production of a subsequent form or aspects of its meaning, which is referred to as the *response* or *target*. Priming is believed to be an implicit process that for the most part occurs with little awareness on the part of individual language users. Its implicit nature makes priming one manifestation of a larger system of human memory—implicit memory. Briefly, implicit memory involves memory for cognitive operations or procedures that are learned through repeated use, and includes memory for skills and habits, and priming. A speaker's sensitivity to previous encounters with language forms and meanings suggests that language use is sensitive to the occurrence of language forms and meanings in the environment. In other words, the exact forms and meanings that speakers use can be affected by the language that occurred in discourse they recently engaged in.

Although the term priming describes all situations in which prior language exposure influences subsequent language processing, different types of priming have been defined in literature. Of the many different kinds of priming, we will focus in this book on three: auditory, semantic, and syntactic (see box 1.1).

Box 1.1 Priming

In technical terms, *priming* is defined as "facilitative effects of an encounter with a stimulus on subsequent processing of the same or a related stimulus" (Tulving, Schacter, & Stark, 1982, p. 336).

Two of the priming phenomena discussed in this book—auditory and syntactic priming—are types of repetition priming. In the context of language use, *repetition priming* refers to facilitation in the processing of language *forms* (e.g. phonological or syntactic) due to language users' previous repeated experiences with these forms (Ellis & Ellis, 1998; Kirsner, 1998). As repetition priming phenomena, auditory and syntactic priming thus appear to provide an index of language users' implicit sensitivity to repeated language forms: phonological and syntactic.

The third priming phenomenon discussed in this book—semantic priming—shares a number of properties with repetition priming. For example, similar to auditory and syntactic priming, semantic priming is also characterized as a largely automatic and implicit process. However, unlike auditory and syntactic priming, which involve facilitation due to repeated exposure to language forms, semantic priming refers to facilitation due to repeated exposure to similar or related *meanings*. As such, semantic priming appears to be an implicit index of semantic relatedness (or, in researchers' parlance, of the extent of "semantic activation") among words in memory.

First, auditory priming refers to the tendency for people to process a spoken word or word combination more quickly and more accurately when they have had previous exposure to that word or word combination in speech. Processing is generally measured as a time or accuracy benefit for repeated spoken words and word combinations as compared to non-repeated spoken words and word combinations. For example, if people listen to a list of words such as *glasses, chair, picture* spoken one at a time and then are asked to listen and repeat words like *mug, printer, chair*, they will repeat the word that appeared on the initial list (*chair*) more quickly and accurately than the words that did not appear on the initial list (*mug* and *printer*). Several factors can influence the processing of previously heard words, including the voice and gender of the person who read the initial word list. Auditory priming, which is one type of repetition priming, and its uses in L2 speech perception and production research are discussed in chapter 2.

Second, semantic priming refers to the tendency for people to process a word more quickly and more accurately when they have been previously exposed to a word that is related in meaning. For example, language users will correctly identify the string *cat* (the target) as a word more quickly if they recently read the word *dog* (the prime) as opposed to an unrelated word, such as *shoe*. By activating the meaning of *dog* in comprehension or production, speakers activate the meaning of *cat* due to the shared meaning between the two. Both words denote animals, and both refer to household pets. This activation is largely automatic (not subject to conscious control), proceeding without speakers' attention or awareness. As such, semantic priming is said to reflect some fundamental properties of the way speakers organize their knowledge of the lexicon and the way they retrieve and use this knowledge. While semantic priming shares many features with repetition priming, it does not involve repeated exposure to the same forms. Semantic priming is discussed in more detail in chapter 3.

Finally, syntactic priming refers to the tendency for a speaker to produce a syntactic structure that appeared in the recent discourse, as opposed to an equally acceptable alternative. Similar to auditory priming, syntactic priming is a type of repetition priming. For example, if a speaker uses a prepositional dative, such as *my husband gave our lawnmower to the neighbor*, later in the conversation her interlocutor is likely to produce another prepositional dative (*my daughter sent a birthday card to her grandmother*) rather than a double-object dative (*my daughter sent her grandmother a birthday card*). This sensitivity to previously experienced sentence structures is not due to similarities in lexical items, surface-level morphology, or metrical patterns, but is attributed to the syntactic structure itself. Syntactic priming and its application to L2 processing and acquisition research are discussed in chapter 4.

In sum, these three types of priming essentially investigate how prior exposure to language impacts subsequent language processing. Experimental priming methods have been used in many areas of psycholinguistics to gain insight into the processes that govern the comprehension and production of language. Prior to outlining potential uses of priming methods in L2 processing and acquisition, we first consider the ecological validity of priming research in the following section.

Is Priming Research Ecologically Valid?

Priming research is typically carried out in order to establish generalizations about language representations and processes that provide insight into the organization of mental processes. However, since it employs tightly-controlled experimental methods, questions have been raised about its ecological validity. The debate concerns the extent to which research that is carried out under conditions that do not reflect real-world language use can be used to draw conclusions about language processing. Although priming researchers rarely address this issue explicitly, Libben and Jarema (2002) outlined three primary factors that may negatively impact the ecological validity of priming research: language, population, and tasks.

In terms of language, researchers are typically interested in identifying general principles of language organization and processing. However, individual languages make demands on language processing as a result of their specific phonological, morphological, orthographic, syntactic, and semantic features. Consequently, it can be difficult to generalize the findings based on the processing of one specific language to other languages or to language in general. This is especially problematic if one particular language, such as English, is widely targeted in priming studies while other languages are rarely (or never) examined.

The second factor that can negatively impact the ecological validity of priming research is the population that the research sample represents. The most commonly-targeted sample in priming research is unimpaired adult native speakers. In order to represent the actual population of language users and allow generalizations to be made to human language use, the samples targeted in priming research should represent a wider variety of language users, such as developing and stable bilinguals, individuals with language impairments (such as aphasia and dysphasia), developing L1 speakers, and L1 speakers from various age groups.

Finally, the third factor that can impact the ecological validity of priming research is the experimental task. For example, priming research to investigate the mental lexicon commonly uses lexical decision tasks that may involve visual rather than aural presentation of stimuli. Furthermore, the stimuli are often presented as individual words or phrases, which is in contrast to real-world language processing where information occurs in linguistically and situationally embedded contexts.

Although Libben and Jarema (2002, 2004) were discussing priming research about the mental lexicon specifically, the factors they outlined are also applicable to priming research about phonological and syntactic forms. Their suggestions for positively impacting the ecological validity of priming research can be summarized as follows:

- Include a wide-variety of target languages and forms.
- Select samples that represent various categories of language users.
- Design experimental tasks that resemble naturally-occurring language use and include multiple experimental techniques and/or new paradigms in priming research such as eye-tracking and neuroimaging.

While they did not explicitly address the issue of ecological validity, Pickering and Garrod (2004) pointed out that many psycholinguistic studies, including priming research, have targeted individual speakers. However, since a great deal of language use occurs in the form of dialogue, the ecological validity of these studies can be enhanced by investigating language processing during conversation.

Besides using a variety of experimental tasks, priming researchers can also positively impact the ecological validity of their studies by adopting a variety of measures. The most commonly used measure in priming research is reaction time (or response latency). This measure is used in psycholinguistic research to reveal insights into how speakers use different types of information during on-line processing of language (e.g. in the form of sentences or individual words), where difficulties in processing occur, and how ambiguities are resolved. Reaction times have also been used to make inferences about the nature of speakers' linguistic knowledge and their access to that knowledge. In priming studies, reaction times are used to assess whether prior exposure to phonological or syntactic forms results in faster subsequent processing, when compared to the processing of forms that were not present in the previous discourse. Similarly, in semantic priming studies, reaction times are used to determine whether prior exposure to a semantically-related word facilitates subsequent processing.

Although the use of reaction times has been widely-accepted in adult L1 speech perception and production research, their use in child L1 and L2 research has been debated. In particular, questions have been raised about whether reaction times can be used as indirect measures of linguistic knowledge for speakers who have not fully acquired the target language (e.g. Crain & Thornton, 1998). L2 studies that have employed multiple measures, such as acceptability judgments to assess speakers' linguistic knowledge, plus reaction times to assess their ability to process linguistic information, have shown a dissociation between knowledge and processing. For example, Murphy (1997) found no significant differences in the reaction times between L1 and L2 speakers, but did find significant differences in their ability to judge grammatical and ungrammatical sentences involving subjacency.

Priming studies have also demonstrated dissociation between reaction times and other measures for bilingual speech production. For example, Kotz (2001) has shown that bilingual speakers' reaction times for priming tasks in the L1 and the L2 are not significantly different, but their event-related brain potentials (ERPs), time-locked measures of electrical activity in the brain, are different for the L1 and the L2. Similarly, studies involving both high and low proficiency L2 speakers have shown that reaction times and ERPs vary differently as a function of language proficiency (e.g. Elston-Güttler & Friederici, 2005; Kotz & Elston-Güttler, 2004).

In sum, researchers can enhance the ecological validity of priming research by including multiple measures to identify similarities and differences in L1 and L2 processing or to clarify proficiency differences in L2 processing that may not be apparent when reaction times are used as the only measure.

What Topics can be Explored Using Priming Methods?

Priming methods can contribute to numerous topics of interest to L2 researchers, including issues related to L2 processing, representation, and acquisition. L2 processing research examines how linguistic information is processed during reading and listening tasks, referred to as *parsing*, and how linguistic information is accessed and assembled during speech production. Researchers interested in the representation of linguistic knowledge often investigate how L1 and L2 linguistic information is stored in mental models, particularly whether the linguistic information of the two languages is stored separately or in a shared fashion. Finally, L2 acquisition researchers typically explore the nature of learners' linguistic knowledge and its development over time.

Although L2 processing, representation and acquisition are often investigated in isolation, each domain contributes to a global understanding of L2 use. For example, once acquired, linguistic information must be integrated into a mental model that includes both L1 and L2 knowledge. L2 learners also must acquire appropriate processing or parsing procedures in order to comprehend and produce L2 input in real time, and this requires access to information that has been acquired and represented in their mental models. While L2 acquisition theories differ in terms of what they regard as linguistic knowledge (such as form–function mappings versus innate principles) and what facilitates the acquisition of that knowledge, they share the premise that linguistic knowledge must be represented and accessed during parsing and production.

In the sections that follow, we outline several topics of interest to L2 researchers that can be investigated using priming methods. Far from exhaustive, this list includes issues related to L2 processing, representation, and acquisition that provide a starting point for developing a wider range of topics that could be explored by using priming methods. For a more general discussion about the use of psycholinguistic techniques in L2 research, see overview articles by Juffs (2001) and Marinis (2003).

Models of Speech Production

There is general consensus among speech production researchers that language production consists of several stages:

1   planning message content (conceptualization);
2   encoding grammatical, lexical and phonological forms (formulation);
3   articulating speech sounds (articulation);
4   checking the appropriateness of the language produced (self-monitoring).

At least two types of models have been put forth to account for these procedures: modular models (e.g. Levelt, Roelofs, & Meyer, 1999) and spreading activation models (e.g. Dell, 1986). As summarized by Kormos (2006), there are two major differences between these two model types. First, whereas modular models state that activation of information can spread across the stages of language production in one direction only, spreading activation models allow for feedback between these stages in any direction. Second, modular models are lexically driven, in that the syntactic information is stored with individual lexical items (words), and the selection of individual words activates their associated syntactic structures. In contrast, spreading activation models assume that speakers begin with sentence constructions whose slots are then filled with individual lexical items.

Priming methods can be used to test both modular and spreading activation models of speech production. For example, modular models predict that activation at the conceptualization stage spreads forward to the formulation stage, from where it then proceeds to activate the relevant word forms and phonemes at the articulation stage. In contrast, spreading activation models allow for the activation at the phoneme level to feed "backwards" to influence the activation at the higher (syntactic and semantic) stages of language production. While both accounts predict that activation spreads in the forward direction (e.g. from the syntactic structure to the relevant phonological information), only the spreading activation account predicts that activation of phonological information could also spread backwards to affect syntactic structure. Syntactic priming tasks have in fact been used to test this prediction of spreading activation models but have not yet yielded evidence in support of it (Cleland & Pickering, 2003).

In terms of L2 speech production, priming research can shed light on whether syntactic and phonological information is stored separately for the L1 and L2 or whether the linguistic information relevant to both languages is shared. Syntactic priming studies have shown that bilingual speakers who are primed in one language produce the same structure in the second language, which supports the shared-syntax account (Hartsuiker, Pickering, & Veltkamp, 2004). Similar cross-language priming methods can be used to determine whether phonological information is also shared between the L1 and L2. In terms of the bilingual lexicon, semantic priming studies can contribute to current debates, such as whether semantic information is stored in a language user's lexicon and whether L1 and L2 conceptual representations are shared.

Models of Speech Comprehension

The discussion of language comprehension (word recognition, to be exact) often involves comparisons between abstractionist and episodic theories (Oldfield, 1966; Tenpenny, 1995). An abstractionist view of word recognition assumes that listeners perceive speech by mapping auditory percepts onto abstract representations of words. Such representations are abstract because they do not include contextual details of speech: information about a speaker's voice, gender, or the specifics of a word's articulation. According to this view, listeners somehow manage to "filter out" these details, being able to map the same word (e.g. *book*) spoken by different speakers (e.g. a child and an adult) onto exactly the same abstract representation despite the obvious differences between these speakers' pronunciations. In contrast, an episodic view of word recognition assumes that listeners encode and store these contextual details of speech in memory, along with other auditory information. They later use these detailed records of their perceptual experience in order to understand words spoken by different speakers, in different accents, with different intonation patterns, etc.

Priming methods have been used to test abstractionist and episodic theories of word recognition. For example, abstractionist theories predict that listeners will not be sensitive to detailed information available in speech, hypothesizing that such information is "discarded" at some point in the recognition process. In contrast, episodic theories predict the opposite, that listeners encode and use all this information. These predictions have been tested in a number of auditory priming studies in which listeners were exposed to repetitions of the same words spoken by the same or different speakers, or to repetitions of the same words spoken in different intonation patterns (Goldinger, 1996a; Schacter & Church, 1992). Findings of these studies have yielded support for episodic encoding of words, showing that listeners access and use detailed context-specific representations to recognize words.

Priming research can also provide insight into word recognition processes in bilinguals and L2 learners. Such research can, for example, determine whether L2 learners create detailed representations of L2 words (Pallier, Colomé, & Sebastián-Gallés, 2001) and what factors might influence the extent to which they do so. Similarly, this research can reveal precisely what kinds of phonological information L2 learners are sensitive to. For example, learners might be overly sensitive to a speaker's voice in word recognition. In other words, these learners (at least under certain circumstances) would not show auditory priming for repetitions of words that were produced by two different speakers (Trofimovich & Gatbonton, 2006). Priming research, particularly studies combining auditory and semantic priming paradigms, can also investigate the interaction of semantic and phonological factors in the comprehension of L2 speech.

Convergence in Dialogue

Conversation is a joint activity in which interlocutors work together to achieve shared understanding of what is being talked about. Throughout a conversation, speakers often demonstrate convergence in that they begin to express themselves in similar ways. For example, Garrod and his colleagues have shown that speakers who are describing abstract mazes to each other converge in their descriptions of the mazes as well as in the lexical expressions used to describe the objects placed in them (Garrod & Anderson, 1987; Garrod & Doherty, 1994). This coordination is believed to facilitate successful communication by increasing the likelihood that a listener will understand a speaker's meaning. In addition, a speaker can re-use an expression whose meaning has been established earlier in the discourse, which reduces the computational demands associated with generating a new expression. While the majority of conversation research has focused on semantic and lexical convergence, recent syntactic priming studies have also explored whether speakers converge or align in their use of syntactic structures.

In an early study that examined syntactic convergence, Levelt and Kelter (1982) demonstrated that shopkeepers' responses to customers' queries had a parallel syntactic structure. For example, when asked *At what time does your shop close?* the shopkeepers answered with a prepositional phrase (*at five*), but when asked *What time does your shop close?*

they answered with a noun phrase (*five*). Inspired by Levelt's work, syntactic priming researchers have investigated how prior exposure to a syntactic structure influences a speaker's subsequent production. The focus of syntactic priming research has been to determine whether repetition of syntactic structure is due to lexical or pragmatic considerations, or whether it is the result of syntax. This line of research has shown that speakers tend to repeat syntactic structures across subsequent utterances despite surface-level differences in lexical items, morphology, or grammatical categories (e.g. animacy).

Priming research contributes to the study of conversation by identifying what factors facilitate convergence in speakers' use of phonological, lexical, and syntactic forms. For example, auditory priming research has shown that besides being sensitive to previously heard lexical items, speakers are also sensitive to contextual details of previously encountered speech, such as voices they have heard before, the gender of their interlocutor, and particular intonation patterns. Similarly, syntactic priming research has shown that speakers are sensitive to the syntactic structures produced by an interlocutor, even when their sentences have no lexical, metrical, or thematic similarities with the sentences spoken by their interlocutor. L2 researchers working within the interaction framework have used priming tasks to explore whether syntactic priming helps account for the beneficial relationship between interaction and L2 development.

Linguistic Knowledge

The goal of linguistic theory is to provide an account of the structural features of language that underlie our mental representations. Several priming researchers have pointed out that priming studies can help inform linguistic theory (Bock, 1995; Pickering & Branigan, 1999), and many linguists have used processing evidence to help confirm or reject linguistic theory. For example, several L2 acquisition researchers have adopted processing measures in order to gain insight into L2 learners' abstract linguistic knowledge and the relationship between knowledge and processing (e.g. Juffs & Harrington, 1995; Montrul, 2004; Murphy, 1997). In addition, Nicol and colleagues have adopted processing measures (e.g. Nicol & Pickering, 1993; Nicol & Swinney, 1989; Vigliocco & Nicol, 1998) to explore the interpretation of coreference assignment and syntactic ambiguities, as well as syntactic dependencies and hierarchical syntactic relationships.

As an example of the contribution of priming research to linguistic theory, consider the syntactic priming studies carried out by Bock and her colleagues (Bock, Loebell, & Morey, 1992). Using a picture recognition and description task, they found that L1 English speakers were more likely to produce a sentence with an animate subject after they had been exposed to a sentence with an animate subject. This sensitivity to the animacy of subjects occurred even if the initial sentence was active while the subsequent sentence was passive. The fact that the speakers categorized the subjects of active and passive sentences similarly provides evidence against any linguistic theory that equates the subject of a passive sentence with the object of an active sentence, and supports those theories that do not emphasize such transformations.

More recently, syntactic priming has been used to explore competing theoretical claims about the nature of thematic roles (semantic relationships such as *agent*, *goal*, or *patient*). While traditional theories of grammar claim that thematic roles are associated with lexical entries, construction-based grammar (Goldberg, 1995) states that they are associated with structural configurations that are independent of individual lexical items. Priming research can contribute to theories of linguistic knowledge by providing insight into the relationships between semantic properties and grammatical relations. For example, Chang and his colleagues (Chang, Bock, & Goldberg, 2003) used a syntactic priming task to test whether thematic roles are a part of grammatical processing and therefore susceptible to priming. For L2 acquisition researchers, priming methods can be used to explore the nature of L2 learners' linguistic representations, supplementing traditional experimental methods such as acceptability judgment tasks.

Incidental Learning

In a recent textbook about theories in second language acquisition, Van-Patten and Williams (2007) compiled a list of observed phenomena that L2 acquisition theories should be able to account for. They included in this list the observation that "a good deal of SLA happens incidentally," by which they mean that learners can "pick up" linguistic features (lexis, syntax, morphology, phonology) while their primary focus of attention is on meaning. While L2 acquisition theories assign varying degrees of importance to incidental learning, several theories argue that the bulk of L2 linguistic knowledge is acquired incidentally. For example, Ellis (2007) has argued that language learning is largely exemplar driven. That is, learners form generalizations about linguistic structures based on abstractions of frequent patterns in the input. While explicit metalinguistic information or explicit instruction may facilitate the initial registration of a structure, integration and synthesis of that pattern occur implicitly, for the most part through exposure to the target language (Ellis, 2005).

As an implicit phenomenon, priming may help facilitate this integration and synthesis by encouraging learners to produce language forms (phonological, lexical, or syntactic) that they may be in the process of acquiring. Although they may initially associate a structure with specific lexical items, exposure to primes that present the structure with a variety of lexical items (or in a variety of voices, accents, or speaking styles) may help facilitate learners' development of a more abstract linguistic representation. Producing responses with the structure modeled by the prime may also strengthen the connections between the structure and the appropriate lexical items (and between the lexical items and their phonological form). Recent L1 acquisition research by Tomasello and his colleagues (Savage, Lieven, Theakston, & Tomasello, 2003, 2006) has found a positive relationship between priming and the acquisition of English passives by young children, while L2 acquisition research has demonstrated that priming is associated with the L2 acquisition of questions (McDonough & Mackey, 2008).

Skill Acquisition

As summarized by DeKeyser (2007) in his skill acquisition theory, learning proceeds from initial knowledge representation to changes in behavior, and eventually results in fluent, effortless, and highly skilled performance. This process occurs in three stages, with the first stage consisting of the acquisition of declarative knowledge. In the second stage, which is the acquisition of procedural knowledge, learners begin to acquire the ability to use their declarative knowledge. In the final stage, gradual automatization of knowledge occurs through repeated, meaningful practice that allows for the behavior to become consistent, fluent, and error-free. Because priming is an implicit phenomenon that does not provide any explicit information about language form, it is unlikely to facilitate the acquisition of declarative knowledge. However, it may contribute to the proceduralization and automatization phases of skill acquisition by providing learners with multiple exemplars of the target structure in the form of primes and by creating opportunities for them to produce those target structures in response to those primes. Priming may facilitate proceduralization both of comprehension through repeated exposure to primes in the input and of production through the elicitation of targets after primes. Measures of automatization, such as reaction time, interference from dual tasks, and accuracy rates, are comparable to measures often used in priming research, particularly auditory priming and semantic priming. Relatively few L2 studies have investigated skill acquisition, and priming methods have potential to contribute to our understanding of how linguistic knowledge becomes proceduralized and automatized.

Neuropsychology of Language Learning and Use

Priming research may offer exciting possibilities for revealing the neurological underpinnings of language learning and use. Although a relatively new area, neuropsychological research on priming has already made significant contributions to the understanding of priming as an implicit memory phenomenon, and has started to uncover neurological correlates of priming. For example, several studies employing such techniques as positron-emission tomography (PET) and functional magnetic-resonance imaging (fMRI) have revealed that priming is associated with decreases in brain activity in parts of the visual cortex (involved in perceptual processing) and in some areas of the frontal lobe (involved in semantic and conceptual processing). However, most of this research has focused on L1 processing and has not extensively investigated L2 processing.

Neuropsychological studies of priming (especially in the L2) would be interesting because they may reveal possible L1–L2 differences in the way that language users process language information. For example, language users may process auditory, semantic, and syntactic information in different cortical locations and to different degrees. In addition, neuropsychological investigations of L2 priming may help answer questions about how different memory processes interact in the bilingual brain. Some of these questions include the effect of declarative (explicit) memory on priming, the influence of processing task on priming, the interaction between automatic and conscious aspects of memory, and the neurological underpinnings of episodic encoding and retrieval.

Investigating these issues in future neuropsychological priming studies will be important for advancing our understanding not only of L2 processing and learning but also of human cognitive capacity. While a detailed discussion of neuropsychological priming studies (whether in L1 or L2) is beyond the scope of this book, an excellent introduction to neuropsychology of language can be found in Pulvermüller (2003), and neuroimaging studies of priming are reviewed in Henson (2003).

Representative L2 Priming Studies

Many studies have examined bilingual language processing in which bilingual participants are exposed to primes in one language and respond in the other language (which is known as *between-* or *cross-language priming*). Fewer studies have explicitly focused on the occurrence of priming in the L2, in which both the primes and responses occur in the participants' L2 (which is referred to as *within-language priming*). In table 1.1 we have compiled a sampling of L2 studies that have adopted auditory, semantic, and syntactic priming to address questions of interest for L2 processing and acquisition. More specific information about these studies, as well as L1 and bilingual priming studies, is provided in the subsequent chapters. As this sampling indicates, only a few tasks within each category of priming research have been used in L2 studies. For example, L2 auditory priming studies have primarily used repetition

Table 1.1 Representative L2 priming studies

Study	Participant language(s)	Priming type & task	Participants	General findings
Bernolet, Hartsuiker, & Pickering, (2007): Ex. 2	Dutch L1, English L2	Syntactic: Scripted interaction	32 university students	Syntactic priming occurred for word order with relative clauses
Bird & Williams (2002)	Various L1s, English L2	Auditory: Familiarity and rhyme judgment	40 university students (2 experiments)	Priming effects were found for known words in familiarity judgment, for novel words in rhyme but not in familiarity judgment
Favreau & Segalowitz (1983)	English L1, French L2 & French L1, English L2	Semantic: Lexical decision	60 adults	Priming effect was similar in L1 and L2 for more proficient learners; priming effect was larger in L1 than L2 for less proficient learners
Frenck-Mestre & Prince (1997)	French L1, English L2	Semantic: Lexical decision	108 university students (2 experiments)	English monolinguals and more (but less) proficient learners showed similar priming effects
Gries & Wulff (2005)	German L1, English L2	Syntactic: Written sentence completion	64 university students	Priming occurred for both double-object and prepositional datives
Kim & McDonough (2008)	Korean L1, English L2	Syntactic: Scripted interaction	76 university students	More passives occurred when the learners' prompts had the same verb produced by the scripted interlocutor
McDonough (2006)	Various L1s, English L2	Syntactic: Scripted interaction	104 university students (2 experiments)	Priming occurred for prepositional datives only

Study	Languages	Task	Participants	Findings
McDonough & Mackey (2008)	Thai L1, English L2	Syntactic: Scripted interaction	46 university students	Priming was associated with question development
Schoonbaert, Hartsuiker, & Pickering, (2007): Ex. 1	Dutch L1, English L2	Syntactic: Scripted interaction	22 university students	Priming occurred with prepositional datives
Trofimovich (2005)	English L1 Spanish L2	Auditory: Repetition task	60 university students (2 experiments)	Priming occurred, but learners overused speakers' voice details in L2 speech processing
Trofimovich & Gatbonton (2006)	English L1, Spanish L2	Auditory: Repetition task	60 university students (2 experiments)	Priming occurred except with low pronunciation ability learners who focused on meaning while listening
Trofimovich (2008)	Chinese L1, English L2	Auditory: Repetition task	52 university students	Priming depended on L2 proficiency and attentional orientation imposed by a task

tasks, L2 semantic priming studies have relied on lexical decision tasks, while L2 syntactic priming studies have used scripted interaction tasks. Hopefully, future L2 research will adopt a wider variety of priming tasks to gain further insight into L2 speech processing and acquisition.

Summary

In this chapter, we have introduced the phenomenon of priming and discussed the potential uses of priming methods to investigate L2 speech processing and acquisition, such as models of speech production and comprehension, convergence in dialogue, linguistic knowledge, incidental learning, automatization, and the neuropsychology of language use. In chapter 2, we focus in more detail on auditory priming, explaining the questions investigated in auditory priming research and describing the three experimental tasks commonly used in auditory priming studies.

Follow-up Questions and Activities

1. In addition to the topics mentioned in this chapter, what other issues in L2 processing and acquisition could be explored using priming methods?

2. Which of the three types of priming introduced in this chapter —auditory, semantic, and syntactic—are you most interested in? Why?

3. As described in this chapter, priming methods have been used to investigate convergence in conversation. In your experience, can you recall a situation in which you and your interlocutor began to use similar expressions, similar pronunciation patterns, or similar grammatical structures? In other recent conversations you may have heard, did you detect any instances of convergence?

4. Locate one of the articles listed in table 1.1 and write a short summary and critique of the study.

5. If you are planning a research project, consider the following questions:

   a) What topic are you interested in?

   b) What previous research about that topic has been done already and how do the findings relate to your proposed project?

   c) What will be your research question(s)?

   d) Which type of priming (auditory, semantic, or syntactic) will you use?

---

   e)   Which aspect of language processing will you target (such as recognition, comprehension, or production) and how will you measure it (such as reaction time, accuracy, use of target structures)?

   f)   What is the purpose of the project (class requirement, qualifying paper, journal article), who is the intended audience (priming researchers, L2 acquisition researchers, L2 teachers), and where do you hope to present and/or publish it?

6.   Consider the data in table 1.2. The table shows how often the participants produced prepositional dative and double-object dative responses after prepositional and double-object dative primes. Their responses were calculated as a proportion based on the number of each dative type divided by the total number of responses. How would you describe the pattern that these data illustrate? Write a short description of the information in the table.

Table 1.2 English L1 speakers' production of dative targets by prime type

Prime	*Target*	
	Prepositional dative	*Double-object dative*
Prepositional dative	.62	.19
Double-object dative	.27	.46

Source: Adapted from table 2 in Kaschak, Loney, & Borreggine, 2006, p. 878.

2

AUDITORY PRIMING

In this chapter, we define auditory priming and describe its uses in L1, bilingual, and L2 processing and acquisition research. We outline the three experimental tasks commonly used in auditory priming research and describe in detail the materials, procedure, and analysis for each task. We then highlight as an example a study that used auditory priming to investigate L2 acquisition, and we point out issues to consider when designing auditory priming experiments. We conclude the chapter with suggestions for additional uses of auditory priming tasks in L2 research.

What is Auditory Priming?

In his 2005 book exploring cognitive underpinnings of common everyday decisions, such as choosing a house for purchase or deciding on a book to read, Malcolm Gladwell drew on a variety of cognitive psychological research to conclude (among other things) that our decision making can be primed, our choices being heavily affected by our past experiences, often quite unbeknownst to us. Gladwell discussed priming in terms of complex (and often unconscious) mental operations that are "taking care of all the minor mental details in [our] life, keeping tabs on everything going on around [us]" (pp. 58–59). Gladwell's metaphor clearly captures two major properties of many priming phenomena, particularly those that are the focus of this book. The first of these properties is the unintentional nature of priming. Most of the time, we are not aware whether and how our behavior is subtly influenced by our past experiences. The second of these properties is our sensitivity to many, often quite minor, details of our past experiences, the details that, once encoded and stored, have the potential to influence our future behavior.

The priming phenomenon discussed in this chapter can also be conceptualized within Gladwell's metaphor. Auditory priming can be described as the mental operations that keep tabs on all the details of a language spoken around us, a language that we speak and comprehend. In speaking and comprehending a language, listeners (often without conscious intention or awareness) appear to encode and store a number of details about what they hear, including, for example, peculiarities of a speaker's voice, pitch height of an utterance, or a specific pronunciation of a word. Circumstances permitting, listeners may then draw on these details later

19

(again, quite unintentionally) and, as a result, may become faster or more accurate at comprehending and speaking a language.

In a broad sense, auditory priming characterizes this phenomenon of unintentional facilitation in auditory (perceptual) processing of spoken language, this facilitation arising due to listeners' previous experience with some aspects of a spoken language (see box 2.1). Auditory priming is a form of repetition priming because listeners essentially benefit from every repeated episode of their experience with speech (see Ellis & Ellis, 1998, and Kirsner, 1998, for an introduction to repetition priming). To use a concrete example, listeners are typically faster and more accurate at recognizing the spoken words they have heard in recent experience (repeated words) than the words they have not heard recently (unrepeated words). The goal of this chapter is to examine this phenomenon in detail.

Box 2.1 Auditory priming

Auditory priming (also known as *auditory word priming* and *long-term auditory repetition priming*) is observed when the processing of a spoken word or word combination is facilitated due to a language user's prior experience with this word or word combination. It is often argued that each experience with a spoken word leaves a long-lasting perceptual "record" that, when accessed later, facilitates a subsequent re-processing of this word (Church & Fisher, 1998). Auditory priming is a form of repetition priming.

Auditory priming needs to be distinguished from at least two related, but not identical, priming phenomena.

Phonological or *phonemic priming* (also known as *form priming*) is observed when the processing of a spoken word is modified due to a language user's prior experience with another word that is phonologically similar in terms of individual segments, syllable onsets or rhymes. For example, relative to an unrelated word (e.g. *city*), a listener may be more or less likely to identify or name the word *great* after having heard the words *goal, grief,* or *grace* (all sharing one, two, and three segments with it, respectively). For more details, see Zwitserlood (1996).

Phonetic priming (also known as *feature priming*) is observed when the processing of a spoken word is modified due to a language user's prior experience with another word that overlaps with it phonetically (in terms of one or more of its phonetic features). For instance, relative to an unrelated word (e.g. *win*), a listener may be more or less likely to identify or name the word *bat* after having heard the word *peel* due to the shared phonetic features between *b* and *p* (both bilabial stops). For more information, see Luce, Goldinger, Auer, and Vitevitch (2000).

Auditory Priming in L1 Processing and Acquisition

Examples of Auditory Priming

As discussed above, auditory priming is defined as unintentional facilitation in auditory processing of language. This facilitation is most often observable as a time and/or accuracy benefit for repeated versus non-repeated spoken words and word combinations. To clear up terminological confusion from the outset, what we term *auditory priming* primarily refers here to the general phenomenon of unintentional facilitation observed in the processing of speech. By extension, the same term can also be used to describe a possible cognitive mechanism underlying this facilitation. We will clearly identify cases when *auditory priming* is used in this sense (i.e. referring to a cognitive mechanism as opposed to a general phenomenon). In turn, what we call an *auditory priming effect* describes the specific, and often measurable, extent or magnitude of facilitation observed in the processing of speech. Thus, for example, if an experimenter were to study auditory priming in listeners' processing of spoken words, he or she could use a word repetition task (discussed in detail below) to determine the magnitude of an auditory priming effect (measured in milliseconds), defined as the extent to which repeated words are produced more rapidly than unrepeated words.

The beneficial effects of listeners' prior experience with spoken language have been observed in a variety of psycholinguistic (processing) tasks: word or sentence identification, lexical decision, repetition (naming), word fragment or word stem completion (all discussed in greater detail below). For example, in a word or sentence identification task, listeners are typically asked to identify previously studied and non-studied words or sentences presented under difficult listening conditions (e.g. with sentences or words masked in background noise), which increase task difficulty for the listeners performing the task (Franks, Plybon, & Auble, 1982; Jackson & Morton, 1984). Auditory priming is demonstrated in this task if listeners appear to be more accurate at identifying the words they have heard previously versus the words they have not heard previously. In one such study, Ellis (1982) demonstrated that a prior experience of hearing words significantly improved listeners' subsequent recognition of the same words presented in noise, but a prior experience of reading words in a conventional or a misspelled form produced either little or no facilitation. For example, the listeners in that study were able to reliably identify the word *fox* presented in noise after they had heard it spoken earlier but not after they had seen it presented in its conventional spelling (*fox*) or phonetically misspelled (*phoks*).

Auditory priming effects are likewise obtained in tasks that require listeners to complete spoken word stems or spoken word fragments. In these tasks, listeners first hear a number of spoken words and, after a short delay, are subsequently instructed to complete spoken word stems or fragments (either related or unrelated to the studied words) with the first word that comes to mind (Bassili, Smith, & MacLeod, 1989; Schacter & Church, 1992). Examples of a word stem and a word fragment to be completed with the first word that comes to mind are *ele____* (to be completed as *elephant* or *elevator*) and *w_ _der* (to be completed as *wonder*). Auditory priming is demonstrated in this task if listeners appear to complete more word stems or fragments with the words they have heard previously versus the words they have not heard previously. Bassili et al. (1989), for example, showed that their participants were indeed more likely to complete word stems with the words that were heard earlier as opposed to the words not previously heard. Although these participants were also more likely to complete word stems with the words that they read earlier, the effect of prior listening experience was significantly larger than the effect of prior reading experience. The findings of both studies described above (Bassili et al., 1989; Ellis, 1982) suggest that auditory priming largely arises as a consequence of auditory (listening) rather than visual (reading) processing.

Properties of Auditory Priming

Auditory priming as a psycholinguistic phenomenon displays a number of characteristics. One of them is its stimulus specific nature. Stimulus specificity of auditory priming refers to the observation that what can be primed in speech processing is not only repeated words or word combinations but also their contextual details. Craik and Kirsner (1974) were among the first to show that a speaker's voice, one contextual detail of speech, can also be primed. In Craik and Kirsner's study, listeners were not only faster and more accurate at recognizing repeated words, but they were also faster and more accurate at recognizing repeated voices. That is, in a word recognition task, repeated words spoken in a "familiar" (i.e. previously heard) voice were recognized more rapidly and accurately than the same words spoken in an unfamiliar voice.

More recent investigations of auditory priming have yielded evidence that, in addition to benefiting from repeated words, listeners also profit from their familiarity with many contextual details of speech: speaker's gender (Schacter & Church, 1992), speaker's voice (Goldinger, 1996a; Sheffert, 1998), the intonation in which a spoken word is uttered (Church & Schacter, 1994), its pitch (Church & Schacter, 1994), and the phonetic context of neighboring vowels and consonants (Fisher, Hunt, Chambers, & Church, 2001). Even more strikingly, listeners also appear to be sensitive to within-category phonetic variation, such as fine-grained differences in consonant voicing (Ju & Luce, 2006) or differences between two allophonic variants of the same phoneme (McLennan, Luce, & Charles-Luce, 2003). What these studies suggest is that the magnitude of an auditory priming effect is largest when two renditions of a spoken word also share one (or more) context specific details. Put differently, it appears that listeners are sensitive not only to repeated spoken words (demonstrating an auditory priming effect for repeated vs. unrepeated words) but also to their form-related, contextual details (demonstrating an additional priming effect for repeated voices, repeated intonation patterns, repeated phonetic contexts, and even repeated phonetic detail of individual sounds).

Another property of auditory priming lies in its rapid, nearly automatic functioning. Indeed, as many experiments have shown, it usually takes a single experience with a spoken word to facilitate its subsequent re-processing (Goldinger, 1996a). Auditory priming occurs even in situations when a language user has no explicit memory of ever experiencing a word before. For example, amnesiacs (individuals with a brain damage who are typically unable to retain explicit memories) show auditory priming for spoken words without having the ability to explicitly remember that they heard these words before (e.g. Schacter, Church, & Treadwell, 1994). Taken together, this evidence suggests that auditory priming arises as a rapid and automatic consequence of word identification (Church & Fisher, 1998).

Another characteristic of auditory priming is its long-lasting nature. Previous research has shown that listeners demonstrate benefits in their processing of a repeated spoken word even though their prior experience with this same word occurred seconds, minutes, hours, or even days before. For example, reliable auditory priming effects have been found after delays of 8 seconds (Cole, Coltheart, & Allard, 1974), several minutes (Church & Schacter, 1994; Schacter & Church, 1992), days, and even weeks (Goldinger, 1996a). It is interesting to note that comparable investigations of visual priming (that is, priming arising as a consequence of readers' experience with written words or sentences) have yielded reliable processing benefits one month (Kolers & Ostry, 1974) and even one year (Kolers, 1976) after participants' initial experience reading words or sentences. These findings argue against the notion that auditory priming is a highly transient phenomenon. Instead, these findings suggest that auditory priming has a long-term memory component.

Yet another characteristic of auditory priming lies in its relative insensitivity to the type of processing in which listeners engage during their initial exposure to spoken words. This is most clearly observable in experimental manipulations of listeners' attentional orientation during their exposure to spoken words (Church & Schacter, 1994; Schacter & Church, 1992; but see Brown & Mitchell, 1994, and Mulligan, Duke, & Cooper, 2007). These studies have shown that the magnitude of auditory priming effects is relatively uniform whether or not listeners are oriented, at the time of their initial exposure to spoken words, to their meaning (i.e. semantic, conceptual characteristics of words) or to their form (i.e. auditory, perceptual characteristics of words). For example, Schacter and Church (1992) reported comparable auditory priming effects in a word stem completion task for two types of repeated spoken words: those that listeners previously heard under the instructions to estimate how many meanings they might have (focus on word meaning) and those that listeners previously heard under the instructions to estimate how clearly they were enunciated (focus on word form). This finding suggests that different encoding manipulations (i.e. particular circumstances accompanying listeners' experience with words) do not seem to affect the extent to which listeners benefit from repeated spoken words. (We will revisit this point in the following sections in relation to L2 users who, unlike L1 speakers, may be affected by encoding manipulations.) At least for L1 speakers, then, auditory priming seems to emerge as a rapid and automatic consequence of identifying auditory (phonological) word forms and appears to rely little on word meaning (Schacter et al., 1994).

Finally, auditory priming effects display a relative constancy in language development; from children (Church & Fisher, 1998) to older adults (Pilotti & Beyer, 2002). Church and Fisher (1998), for example, examined auditory priming in very young monolingual children (see also Carlesimo, Vicari, Albertoni, Turriziani, & Caltagirone, 2000). In their studies, children as young as two years of age showed robust processing facilitation in their identification of previously studied words. This finding underscores the involvement of auditory priming in the processing of speech in both adults and children.

Relevance of Auditory Priming to L2 Processing and Learning

As the preceding discussion suggests, auditory priming emerges as a modality-specific (auditory as opposed to visual), context-sensitive, long-lasting, non-semantic, and apparently developmentally constant phenomenon, a characterization which perhaps accentuates its important role in speech processing by children and adults. In fact, Church and Fisher (1998) identified the processing operations giving rise to auditory priming as a likely mechanism supporting spoken word processing and learning. More specifically, they argued that these processing operations appear to represent just the right mechanism for aiding children in their learning of spoken words. In this sense, therefore, *auditory priming*, as a term, refers not only to a general psycholinguistic phenomenon, but also to a cognitive mechanism underlying it.

Children acquiring their L1 should be able to accomplish at least two related learning tasks. One such task is for children to be able to register repeated uses of spoken words as repeated sound patterns or phonological forms, without attaching a separate meaning to each individual instance of a spoken word heard (e.g. *cat* as spoken by a mother and a grandfather). This ability to identify spoken word forms in a variety of different contexts (e.g. when words are spoken in isolation or in sentences, at different speaking rates, or in different voices) should help children accumulate evidence about the range of variability inherent in different uses of spoken words and, as a result, should help them associate words with their meanings consistently in a variety of contexts (see Fisher, Hall, Rakowitz, & Gleitman, 1994, Pinker, 1984, and Waxman & Markow, 1995, for theoretical justifications).

A closely related learning task is for children to be able to represent spoken words with sufficient acoustic and contextual detail in order to subsequently recognize them in a variety of situations (Jusczyk, 1997; Ryalls & Pisoni, 1997; Saffran, Aslin, & Newport, 1996). Put differently, children need to be able to store enough detail about a spoken word to be able to recognize it when it is used under slightly different circumstances (e.g. whispered or sung) or in a different linguistic context (e.g. embedded in a sentence or spoken in isolation). In essence, children's phonological representations of words should be sufficiently detailed to identify instances of the same word in different contexts (e.g. *ball* spoken by a father and a mother) and to distinguish a word from phonologically similar ones (e.g. telling *ball* and *Paul* apart).

According to Church and Fisher (1998), auditory priming is a mechanism that allows children to accomplish these learning tasks. First, because auditory priming does not require access to word meaning, it may reflect the process whereby children build and use phonological (form-related) representations of words. Second, because the magnitude of auditory priming effects depends on the perceptual match between words, auditory priming most likely arises as a consequence of creating and using context-specific phonological representations of words (Goldinger, 1996a). Finally, the long-lasting and developmentally constant nature of auditory priming renders it an automatic mechanism for the encoding and retrieval of phonological word representations. Thus, auditory priming may provide the necessary support for just what children need to do in early stages of language learning: to build a *spoken* lexicon of their native language (Church & Fisher, 1998).

Is auditory priming, as a learning mechanism, involved in L2 acquisition in a similar way to how Church and Fisher hypothesized it is in L1 development? It is certainly appealing to suppose that auditory priming also supports spoken L2 word processing and learning. Although there are a number of differences between L1 acquisition and L2 learning beyond infancy (most significant being the fact that most L2 learners, whether child or adult, already have a command of at least one language), L2 learners need to accomplish the same learning tasks faced by infants acquiring their L1. In other words, learners need to learn to associate the phonological form of an L2 word with its meaning and to consistently recognize this word, regardless of the linguistic or non-linguistic contexts in which it is encountered. For example, native English speakers learning Spanish need to associate the Spanish word *ventana* with its meaning (window) and to recognize this word as such when it is spoken in isolation or in a sentence, when it is whispered or shouted, or when it is uttered by their classroom teacher or an unknown person.

On the other hand, however, auditory priming may *not* play a prominent role in L2 development or it may be involved differently in L1 versus L2 spoken word processing and learning. For example, auditory priming may be mediated or altogether eliminated in situations when learners' attention is directed away from the perceptual details of spoken L2 words. In fact, such situations may not be uncommon in those L2 learning contexts where the formal (i.e. phonological, grammatical) properties of an L2 are not emphasized to the same extent as are its meaningful (i.e. semantic, conceptual) properties (e.g. Turnbull, Lapkin, Hart, & Swain, 1998). Auditory priming may be involved differently in L2 spoken word processing due to learners' limited processing capacity, at least in the initial stages of L2 learning (Chincotta & Underwood, 1998). In addition, auditory priming may depend on the degree of learners' proficiency and dominance in, or amount of use of, a language they are learning. Whatever their underlying source, such differences (if demonstrated) may help us gain a better understanding of L2 spoken word processing and learning, yielding possible answers to complicated questions such as this: Why is it that most L2 learners are able to learn the meaning of a previously unknown L2 word (e.g. Horst & Meara, 1999; Weber-Fox & Neville, 1996) but are often unable to accurately perceive and produce it (e.g. Flege, Yeni-Komshian, & Liu, 1999)? We will review this and other related issues in the following section.

Questions Addressed in L2 Auditory Priming Research

Although the priming paradigm has been used extensively in bilingual and L2 research, *auditory* priming has merited surprisingly little attention in investigations of L2 learning and bilingualism. In essence, the study of L2 processing and learning (including bilingual language processing) has to date predominantly relied on visual rather than auditory processing. Among many questions that can be investigated in L2 priming research, one of the most basic is whether and to what extent auditory priming, as a phenomenon and (by extension) as a mechanism, is involved in an L2. We review this question first.

Auditory Priming with L2 Speakers

One of the first demonstrations of auditory priming in an L2 appeared in investigations of word processing in bi-dialectal speakers of the standard and the Maastricht dialects of Dutch (de Bot, Cox, Ralston, Schaufeli, & Weltens, 1995; Woutersen, de Bot, & Weltens, 1995; Woutersen, Cox, Weltens, & de Bot, 1994). The goal of these studies, employing a primed lexical decision task (discussed in greater detail in chapter 3, see pp. 74–77), was to determine how bi-dialectal speakers organize their lexicons. (The Maastricht dialect of Dutch is hardly ever written; hence, presenting words visually in two dialects was impossible.) These researchers tested their participants in between-dialect conditions, asking them to decide whether or not the presented word is a real word in Dutch or its Maastricht dialect. For example, participants would first respond to the standard Dutch word *ziek* (sick) and then, after a delay, to its Maastricht dialect equivalent *kraank*. For comparison purposes, the researchers also tested their participants in within-dialect conditions, where words in only one dialect were used. For example, participants would first respond to the Maastricht dialect word *tas* (cup) and then, after a delay, would do so again. An analysis of response times in these within-dialect conditions revealed that bi-dialectal speakers benefited from repeated words in each dialect, showing an auditory priming effect (Woutersen et al., 1994; see also de Bot et al., 1995; Woutersen et al., 1995). That is, the speakers were faster at responding to a word spoken in standard Dutch having heard it previously in standard Dutch. They were also faster at responding to a Maastricht dialect word having heard it previously in this dialect. More recently, Pallier et al. (2001) demonstrated a very similar effect in Spanish-Catalan and Catalan-Spanish bilinguals. These bilinguals demonstrated auditory priming effects in both of their languages.

Do language learners, like bilinguals (Pallier et al., 2001) and bi-dialectal speakers (Woutersen et al., 1994), demonstrate auditory priming as well? Few studies have to date examined auditory priming in L2 learners (Bird & Williams, 2002) and only a handful have done so in detail (Trofimovich, 2005, 2008; Trofimovich & Gatbonton, 2006; see also Ju & Church, 2001). The conclusion that emerges from these studies is that L2 learners, too, benefit from auditory priming. In a study investigating the effects of within-language subtitling (simultaneously presenting auditory and textual information to learners as an aid to L2 listening comprehension), Bird and Williams (2002) tested advanced L2 learners of English in several priming conditions. Of particular interest here is one of these conditions consisting of a study and a test task. In the study task, participants listened to a list of L2 words and indicated which words were familiar to them (this task is a variant of a lexical decision task, discussed in detail in chapter 3, see pp. 74–77). In the subsequent

27

test task, they heard another word list (containing words previously heard and those not previously heard) and were instructed to perform the same task: to indicate which words were familiar to them. Recall that listeners demonstrate auditory priming if in the test task they are faster at making word familiarity judgments for the words they heard previously in the study task as opposed to the words not heard previously in the study task. The learners indeed demonstrated auditory priming. This showed that a previous experience with a set of spoken L2 words enabled advanced L2 learners to be faster and more accurate at responding to these same words later.

In a detailed investigation of auditory word priming in L2 learners, Trofimovich (2005) also showed that low-intermediate L2 learners of Spanish overall appear to benefit from their experience with spoken words, demonstrating auditory priming effects. This finding suggests that even relatively low-proficiency L2 learners, just like fluent bi-dialectal speakers and bilinguals (Pallier et al., 2001; Woutersen et al., 1994), are able to encode the phonological information in spoken words and to bring this information to aid in subsequent word processing. Assuming that auditory priming exemplifies a likely mechanism supporting the processing and learning of an L1 (Church & Fisher, 1998), the results of this study, coupled with the findings of other investigations (Bird & Williams, 2002; Ju & Church, 2001), suggest that this mechanism also supports L2 processing and learning.

Task Effects

Although the evidence presented thus far suggests that L2 learners benefit from auditory priming as a learning mechanism, demonstrating sensitivities to repeated L2 phonological information, it is not clear whether they do so at all times, in all processing tasks. Language processing, including that typical of L2 learning contexts, normally requires attention to both the form and the meaning of L2 input (VanPatten, 1990). For example, upon hearing a question posed in an L2, *Vous avez l'heure?* (Do you have the time?), learners need not only to recognize each individual spoken word but also to understand the meaning of the entire utterance and, ultimately, to respond to it appropriately. Do L2 learners benefit from auditory priming, as a potential mechanism of spoken word processing and learning, when they attend to meaning- and form-related aspects of language? If not, in what circumstances are they most likely to experience auditory priming benefits?

We already know that auditory priming in an L1 is relatively insensitive to the nature of a processing task, that is, whether listeners' attention is directed to the meaning or form of spoken words. This finding is robust, documented in both adults (e.g. Church & Schacter, 1994) and children (e.g. Church & Fisher, 1998). However, there exists some evidence that auditory priming in an L2 depends on the processing task. It appears that priming effects may be effectively abolished, even under the most favorable conditions, when a task requires L2 learners to attend to meaningful (semantic, conceptual) aspects of an L2. Put differently, an explicit emphasis on meaning-based properties of L2 input may eliminate auditory priming effects, processing benefits arising as a consequence of repeated word forms.

Previous research (albeit not specific to auditory priming) has yielded several findings supporting this claim. For instance, it appears that a meaningful, conceptual task can have a negative impact on priming. Heredia and McLaughlin (1992) tested this possibility in a visual word priming study with Spanish-English bilinguals. These researchers first asked bilinguals to study words in English, their L2. Then, they tested these bilinguals in two different tasks. One group of bilinguals completed English word fragments. For example, upon seeing the English word fragment gla____, bilinguals would complete it with the English word glasses. The other group used the same English word fragments as a cue to produce Spanish translations of English words. In this case, upon seeing the same fragment, bilinguals would produce the Spanish word gafas (glasses). In both tasks, the bilinguals could complete half of the presented fragments with the words they had actually seen earlier in the experiment and half with the words they had not previously seen. Heredia and McLaughlin reported that only the bilinguals who completed English word fragments in English actually showed a visual priming effect, benefiting from their previous experience with L2 words. By contrast, the bilinguals who generated Spanish translations showed no such benefit. In essence, for these bilinguals, visual priming effects in English were markedly attenuated because a translation task likely encouraged meaningful, conceptual processing of English words and eliminated any form-related processing benefits associated with actually having seen these words before (see also Smith, 1991, for evidence suggesting that a meaningful textual context can also have a negative impact on priming).

Taken together, these studies suggest that a rich context surrounding a task (Smith, 1991) or the meaningful nature of a learning task (Heredia & McLaughlin, 1992) encourages a meaningful, conceptual processing of words and, as a result, may obliterate any benefits of previous experience with word form. Would conceptual, meaningful tasks have a negative effect on auditory priming in an L2 as well? Trofimovich and Gatbonton (2006) investigated this issue in detail. These researchers used a repetition task to test low-intermediate L2 learners of Spanish who differed in degree of L2 pronunciation ability (low vs. high). In the study phase of the task, the learners listened to L2 words and were asked, depending on the condition, to do one of two things. Half of the learners rated how pleasant each word's meaning was on a 7-point scale (1 = *word meaning is unpleasant*; 7 = *word meaning is pleasant*). The other half of the learners rated how clearly each word was enunciated on a 7-point scale (1 = *word does not sound clearly enunciated*; 7 = *word sounds clearly enunciated*). Used in studies investigating depth of processing (e.g. Schacter & Church, 1992), instructions to rate word pleasantness increase the likelihood that language users access word meaning during processing. Instructions to rate word clarity (e.g. Church & Schacter, 1994), by contrast, increase the likelihood that language users attend to more "superficial" auditory (phonological) characteristics of words. In the test phase of the task, the learners were asked to listen to a number of words (of which half were previously heard and half were new to the task) and to repeat these words responding as quickly as possible.

Analyses of reaction times (how quickly the learners repeated the spoken words) revealed several findings. In the enunciation clarity rating (auditory) condition, all learners showed significant auditory priming effects in their L2 (Spanish), and these effects appeared to be equivalent for learners with high and low pronunciation accuracy. By contrast, in the pleasantness (semantic) condition, the mean priming effect virtually disappeared for learners of low L2 pronunciation ability. That is, these learners were unable to benefit from their previous exposure to spoken L2 words when these learners' attention was drawn, at the time of first exposure to words, to their meaning (cf. Barcroft, 2003). Trofimovich (2008) found a similar result for Chinese learners of English whose experience with English (their L2) in Canada was relatively brief. These findings suggest that L2 learners may not benefit from repeated experiences with spoken words, at least early in their L2 development or after a relatively brief experience with the L2, when they engage in a meaningful, semantic processing of words. Several possible explanations for these findings can be found in Trofimovich (2005, 2008) and Trofimovich and Gatbonton (2006). See box 2.5 for a detailed description of this study.

Sensitivity to L2 Speech Features

If L2 learners show auditory priming as a phenomenon and (by extension) benefit from it as a potential learning mechanism, at least in some situations, then it is important to determine what these benefits are. What exactly are learners benefiting from as they process repeated spoken words? One way to determine the nature of word priming benefits is to examine priming effects for words that differ in degree of perceptual specificity. Previous research has shown that listeners are sensitive to both relatively abstract and relatively specific perceptual information available in spoken words. That is, listeners not only demonstrate a processing benefit when the same word is repeated (benefiting from an "abstract" word identity match) but also gain an additional processing benefit when "specific" details of spoken words (e.g. a speaker's voice, or intonation of an utterance) are repeated. For example, listeners identify more accurately and/or process more rapidly a word they have heard than a word they have not heard in recent experience; they appear to do so even more accurately and/or rapidly when such a word is spoken in a familiar as opposed to an unfamiliar voice. In other words, both repeated words and repeated voices prime (facilitate) the processing of spoken words. That is, listeners are sensitive to both abstract and specific phonological information available in spoken words.

Although listeners may indeed be sensitive to both abstract and specific information available in spoken words as they use auditory priming in their L1, they may be less likely to do so in their L2. For example, learners may be less sensitive in their L2 than in their L1 to context-specific characteristics of spoken words (Bradlow & Pisoni, 1999), failing to encode detailed perceptual information available in L2 words. Learners may also be less sensitive in their L2 than in their L1 to abstract word-identity matches (Bradlow, Pisoni, Akahane-Yamada, & Tohkura, 1997; Lively, Pisoni, Yamada, Tohkura, & Yamada, 1994), failing to general-ize across multiple, context-specific instances of the same word. Taken together, such L1–L2 differences may help explain why adult learners often fail to learn robust phonological representations for L2 sounds (Flege et al., 1999) and therefore may indicate why learning L2 phonology often poses a considerable task for L2 learners.

The question of what types of information L2 learners are sensitive to was investigated by Trofimovich (2005; see also Trofimovich, 2008). In this study, low-intermediate L2 learners of Spanish were tested in an auditory repetition task. First, the learners listened to one set of L2 words. Then, they listened to another set of L2 words (of which half were previously heard and half were new to the task) and repeated the words as rapidly and as accurately as possible. What is important is that half of the previously heard words were spoken by the same speaker (in exactly the same voice), the other half were spoken by a different speaker. If learners are sensitive to both abstract and specific information in spoken L2 words, then they should repeat both these types of words (showing auditory priming effects) more rapidly than those words that were not heard previously.

Results revealed that the learners showed priming effects *only* for those words that were spoken in the same voice. This finding suggested that the learners were sensitive to specific information in spoken L2 words, being able to encode specific perceptual information about spoken L2 words and to bring this information to aid in subsequent spoken word pro-cessing (Bradlow & Pisoni, 1999). This finding also suggested that the

31

learners were not sensitive to abstract information in spoken L2 words. Apparently, when specific characteristics of spoken words (i.e. a speaker's voice) were not preserved, the learners treated such repeated words as being "new", engaging in what can be termed as *speaker-specific* (or *teacher-specific*) word processing strategy. Thus, the ability to disregard variability in a speaker's voice (and perhaps in other context specific details in speech) may not easily transfer from learners' L1 to their L2, at least in relatively early stages of L2 learning. In these stages of L2 development, learners appear to over-rely in their L2 processing on context specific characteristics of spoken words. These findings both validate and, in fact, encourage exposing L2 learners in language teaching to a variety of speakers. Exposing L2 learners to a highly variable input may thus help them avoid the type of learning that is specific to an individual speaker and an individual learning situation.

As the preceding discussion has illustrated, a variety of auditory priming tasks have been used in L1 and L2 speech processing and acquisition. Both asking and answering interesting questions about the role of auditory priming in L2 learning clearly hinges on using appropriate methods and carefully constructed materials. We introduce methods and materials typically used in auditory priming research in the following section.

Tasks Used in Auditory Priming Research

Logic of Auditory Priming Experiments

The logic of auditory priming experiments is based on the idea that auditory priming effects are repetition effects. Defined even more precisely, auditory priming effects are *within-language* repetition effects, arising as a consequence of language users' repeated experience with words in that same language. Auditory priming experiments, therefore, are designed to examine how language users process (comprehend or produce) some aspects of language (e.g. words or short phrases) that are repeated as opposed to those that are encountered for the first time in the course of the experiment. For example, a researcher may find evidence of an auditory priming effect if a presentation of a word on one occasion facilitates subsequent reprocessing of the same word presented on another occasion. At least one goal of auditory priming experiments is thus to measure the extent of this facilitation for repeated spoken words (or word combinations), relative to participants' performance on unrepeated spoken words in a given language.

Suppose, for example, that in an auditory repetition task (described on pp. 41–44), participants took on average 856 milliseconds to respond to L2 words previously heard in the course of the experiment (repeated words), but required 901 milliseconds to respond to L2 words not previously heard in the course of the experiment (unrepeated words). In this case, a researcher may conclude that the participants' prior experience with repeated spoken words somehow enabled them to respond to these words faster than to unrepeated words. A researcher may then estimate the extent of this facilitation, or the magnitude of the auditory priming effect, at 45 milliseconds (901–856). Of course, what exactly is facilitated in terms of processing due to repetition clearly depends on the task that participants are asked to perform. For example, if a task requires participants to identify spoken words, then the auditory priming effect will be measured as the extent to which repeated words are identified more accurately than unrepeated words. This effect will then be measured as the proportion of words identified correctly rather than as speed of response in milliseconds.

Typically, auditory (repetition) priming experiments consist of two phases: the study phase and the test phase. In the study phase, participants perform a language processing task. Following a short delay or a distractor task, they perform an identical or similar task in the test phase. In this task, some of the presented words are identical to the words heard in the study phase, and some other words are those that were not previously heard in the study phase, usually with an equal number of each. As discussed earlier, *auditory priming* refers to the processing facilitation, defined as faster and/or more accurate responses for words repeated between the study and the test task, relative to words presented only in the test task.

What are some of the processing tasks that may be used as the study and test tasks of an auditory priming experiment? It appears that some processing tasks are more suited than others for detecting and measuring auditory priming effects. We turn to this issue next.

In descriptions of processing tasks used in priming (and other) research, a frequently drawn distinction is that between perceptual (data driven) and conceptual (conceptually driven) memory tests (Blaxton, 1989; Roediger, Weldon, & Challis, 1989; Tulving & Schacter, 1990). Perceptual tests of memory are those that largely require a language user to rely on form-related, perceptual characteristics of verbal or non-verbal stimuli to perform a task. Examples of perceptual tasks include tests of word identification, especially under degraded listening or viewing conditions (e.g. when words are masked in background noise), or word fragment completion (e.g. e_e_h_ _t to be completed as *elephant*). To complete these tasks successfully, language users need to attend more to the auditory properties of a spoken word or to the orthographic properties of a word fragment than to its semantic, conceptual properties. Thus, language users' performance on perceptual tasks is largely contingent on their ability to resolve form-related, perceptual details of verbal or non-verbal stimuli.

On the other hand, conceptual tasks largely appeal to language users' ability to establish or activate semantic or conceptual relations between the studied event and the already-known information. Exemplifying conceptual tasks of memory are tasks requiring language users to generate an instance of a specific semantic category, to translate a word, or to answer a general-knowledge question. Examples of conceptual tasks include word-association tests in which participants are asked to produce the first word that is associated in their minds with a given word (e.g. *salt*—?) or tests requiring participants to answer a general-knowledge question, such as, *What animal did Hannibal use to help him cross the Alps in his attack on Rome?* (Blaxton, 1989). To complete these tasks successfully, language users need to rely more on semantic, conceptual properties of the given linguistic information than on its perceptual or auditory (or orthographic) properties. Thus, language users' performance on conceptual tests depends on their ability to establish and maintain semantic or conceptual details of verbal or non-verbal stimuli.

Although, in actuality, any given task does not involve pure perceptual or conceptual processing (Craik, Moscovitch, & McDowd, 1994), but instead exemplifies a complicated interaction between the two (Challis, Velichkovsky, & Craik, 1996), the perceptual–conceptual task distinction is nevertheless relevant to describing priming phenomena. This distinction is relevant because auditory priming (as many other repetition priming phenomena) mainly resides at the level of perceptual, form-related, data-driven processing, its effects being most prominent when perceptual or form-related properties of spoken words are maintained across episodes of experience (Goldinger, 1996a; Kirsner & Dunn, 1985). Therefore, to estimate auditory priming effects, which are perceptual in nature, a researcher would have to employ tasks that require participants to engage in perceptual processing. This match between the processing operations called on by a task and the processing operations being measured in an experiment, as many would argue (Franks, Bilbrey, Lien, & McNamara, 2000; Morris, Bransford, & Franks, 1977), is crucial for the study of auditory priming.

In the remainder of this section, we briefly describe three auditory processing tasks that, to a greater or lesser extent, rely on perceptual processing and are therefore suitable for detecting and measuring auditory priming effects. In describing each task, we outline the materials, variables, and analyses associated with it.

Word Stem/Fragment Completion Task

Materials and procedure. Auditory word stem or fragment completion tasks have been used in several investigations of auditory priming, albeit thus far only in the L1 (Bassili et al., 1989; Church & Schacter, 1994;

Habib & Nyberg, 1997; Mulligan et al., 2007; Pilotti et al., 2000; Schacter & Church, 1992). These tasks consist of two subtasks: study and test. In the study task, listeners hear individually presented spoken words at a pre-defined presentation rate (e.g. every 5 seconds). In the test task, they hear a set of word stems (usually the first syllable of a word; e.g. *won* for *wonderful*) or a set of word fragments (e.g. *wo____er_ul* for *wonderful*, where _ designates an amount of silence equivalent to the deleted portion of the word). Word stems and fragments are created in speech editing software (e.g. *Audacity, CoolEdit 2000*) by deleting certain portions of the word or by replacing them with silence. Some of the presented word stems or fragments represent words that were previously heard in the study task, others represent words not heard previously in the study task. Upon hearing each word, listeners complete the presented word stem or word fragment with the first word that comes to mind by writing it down on paper, by typing it into a box on a computer screen, or by saying it out loud. A schematic illustration of this task appears in figure 2.1.

Dependent variables. Dependent variables (also known as *response variables*) are those variables that are being measured in the course of an experiment. The dependent variable commonly used in the test phase of a word stem/fragment completion task is word completion accuracy, measured as a proportion of completed stems (or fragments). A researcher typically computes two proportions for each participant. One proportion represents the ratio of the number of stems (or fragments) for repeated words completed correctly to the total number of stems (or fragments)

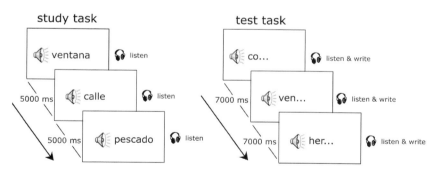

Figure 2.1 A schematic illustration of a word stem completion task in Spanish (modeled after Schacter & Church, 1992). This illustration depicts the following sequence of events: (1) in the study task, participants listen to words presented one at a time with a 5-sec interval, (2) there is a short break between the study and the test task, (3) in the test task, participants listen to word stems presented one at a time with a 7-sec interval; upon hearing each stem, they complete it with the first word that comes to mind. Word fragments (*co, ven, her*) represent a repeated word *ventana* (window) and unrepeated words *cocina* (kitchen) and *hermosa* (pretty).

for repeated words. The other represents the ratio of the number of stems (or fragments) for unrepeated words completed correctly to the total number of stems (or fragments) for unrepeated words (Bassili et al., 1989; Church & Schacter, 1994; Habib & Nyberg, 1997; Pilotti et al., 2000; Schacter & Church, 1992).

Independent variables. Independent variables (also known as *manipulated variables*) are those variables that are selected by a researcher to determine their relationship to a dependent variable. One set of independent variables that a researcher may employ to explore auditory priming in stem/fragment completion tasks (and in other tasks reviewed later in this chapter) involves some contextual characteristics of the study phase of the task. These characteristics are usually described in terms of the *processing orientation* (also known as *encoding manipulation*) that listeners engage in during their initial exposure to spoken words in the study phase of the task. The important assumption here is that auditory priming may differ for words that listeners experience under the instructions to attend to word meaning (conceptual encoding manipulation) versus words that listeners experience under the instruction to attend to word form (perceptual encoding manipulation). Underlying this assumption is the idea that the precise nature of the "learning" experience listeners engage in may have an impact on the degree to which they benefit from spoken words.

Researchers typically manipulate processing orientation in auditory priming tasks by asking listeners to rate spoken words in the study phase of the task for a number of properties. For example, a researcher may ask listeners to rate spoken words for the perceived degree of pleasantness or clarity on 7-point scales (see pp. 29–30 for details of one such task). A summary of variables used to explore encoding manipulation in a selection of published auditory priming studies appears in table 2.1. Sample results form a word stem/fragment completion task are provided in box 2.2.

Identification Task

Materials and procedure. An auditory identification task has been used in several previous investigations of auditory priming in both L1 (Church & Schacter, 1994; Goldinger, 1996a; Mulligan et al., 2007; Schacter & Church, 1992; Sheffert, 1998) and L2 (Ju & Church, 2001). This task consists of two subtasks as well. In the study task, listeners hear individually presented spoken words at a pre-defined presentation rate (e.g. every 5 seconds). In the test task, listeners hear another set of spoken words that contains words previously heard in the study phase and words not previously heard in the study phase. Upon hearing each word, listeners identify (recognize) the word by writing it down on paper, by typing it into a box on a computer screen, or by saying it out loud. A schematic illustration of an auditory identification task appears in figure 2.2.

Table 2.1 Encoding manipulation variables in published auditory priming studies

Conceptual encoding	L1 Studies	L2 Studies
Counting of word meanings	Schacter & Church (1992): Ex. 4, 5; Church & Schacter (1994): Ex. 3	
Word pleasantness rating	Schacter & Church (1992): Ex. 3; Habib & Nyberg (1997): Ex. 1	Trofimovich (2005): Ex. 2; Trofimovich & Gatbonton (2006); Trofimovich (2008)
Word familiarity rating	Pilotti et al. (2000)	
Classification (e.g. noun vs. adj.)	Schacter & Church (1992): Ex. 1, 2; Goldinger (1996a): Ex. 3	
Perceptual encoding	*L1 Studies*	*L2 Studies*
Pitch rating	Schacter & Church (1992): Ex. 1–3	
Loudness rating	Habib & Nyberg (1997): Ex. 1	
Initial phoneme classification	Goldinger (1996a): Ex. 3	
Speaker's gender classification	Goldinger (1996a): Ex. 3	
Enunciation clarity rating	Schacter & Church (1992): Ex. 4, 5; Church & Schacter (1994); Pilotti & Beyer (2002): Ex. 1, 2	Trofimovich (2005): Ex. 2; Trofimovich & Gatbonton (2006)

Note: Ex. = Experiment.

This design of an auditory identification task may not be the most ideal, however. This is because simply writing down words that are played back one at a time may turn out to be a very easy task for native speakers and proficient L2 learners alike. If so, then a researcher may find it very hard to detect any processing benefits due to auditory priming, not because these benefits are not there but because they are "masked" by participants' very accurate (and fast) performance. Psychologists term such performance as *ceiling performance* or a *ceiling effect*. A ceiling effect refers to a situation in which participants perform a task so well (close to the asymptote, or their best possible performance in accuracy or speed) that the task does not allow for any "resolution" to determine how participants' performance on the task might differ.

In order to avoid ceiling effects in an auditory identification task, researchers typically make the test phase of this task more challenging. This is usually accomplished in two ways: by masking spoken words in

Box 2.2 Sample results from an auditory word stem completion task

The results of an auditory word stem (or fragment) completion task can be reported in a tabular format. The following table (adapted from Experiment 3 in Schacter & Church, 1992) shows word stem completion rates for native English listeners who heard English words in the study phase of the task in two different encoding conditions: pleasantness rating (pleasant–unpleasant) and pitch rating (high–low).

Mean proportion of completed word stems as a function of encoding task

Encoding task	Repeated words	Unrepeated words
Pleasantness rating	.39	.14
Pitch rating	.27	.14
M	.33	.14

Overall, listeners appeared to be more likely to complete word stems for repeated words ($M = .33$) than for unrepeated words ($M = .14$). Listeners also appeared to be more likely to complete word stems for repeated words after pleasantness rating, a conceptual encoding task ($M = .39$) than after pitch rating, a perceptual encoding task ($M = .27$).

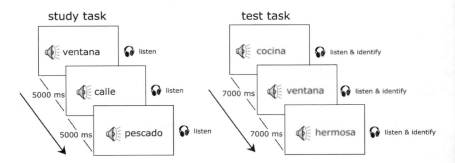

Figure 2.2 A schematic illustration of an auditory word identification task in Spanish (modeled after Schacter & Church, 1992). Words printed in blurred letters represent degraded spoken words (masked in noise or low-pass filtered): a repeated word *ventana* and unrepeated words *cocina* and *hermosa*. This illustration depicts the following sequence of events: (1) in the study task, participants listen to words presented one at a time with a 5-sec interval, (2) there is a short break between the study and the test task, (3) in the test task, participants listen to degraded spoken words presented one at a time with a 7-sec interval; upon hearing each word, they attempt to identify it.

background noise (Ex. 2 in Goldinger, 1996a; Ex. 1, 2 in Schacter & Church, 1992; Ex. 2 in Sheffert, 1998; Pilotti et al., 2000) or by low-pass filtering spoken words (Ex. 1–3 in Church & Schacter, 1994; Mulligan et al., 2007; Ex. 1, 2 in Pilotti & Beyer, 2002; Pilotti et al., 2000; Ex. 2 in Sheffert, 1998). Background noise (also called *white noise*) adds a constant level of static noise to the speech signal. White noise, termed by analogy with white light (light that comprises all colors of the rainbow), is a complex sound that usually incorporates equivalent amounts of all audible tones. Words masked in white noise sound as if they were played over a radio with a fair amount of hissing static noise. An illustration of a sound masked in background noise appears in figure 2.3.

Low-pass filtering, in turn, refers to physical alteration of a speech signal by means of speech editing software (e.g. *CoolEdit 2000*, *Praat*) whereby all energy components of the speech signal above a specific frequency value (specified in Hz) are removed. Low-pass filtering typically preserves suprasegmental aspects of the speech signal, including intonation (F0 contours or contours in lower-frequency harmonics) and stress timing information, while removing most of its segmental content (see Trofimovich & Baker, 2006, 2007, for uses of low-pass filtering in L2 research). Low-pass filtered words usually sound muffled, as if spoken in an adjacent room, just out of earshot (e.g. Munro, 1995). An illustration of a low-pass filtered word appears in figure 2.4.

Dependent variables. A dependent variable typically used in the test phase of an auditory identification task is word identification accuracy, measured as the proportion of words identified correctly. Two proportions are usually computed for each participant. One proportion represents the ratio of the number of repeated words identified correctly to the total number of repeated words. The other represents the ratio of the number of unrepeated words identified correctly to the total number of unrepeated words.

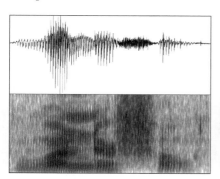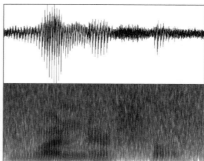

Figure 2.3 A waveform and a spectrogram of the word *wonderful* spoken in the clear (left panel) and of the same word spoken against background noise (right panel).

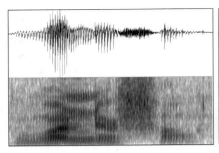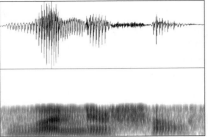

Figure 2.4 A waveform and a spectrogram of the word *wonderful* spoken in the clear (left panel) and of the same word after low-pass filtering (right panel). Low-pass filtering removed all energy components at frequencies above 2,000 Hz (2 kHz).

Independent variables. Some independent variables that a researcher may use to examine auditory priming in an identification task (and in other tasks as well) involve various auditory properties of words: (a) speaker's gender (male vs. female), (b) speaker's voice (e.g. male vs. another male, female vs. another female), (c) intonation (e.g. angry, happy, questioning or statement intonation), (d) pitch (e.g. high–low), or (e) loudness (loud–soft). The assumption here is that auditory priming may differ for repeated words that are exact replicas of each other versus repeated words that are not exactly the same (*ventana* spoken by a male, or in an angry intonation in the study task and *ventana* spoken by a female or in a neutral intonation in the test task). This assumption is central to auditory priming. Suppose, for example, that auditory priming effects are found in both these cases: a slightly larger effect for exact repetitions of spoken words and a somewhat smaller (albeit significant) effect for non-exact repetitions of spoken words (e.g. same words that nonetheless differ in speaker's gender, voice, pitch, etc.). In this case, a researcher can claim that listeners make both *abstract* and *specific* matches among spoken words. That is, listeners appear sensitive not only to repeated words, but also to their contextual details (speaker's voice, gender, pitch), being thus capable of benefiting from *both* sources of information (repeated words and repeated voices, for instance) in their processing of spoken words.

Researchers typically manipulate auditory properties of words by creating several sets of spoken words as stimuli in their experiments. For example, researchers can record the same words spoken by several speakers (e.g. several females, or males and females). Researchers can also record spoken words uttered in different intonation patterns (e.g. happy vs. sad, statement vs. questioning). Likewise, researchers can manipulate audio recorded spoken words in speech editing software by increasing or decreasing their loudness or altering slightly their pitch. The resulting words are then carefully combined in counterbalanced experimental lists and are prepared for presentation to listeners. The goal here is to determine if listeners would demonstrate auditory priming effects both for identical, exact repetitions of words and for their non-identical repetitions (i.e. when the same word is later spoken in a different voice or in a different intonation). A summary of variables used to explore various auditory properties of spoken words in a selection of published auditory priming studies appears in table 2.2, and sample results of an identification task are illustrated in box 2.3.

Repetition (Naming) Task

Materials and procedure. Auditory repetition tasks have been used in several investigations of auditory priming in both L1 (Goldinger, 1998; McLennan et al., 2003; Mullenix, Pisoni, & Martin, 1989; Onishi, Chambers, & Fisher, 2002; Ryalls & Pisoni, 1997) and L2 (Trofimovich, 2005, 2008; Trofimovich & Gatbonton, 2006). These tasks also consist of two subtasks. In the study task, listeners hear individually presented spoken words at a pre-defined presentation rate (e.g. every 5 seconds). In the test task, they hear another set of spoken words that contains both words previously heard in the study phase and words not previously heard in the study phase. Upon hearing each word, listeners repeat it out loud as quickly and as rapidly as possible by speaking into a microphone connected to an audio recorder or to a voice-activated timer. A schematic illustration of this task appears in figure 2.5.

Dependent variables. The dependent variables commonly used in the repetition task are measures of response latency or reaction time (RT). Response latency provides a measure of processing time, or the amount

Table 2.2 Auditory properties manipulated in auditory priming tasks

Auditory properties	L1 Studies	L2 Studies
Speaker's gender	Schacter & Church (1992); Church & Schacter (1994): Ex 1; Pilotti et al. (2000); Pilotti & Beyer (2002): Ex. 1, 2	Ju & Church (2001); Trofimovich (2005); Trofimovich & Gatbonton (2006); Trofimovich (2008)
Intonation	Church & Schacter (1994): Ex. 2	
Pitch	Church & Schacter (1994): Ex. 3, 4	
Speaker's voice (same gender)	Sheffert (1998): Ex. 1, 2	
Loudness	Church & Schacter (1994): Ex. 5	

Note: Ex. = Experiment.

Box 2.3 Sample results form an auditory identification task

The results of an auditory identification task can be reported in a tabular format as well. The following table (adapted from Experiment 1 in Church & Schacter, 1994) shows identification rates of low-pass filtered words for native English listeners. Half of the words repeated in the test task are spoken by the same speaker as in the study task (same voice); the other half are spoken by a different speaker (different voice).

Mean proportion of identified words as a function of speaker's voice

	Repeated words		Unrepeated words
Same voice	Different voice	M	
.80	.72	.76	.59

Overall, listeners are more likely to identify repeated words (*M* = .76) than unrepeated words (*M* = .59); they are also more likely to do so when repeated words are spoken in the same voice (.80 vs. .59) than when they are spoken in a different voice (.72 vs. .59).

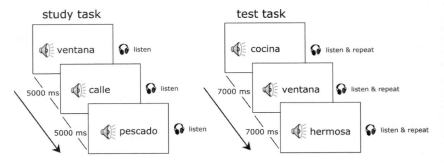

Figure 2.5 A schematic illustration of a repetition task in Spanish (modeled after Trofimovich, 2005). This illustration depicts the following sequence of events: (1) in the study task, participants listen to words presented one at a time with a 5-sec interval, (2) there is a short break between the study and the test task, (3) in the test task, participants listen to words presented one at a time with a 7-sec interval; upon hearing each word, they repeat it as rapidly and as accurately as possible.

of time the listener needs to recognize the spoken word and to initiate its repetition (see Sternberg, 1966, 1969). By comparing response latencies for repeated and unrepeated words a researcher could determine whether repeated words require less processing time than unrepeated words. Two response latency measures are commonly used in repetition tasks. A schematic representation of these variables appears in figure 2.6.

The first measure is *total latency*, defined as the length of time (in milliseconds) between the onset (beginning) of the stimulus word and the onset of the repetition (see Mullenix et al., 1989). This measure includes *both* the duration of the stimulus word and the time that it takes the listener to repeat it. Researchers should be careful about using this measure if speaking rate is not controlled as a variable in the construction of stimulus materials. The reason for this is that stimulus words spoken at a faster rate are shorter than words spoken at a slower rate. Therefore, total latency will vary not only as a function of how quickly the participant can process spoken words but also as a function of how short the stimulus words are. Obviously, the processing of a shorter word will begin earlier than the processing of a longer word. A careful researcher would want to minimize this second contribution to total latency by ensuring that, across all experimental lists, all stimulus words are approximately the same in spoken duration. The second measure is *offset-to-onset latency*, defined as the length of time between the offset (end) of the stimulus word and the onset of the repetition (see Onishi et al., 2002; Ryalls & Pisoni, 1997; Trofimovich, 2005). This measure does not include the duration of the stimulus word and, therefore, is insensitive to differences in how quickly or slowly stimulus words are pronounced. A sample auditory priming study using a repetition task is presented in box 2.5.

Independent variables. Other independent variables that a researcher may use to examine auditory priming in any auditory priming task involve various lexical characteristics of words: word frequency (the relative frequency of occurrence of words in a given language), word neighborhood density (the extent to which words have similar-sounding lexical "neighbors" in a language), word length (measured as number of syllables per word or as the actual time, in milliseconds, it takes a speaker to articulate the word), or word familiarity (the extent to which the participants are familiar with words or know them well). The assumption here is that auditory priming effects may differ, for instance, for words that are more

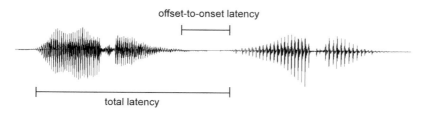

Figure 2.6 A schematic illustration of response latency measures used in a repetition task. The two waveforms represent the stimulus word *water* spoken by a female speaker and repeated by a male speaker.

versus less frequent, for words that have many similar-sounding neighbors (e.g. *hoot, mace, moan*) versus those having few (e.g. *work, long, both*), for longer versus shorter words, or words that participants are more versus less familiar with.

Researchers typically manipulate lexical properties of words by creating several sets of spoken words as stimuli in their experiment. For example, researchers can record words that are more frequent and those that are less frequent in the language. Researchers can also manipulate word familiarity by presenting their participants with words they know and those they do not know (effectively, novel words). The goal here is to determine whether listeners will demonstrate auditory priming effects both for more frequent and less frequent words, or for words they know and for words they do not. To date, very few auditory priming studies have explicitly manipulated lexical variables. Among notable exceptions are Goldinger's (1998) and Ju and Luce's (2006) studies. Word frequency was manipulated as a variable in Experiment 1 in Goldinger (1998) and in Experiment 3 in Ju and Luce (2006); word familiarity (word/nonword) was manipulated as a variable in Experiments 2 and 3 in Goldinger (1998; see also Bird & Williams, 2002). Sample results from a repetition (naming) task are provided in box 2.4, and a representative L2 auditory priming study is summarized in box 2.5.

Issues to Consider in Auditory Priming Research

Selecting an Appropriate Task

Each of the auditory priming tasks discussed above is based on certain assumptions. As was discussed above (see pp. 32–34), one assumption common to all tasks is that they largely rely on perceptual rather than conceptual processing of auditory information. Besides this important assumption, the tests differ in several other respects, including the psycholinguistic (processing) demands they place on a participant, the nature of the data they yield, and the types of data analyses possible. For example, auditory stem/fragment completion and auditory identification tasks typically yield only accuracy measures. By contrast, naming tasks yield both accuracy and reaction time (processing speed) measures. If a researcher is interested in making claims about the speed of auditory processing, using an auditory priming paradigm, then naming tasks may be chosen over other priming tasks.

Another consideration important for deciding among tasks pertains to the nature of the processing operations involved in each task. Auditory identification tasks, for example, rely on perceptual processing. In contrast, naming tasks ostensibly involve both perceptual and articulatory (production) components.

Box 2.4 Sample results from a repetition (naming) task

The results of auditory priming tasks (including repetition tasks) can also be reported in a graphical format. The following figure (adapted from figure 1, Experiment 1 in Trofimovich & Gatbonton, 2006) depicts mean priming effects for two learner groups in English (L1) and Spanish (L2). Mean priming effects were calculated by subtracting mean offset-to-onset latency for repeated words from mean offset-to-onset latency for unrepeated words (the higher the bar, the more processing facilitation).

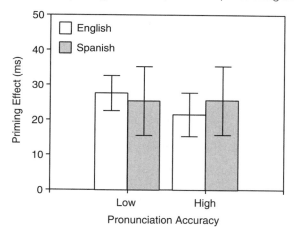

Mean priming effects in English and Spanish as a function of learner pronunciation accuracy. Brackets enclose ± 1 SE.

Sample L2 Auditory Priming Study

Box 2.5 Sample L2 auditory priming study

Trofimovich, P., & Gatbonton, E. (2006). Repetition and focus on form in processing L2 Spanish words: Implications for pronunciation instruction. *The Modern Language Journal, 90*, 519–535.

Background: Previous research has demonstrated that repetition and focus on form (explicit attention to linguistic features in the input directed to the learner) are important factors in L2 learning. The objective of this paper is to discuss the role of these two factors in learning L2 pronunciation from information-processing and pedagogical perspectives.

Research questions: Do L2 learners benefit from repeated experiences with spoken L2 input? Do such benefits depend on learners attention to such input?

(Box 2.5 Continued)

Box 2.5 Continued

Participants: 60 L2 learners of Spanish (low-intermediate level), all L1 speakers of English. Half had a higher and half had a lower pronunciation ability in Spanish.

Materials: 72 English and 72 Spanish words. All Spanish words were familiar to the learners, as determined in a word translation task. The English words were recorded by 6 native English speakers from the United States and the Spanish words by 6 native Spanish speakers from Spain.

Procedure: In Experiment 1, 20 learners completed an auditory repetition task. They first listened to 36 English (or Spanish) words. They then listened to 72 English (or Spanish) words and repeated them as rapidly and as accurately as possible. Half of the words were previously heard, the other half were not. In Experiment 2, 40 participants completed the same task, with one exception. As the learners listened to 36 English (or Spanish) words, their attention was drawn to either word form (focus on form) or word meaning (focus on meaning). Auditory priming is established in this task if participants repeat words that were previously heard more rapidly than those that were not heard previously.

Analysis: The dependent variable was offset-to-onset response latency. Response latencies were calculated as a function of participant pronunciation ability (high, low), language (English, Spanish), and (in Experiment 2) attentional orientation (focus on form, focus on meaning).

Results: In Experiment 1, equivalent auditory priming effects were found in English and Spanish for all participants. In Experiment 2, auditory priming effects were found in all conditions, except in Spanish for the low pronunciation ability participants who focused on meaning.

Discussion: L2 learners appear to benefit from repeated L2 phonological information. However, this benefit may be minimal under instructions to attend to the meaning of spoken input, especially for low pronunciation ability learners. Sensitivity to repeated L2 phonological information may require an individuation of form-related properties in L2 input, at least for low pronunciation ability learners.

Implications: One pedagogical application of these findings may involve creating and using tasks (and, on a larger scale, designing L2 learning contexts) that include comparable information-processing requirements at the time of language learning and of use (for examples, see Gatbonton & Segalowitz, 1988, 2005, and Lightbown, 1998).

Yet another issue important to consider in deciding among the tasks, particularly in planning an L2 auditory priming study, is how naturalistic and doable a given task is for a given population of L2 learners. For instance, completing word stems or fragments may be a slightly less common task than repeating words out loud. To give another example, if a researcher chooses an auditory identification task in which spoken words are degraded by low-pass filtering or by adding white noise, then this researcher should consider whether L2 learners would have more difficulty with this task than would native speakers. Such a difference in task difficulty may have negative consequences for the validity of an auditory priming experiment. Some of the factors to consider when deciding among the three auditory priming tasks are listed in table 2.3.

Counterbalancing of Task Materials

An important issue to be considered in designing any auditory priming task involves counterbalancing of task materials. Counterbalancing refers to rotating materials across experimental conditions (e.g. repeated vs. unrepeated words, words spoken by a male vs. a female). Counterbalancing of task materials is important because it helps reduce potential idiosyncratic (negative) effects of task materials on task outcomes. Suppose, for example, a researcher wishes to compare identification accuracy for repeated versus unrepeated words and asks *all* participants to recognize one set of repeated words (e.g. *work, long*) and another set of unrepeated words (e.g. *hoot, moan*). The results of this experiment obviously would not be valid because the words that the participants encountered as repeated (*work, long*) are somehow easier (i.e. more frequent, less confusable with similar-sounding words) than those that the participants

Table 2.3 Factors to consider when deciding among auditory priming tasks

Consideration	Appropriate task(s)
Both accuracy and response latency data	Repetition (naming)
Accuracy data only	Word stem/fragment completion, identification
Comprehension processes involved	Word stem/fragment completion, identification
Both comprehension and production processes involved	Repetition (naming)
Modification of materials (low-pass filtering or noise) needed to increase task difficulty, less "natural" task	Word stem/fragment completion, identification
No modification of materials needed, more "natural" task	Repetition (naming)
Easy scoring	Word stem/fragment completion, identification
Tape recorder or voice-activated millisecond timer required	Repetition (naming)

encountered as unrepeated (*hoot, moan*). Thus, the participants' identification rates will likely have little to do with auditory priming. Instead, they probably will reflect the specific properties of the words the participants encountered as repeated and unrepeated. Counterbalancing of task materials could help a researcher avoid this bias. In a counterbalanced experiment, participants encounter an equal number of easier and harder words in all experimental conditions (e.g. repeated and unrepeated).

The following example illustrates how to counterbalance materials for a simple auditory priming experiment. The goal of this experiment is to examine auditory priming for repeated and unrepeated words spoken by two different speakers: a male and a female. The researcher, therefore, needs to counterbalance (rotate) all of the materials in this experiment so that they appear in all conditions defined by the two variables: word type (repeated vs. unrepeated) and speaker's gender (male vs. female). For illustrative purposes, the materials in this sample experiment consist of eight words, recorded by a male and a female speaker (see table 2.4).

To counterbalance these experimental materials, the researcher should first divide the eight words into two equal sets. These sets are depicted as Set 1 and Set 2 in table 2.5. Then, the researcher should split each set again into two equal subsets. These subsets are designated in table 2.5 by capital letters (A, B, C, etc.). At this point, the researcher is ready to start constructing several versions of the study and test lists. Recall that the test list is usually twice as a long as the study list. The test list contains all of the words from the study list (repeated words) plus the same number of unrepeated words.

The rules here are simple. First, the researcher should strive to get an equal number of words spoken by a male and a female speaker to appear on the study lists (e.g. word sets AD, BC, EH, or FG satisfy this requirement). Second, the researcher should try to get an equal number of repeated and unrepeated words to appear on the test lists (e.g. word sets AD + EH or BC + FG satisfy this requirement). For example, the

Table 2.4 Sample word stimuli for a simple auditory priming study

Male speaker	Female speaker
street	street
car	car
jam	jam
door	door
pen	pen
lamp	lamp
plane	plane
fox	fox

Table 2.5 Sample word sets for a simple auditory priming study

Set 1				Set 2			
Male speaker		Female speaker		Male speaker		Female speaker	
street car	A	pen lamp	C	pen lamp	E	street car	G
jam door	B	plane fox	D	plane fox	F	jam door	H

Table 2.6 Counterbalanced list versions

List versions	Study list	Test list	
		Repeated	Unrepeated
Version 1	AD	AD	EH
Version 2	BC	BC	FG
Version 3	EH	EH	AD
Version 4	FG	FG	BC

researcher can choose the word sets AD as one version of the study list (4 words) and can match this list with the sets AD and EH as the test list (8 words). The researcher can then choose the word sets BC as another version of the study list (4 words) and can match this list with the sets BC and FG as the test list (8 words). Table 2.6 presents four such possible study and test list versions. In each version, the study list consists of four words; the test lists consists of eight words (half repeated, half unrepeated). In each list, exactly half of the words are spoken by a female and half are spoken by a male. The experimental materials are now counterbalanced. What this means is that, across all four versions, the study and test lists contain an equal number of words spoken by a male and a female speaker, and each word appears equally frequently in the study and test lists.

Now that the counterbalanced lists of study materials are ready, the researcher needs to ensure that two more requirements are met prior to conducting this experiment. The first requirement is that the words in each study list and test list are randomized. Randomization helps minimize unwanted order effects. Suppose that the repeated words on the test list were presented in the same order as in the study list. It is likely that the participants' memory for these repeated words would be enhanced just because they appear in both lists in a fixed order. The second requirement is that an equal number of participants should be randomly assigned to each of the study-test list versions. Random assignment of participants to study-test list versions will ensure that no subset of participants will be exposed to any list version more often than to others.

Equal Baseline Performance

An important issue to be considered in designing auditory priming tasks that include words presented in noise or words that are low-pass filtered (namely, auditory identification tasks) concerns deciding exactly how much noise to add to spoken words or how extensively to low-pass filter them. The purpose of degrading speech by adding noise or by low-pass filtering is to make the identification task harder for the listener. It does not mean, however, that a certain amount of noise or a particular degree of low-pass filtering will make the task *equally* hard for all listeners. For example, older adults may require slightly less degraded spoken words than younger adults to demonstrate comparable levels of word identification accuracy (Pilotti & Beyer, 2002). Similarly, adult speakers of a language may tolerate more noise or a more severe degree of low-pass filtering than child speakers (Church & Fisher, 1998) or L2 learners.

Why is establishing equal task difficulty important then? Suppose, for example, that a researcher wishes to compare auditory priming effects in native speakers and L2 learners. To do so, the researcher tests native speakers and L2 learners in an auditory identification task, with words in the test phase of the experiment presented in noise. If the same degree of noise added to spoken words overall makes this task much harder for L2 learners than for native speakers (presumably because L2 learners are less skilled than are native speakers at perceiving L2 words), this researcher would then likely estimate auditory priming effects inaccurately. L2 learners may, in fact, show a disproportionately large auditory priming effect in comparison to native speakers because the task is overall much harder for them (see Chapman, Chapman, Curran, & Miller, 1994, for theoretical justifications). This large priming effect would thus be an artifact of the procedure used and would not reflect a genuine difference (whatever it may be) between L2 learners and native speakers. This hypothetical example illustrates an important consideration to be taken into account in designing tasks to measure auditory priming (not necessarily an auditory identification task): the task should be equally difficulty for all listeners.

One way to ensure that the task is equally difficult for both L2 learners and native speakers is to compare identification accuracy for unprimed (unrepeated) words. Listeners' performance on these words serves as a baseline for estimating priming effects. If L2 learners and native speakers are equally accurate in their identification of unprimed (unrepeated) words, then the task is equally difficult for them. In practical terms, this means that a researcher wishing to use an auditory identification task to measure auditory priming needs to do a fair amount of pilot testing to ensure comparable levels of word degradation for native speakers and for L2 learners. This also means that a researcher would need to create two sets of materials for the study phase of the auditory identification task: one (more mildly degraded) for low-proficiency L2 learners and the other (more severely degraded) for high-proficiency L2 learners and native speakers, for example. Table 2.7 summarizes the values that have been used in previous investigations of auditory priming to determine the amounts of noise added to spoken words and the extent of low-pass filtering applied to them. A value of noise degradation most commonly used in previously published studies is –5 decibel (dB) signal-to-noise ratio. This means that the level of noise is 5 dB louder than that of the original words masked in it. Values of low-pass filtering commonly used in previously published studies range between a very severe value of 0.8 kHz (Pilotti & Beyer, 2002) to a less severe value of 2.5 kHz (Sheffert, 1998).

Matching Test Materials

Lexical variables deserve lots of attention in designing auditory priming tasks even if they are not manipulated directly. Even if researchers do not wish to determine auditory priming effects for high versus low frequency words, for example, they should still match all test materials for word

Table 2.7 Values for amounts of noise and degrees of low-pass filtering

Degradation	Values	Studies
Noise	–5 dB SPL signal-to-noise ratio	Goldinger (1996a): Ex. 2; Sheffert (1998): Ex. 1; Pilotti et al. (2000)
	0 dB SPL signal-to-noise ratio	Ryalls & Pisoni (1997): Ex. 2
Low-pass filtering	0.8 kHz for young adults	Pilotti & Beyer (2002)
	1.6 kHz for older adults	Pilotti & Beyer (2002)
	1.0 kHz for adults	Pilotti et al. (2000); Mulligan et al. (2007)
	2.0 kHz for adults	Church & Schacter (1994): Ex. 1, 2, 3
	2.5 kHz for adults	Sheffert (1998): Ex. 2
	"mild" low-pass filtering for children	Church & Fisher (1998)
	"severe" low-pass filtering for adults	Church & Fisher (1998)

Note: Ex. = Experiment.

frequency and (preferably) some other lexical variables. That is, they should ensure that the words that appear in the study and test tasks are comparable in terms of their mean frequency counts, neighborhood density estimates, syllable length, and participants' familiarity with these words. Suppose a researcher used only highly frequent (or very familiar) words in the study task (then repeating half of them in the test task) but included only low-frequency (or highly unfamiliar) words as unrepeated words in the test task. In this case, priming effects will be measured inaccurately because the infrequent or unfamiliar words would be harder to process than very frequent or familiar words regardless of any priming benefits.

There are numerous sources to consult for word frequency counts. These include, for example, the Brown corpus (Kucera & Francis, 1967), the CELEX database, or the BNC (British National Corpus). Several corpora now offer spoken frequency counts in addition to written frequency counts (e.g. BNC). It is quite likely that spoken frequency counts, as opposed to written frequency counts, provide a more precise estimate of how frequently listeners may be exposed to spoken words. Neighborhood density may be estimated using a simple computational metric, described in detail by Vitevitch (2002, see also Luce & Pisoni, 1998). Briefly, neighborhood density is counted for a given word by estimating how many real words can be created by the substitution, addition, or deletion of any single phoneme in this given word. For example, the words *bat*, *cab*, and *kit* (among many others) are neighbors of the word *cat*. A word is said to come from a dense neighborhood if it has many neighbors; a word is considered to come from a sparse neighborhood if it has few neighbors. Word familiarity for native English speakers can be checked by consulting word familiarity ratings found in Nusbaum, Pisoni, and Davis (1984). Non-native speakers' familiarity with L2 words can be checked directly by asking the participants themselves to rate their familiarity with words (e.g. using a Likert scale) or to translate words into their L1, preferably after they complete the priming experiment. Alternatively, word familiarity ratings can be obtained from the same population of non-native speakers, for example, those drawn from the same proficiency-level courses.

Additional Uses of Auditory Priming Methods

As discussed in chapter 1 (see pp. 4–6), language, population, and task are the factors that influence the ecological validity of priming research. Therefore, at least one of the goals of future auditory priming studies should be to extend the uses of priming methods to various languages, different populations of language users, and diverse tasks. To date, auditory priming research has predominantly focused on English and has targeted native speakers: children (Church & Fisher, 1998), younger and older adults (Pilotti & Beyer, 2002), and individuals with neurological disorders or brain damage (Swick, Miller, & Larsen, 2004). To extend the findings of these studies to bilingual and L2 processing and learning, various populations of participants (e.g. learners of different ages, stable bilinguals, multilinguals) should be investigated. In addition, in order to positively impact the ecological validity of priming research, future L2 auditory priming studies should ideally test participants in several priming tasks within the same study (e.g. Pilotti et al., 2000). In the following sections, we describe several areas of future research. Research in these areas will not only extend what we know about auditory priming but could also positively impact the ecological validity of auditory priming methods.

Studying Auditory Priming for Novel versus Known Words

There are several avenues of research to be explored using auditory priming methods. One of these is studying L2 learners' sensitivity to phonological information in novel L2 words. Previous research on auditory priming has focused thus far solely on the processing of words that are familiar to the learners (e.g. Trofimovich, 2005, 2008; Trofimovich & Gatbonton, 2006). If auditory priming is indeed a mechanism of L2 spoken word processing and learning, then it is important to investigate whether L2 learners benefit from their experience with novel, unknown L2 words and whether such benefits (if any) differ as a function of learners' L2 proficiency. Are learners sensitive to phonological information available in spoken L2 words as they are encountering them in speech for the first few times? Do such sensitivities depend on the number of encounters with spoken words, on learners' proficiency, on the precise nature of such encounters (i.e. whether a word is spoken all the time by the same speaker or by multiple speakers)? There is some evidence (see Barcroft & Sommers, 2005; Sommers & Barcroft, 2007) that L2 vocabulary learning requires exposure to multiple instances of words spoken by multiple speakers or even in multiple voice types (nasal, whispered, or articulated at a fast speech rate). An auditory priming study of new L2 word learning could extend these findings by investigating whether auditory word priming, as an implicit learning mechanism, indeed supports new L2 word learning.

Auditory Priming in Meaningful Contexts

Another topic to be explored using auditory priming tasks concerns L2 learners' sensitivity to the phonological information that is available in contexts that are longer than individual spoken words. Although the processing of individual spoken words is informative of the kinds of information listeners might be sensitive to in speech, such processing is clearly not representative of what is typical of normal, everyday language use. Indeed, speakers and listeners communicate by encoding and decoding complex messages as part of larger units of discourse, for example, when engaging in dyadic or multi-speaker conversations, when telling stories, or listening to university lectures. Thus, it is important to investigate whether L2 learners benefit from their experience with spoken language as part of larger, meaningful discourse. Are learners sensitive to phonological information available in L2 speech in a meaningful (e.g. sentential) context? Does a meaningful context reduce or obliterate processing benefits for spoken language (see Heredia & McLaughlin, 1992; Smith, 1991), making it harder for L2 learners to encode particular details of L2 phonology? To answer these questions, instead of single words, researchers may need to employ contextualized materials (e.g. a short dialogue, a brief story) in future auditory priming studies. The findings of such studies could yield answers suggesting whether and to what extent learners are sensitive to phonological information in contexts that emphasize sound-based properties of L2 input (e.g. presentation of individual words) versus those that emphasize their meaning-based properties (e.g. sentences or stories). Put in a larger perspective, such findings may reveal how form and meaning factors interact in L2 processing (cf. VanPatten, 1996) and what information learners could "extract" from the spoken input at any given time in their L2 development.

Auditory Priming and L2 Learning in Classroom Contexts

Perhaps one of the most interesting avenues of research to be pursued in future auditory priming studies relates to investigations of speech processing in the context of language learning and teaching. One example of such research may include investigations into the effectiveness of L2 pronunciation training using tasks that recognize the importance of learners gaining experience with spoken L2 input that is highly variable in nature (e.g. spoken in a variety of dialects, voices, intonation patterns, or speaking rates). An example of such learning tasks can be found in pronunciation training studies (e.g. Bradlow et al., 1997; Lively et al., 1994) that used numerous naturally produced words spoken by multiple speakers to train Japanese learners of English to discriminate English /r/ and /l/ (as in *right–light*), a difficult contrast for these learners. Another example includes the procedure used by Barcroft and Sommers (2005) to teach L2 vocabulary using multiple instances of words spoken by different speakers in several voice types (e.g. nasal, high pitched, whispered). Central to both these procedures is the claim that learners' experience with highly variable spoken input may help them generalize across multiple (non-identical) tokens of spoken L2 words to arrive at robust, native-like L2 phonological representations (see Goldinger, 1998, and Pisoni, 1997, for details). Future studies of auditory priming conducted in the context of such learning tasks may suggest whether and to what degree L2 learners can benefit from repeated (yet variable) input available to them.

Another example of such research may include investigations of speech processing in communicative language learning contexts, particularly those that capitalize in L2 teaching on repetition and the formulaic nature of language. One example of such communicative framework of L2 teaching was offered by Gatbonton and Segalowitz (1988, 2005). This framework—termed ACCESS (Automatization in Communicative Contexts of Essential Speech Segments)—involves an instructional process engaging the learner in activities that are genuinely communicative (involve an authentic need to exchange information), inherently repetitive (require repeated use of language to attain the task goal), and functionally formulaic (include language with high re-use potential in everyday interactions). The formulaic language used repetitively within a communicative exchange in ACCESS refers to the targeted set of L2 utterances (*essential speech segments*) that are elicited and practiced (hence, *automatization*) in genuinely *communicative contexts* so that they can be produced with greater accuracy and fluency. The genuinely communicative, inherently repetitive, and functionally formulaic requirements of ACCESS appear most appropriate for the teaching of L2 pronunciation, which should ideally include (besides a meaningful context) repetition and a focus on form (see Trofimovich & Gatbonton, 2006, for details).

How does a pedagogical framework like ACCESS relate to auditory priming research? Inherent in ACCESS is the requirement that communication involves repeated use of formulaic language. Repeated experiences with formulaic utterances ensure that learners experience numerous repetitions of reusable utterances, which promotes cognitively more efficient information processing in perception and production (Schneider & Chein, 2003). Repeated experiences with formulaic utterances also increase the likelihood that learners will notice the relationship between the form and function of utterances (Gass, Mackey, Alvarez-Torres, & Fernández-García, 1999; Jensen & Vinther, 2003), suggesting that repetition itself may serve as a form-focusing device underlying learning. Auditory priming research can be used to investigate this assumption so as to understand why a teaching framework like ACCESS, with its emphasis on *meaningful* communication, is not detrimental to the form-based processing benefits that underlie auditory priming. In other words, learners' accruing experiences with L2 speech within ACCESS should result in increasingly less emphasis on its meaning-related properties (as the meaning of each utterance used becomes progressively more familiar with its every repetition) and in increasingly more emphasis on its form-related properties, leading ideally to more form-based processing benefits. Auditory priming research could be instrumental in exploring this (and similar) hypotheses. All in all, future auditory priming studies conducted within communicative teaching contexts like ACCESS can help qualify and quantify the processing benefits of this type of communicative instruction.

Summary

In this chapter, we introduced auditory priming and the topics that have been explored in L1, bilingual and L2 research using auditory priming methods. We described the three experimental tasks used in auditory priming research (word stem/fragment completion, identification, and repetition) and pointed out some issues that researchers might consider when designing such tasks. Finally, we suggested some additional uses of auditory priming for L2 research. In the next chapter, we focus in more detail on semantic priming.

Follow-up Questions and Activities

1. Locate a published empirical study that investigated auditory priming in L1, bilingual, or L2 speech processing or acquisition and answer the following questions:

    a) What question(s) does the study attempt to address by using an auditory priming task?
    b) What specific task is used in this study? Is that task appropriate for the stated question(s)?
    c) What dependent and what independent variables do the researchers use to address their question(s)?
    d) Do the researchers make sure that there is equal baseline performance in all experimental conditions?
    e) How did the researchers control lexical variables?

2. For the following research questions, explain which auditory priming task would be the most appropriate.

    a) Do bilinguals use auditory priming in processing speech in both of their languages?
    b) Are L2 learners less likely to benefit from auditory priming in their L2 than in their L1?
    c) Do listeners benefit from auditory priming when they are exposed to speech that is longer than individual words?
    d) Do L2 learners of different proficiency levels differ in the extent to which they benefit from auditory priming?

e) Are learners more sensitive to repetitions of words or repetitions of other details of speech (voices, intonation patterns, etc.)?

f) Do listeners benefit from both repeated words and the repeated context in which these words occur? In other words, is there auditory priming for individual words (e.g. *beans*) and for formulaic sequences in which such words are often embedded (e.g. *spill the beans*)?

3. Besides those mentioned in the chapter, what other topics might L2 researchers use auditory priming tasks to investigate?

4. In terms of their materials development, procedure, and analysis, which tasks seem to be the easiest to implement? Which ones seem more difficult?

5. Consider the hypothetical auditory priming data in table 2.8. It shows the mean proportion of completed word stems in an auditory word stem completion task for two listener groups: native speakers of French and L2 learners of French. In the study phase of this task, the listeners heard a number of words spoken with a neutral intonation. All of these words were later repeated in the test phase of the task. Half of the repeated words were spoken with the (same) neutral intonation, while the other half was spoken with a (different) rising intonation. The remainder of the test phase words were unrepeated (baseline control) words spoken with a neutral intonation. How would you describe the pattern that these data illustrate? Write a short description of the information in the table.

Table 2.8 Mean proportion of completed word stems as a function of encoding task

	Repeated words		Unrepeated words
	Same intonation	Different intonation	
L1 French speakers	.78	.61	.45
L2 French speakers	.59	.43	.38

3

SEMANTIC PRIMING

In this chapter, we define semantic priming and describe how semantic priming methods have been used in L1, bilingual and L2 processing and acquisition research. We present the three experimental tasks used in semantic priming research and describe in detail the materials, procedure and analysis of each task. We highlight an example study that used semantic priming to investigate L2 acquisition, and we outline several methodological issues to consider when designing semantic priming studies. We conclude the chapter with suggestions for additional uses of semantic priming tasks in L2 research.

What is Semantic Priming?

Semantic priming refers to a general tendency for language users to show facilitation in their processing of words due to a previous experience with words similar in meaning. Like auditory priming discussed in the previous chapter, semantic priming also fits well within Malcolm Gladwell's popular description of priming phenomena (see p. 19). Semantic priming can be described as mental operations that, in this case, keep tabs on *semantic* (conceptual, meaning-related) details of a language used around us. When speaking and comprehending a language, language users access (or, in researchers' parlance, "activate") the meanings of words heard or seen. For example, when two family members discuss who is going to walk their dog, they would invariably activate the meanings of words like *dog* and *walk*. These same speakers would be faster or more accurate at producing and comprehending the word *cat* should they happen to later talk about their neighbors' new cat, even if this word has not been recently spoken or heard (see box 3.1).

Box 3.1 Semantic priming

Semantic priming is observed when the processing of a stimulus, such as a word or a picture, is facilitated due to a language user's prior experience with a semantically (meaningfully) related word or picture. For example, a language user may respond more rapidly or more accurately to the word *table* (target word) when it is preceded by the semantically related word *chair* (prime word) relative to when it is preceded by the semantically unrelated word *sun*. For more information, see McNamara (2005) and Neely (1991).

(Box 3.1 Continued)

Box 3.1 Continued

Semantic priming needs to be distinguished from a related phenomenon, associative repetition priming.

Associative repetition priming (also known as *episodic priming* or *priming for new associations*) is observed when responses to pairs of words that were studied together are facilitated relative to responses to pairs of words that were not studied together. For example, language users may respond more rapidly to a pair of words that they have previously seen or heard in the course of an experiment (e.g. *beach-fork*) than to a pair of words that they have not seen or heard previously (e.g. *pillow-crab*). For more information on associative repetition priming, see Zeelenberg, Pecher, and Raaijmakers (2003).

Why would these speakers be faster and more accurate at activating the meaning of the word *cat* after speaking or hearing the word *dog*? The reason is that both words are similar in meaning: both denote animals, both refer to household pets. By activating the meaning of *dog*, speakers activate the meaning of *cat* due to the shared meaning between the two. As a result, they become faster and more accurate at comprehending and producing *cat*. In a broad sense, then, semantic priming characterizes this phenomenon of facilitation in language processing, with facilitation arising due to language users' previous experience with words with related or shared meanings (see McNamara, 2005, for an in-depth review of semantic priming). The goal of this chapter is to examine this phenomenon in detail. We first characterize the role of semantic priming in both L1 and L2 processing and learning. We then describe possible cognitive operations underlying it, and discuss ways of measuring it. We conclude by outlining possible methodological advantages and limitations of using semantic priming methods in research on language processing and learning.

Semantic Priming in L1 Processing and Acquisition

Examples of Semantic Priming

As was discussed above (see box 3.1), semantic priming is defined as a facilitation in the speed or accuracy of processing a word (e.g. *table*) when it is preceded by a semantically related word (e.g. *chair*) relative to when it is preceded by a semantically unrelated word (e.g. *sun*). To clarify our terminology from the start, what we term *semantic priming* refers here to the general phenomenon of facilitation observed in the processing of semantically related words. By extension, semantic priming also refers to possible cognitive mechanisms underlying this facilitation. In turn, what we call a *semantic priming effect* describes the specific and often measurable extent or magnitude of this facilitation.

Although semantic priming is observed in a variety of psycholinguistic (processing) tasks, such as semantic classification or naming, the classic demonstrations of semantic priming come from lexical decision tasks (see pp. 74–77). In one of the first demonstrations of semantic priming using a variant of the lexical decision task, Meyer and Schvaneveldt (1971) presented their participants with several pairs of words. Some pairs were semantically associated words (e.g. *bread-butter, nurse-doctor*), other pairs did not bear any obvious association (e.g. *nurse-butter, bread-doctor*), yet other pairs, used for control purposes, were word-nonword pairs (e.g. *chair-marb*). Upon seeing each pair, the participants pressed a *yes* button if both were words, and pressed a *no* button if both were non-words. Results revealed that the participants were on average 85 milli-seconds faster in responding to the associated word pairs (*nurse-doctor*) than to the unassociated ones (*nurse-butter*).

This example of semantic priming illustrates two important points about this phenomenon. It shows that the relationships among words have a powerful influence on how they are stored and processed in the human mind. In Meyer and Schvaneveldt's experiment, the participants needed to access the meaning of both words to decide that they were real words. Clearly, some word associations (e.g. between *nurse* and *doctor*) were more helpful to the participants in making this decision than others (e.g. between *nurse* and *butter*). At a broad level, this finding suggests that strongly associated words (e.g. *nurse-doctor*) are stored together or are somehow "linked" in the mind of a language user and that both get acti-vated by virtue of having such links (e.g. Collins & Loftus, 1975; Neely, 1991).

This demonstration also raises an important question about the pre-cise nature of the relationship between words that give rise to this kind of processing facilitation. In Meyer and Schvaneveldt's experiment, the words *nurse* and *doctor* were strongly associated. A strong associative rela-tionship between two words implies that individuals are more likely to produce the word *doctor* as a first word that comes to mind after seeing or hearing the word *nurse*. In addition, however, the two words were also categorically related. Both *doctor* and *nurse* are members of the same semantic category: both refer to humans who work with patients in health care settings, who treat illnesses, who administer medications, etc. In designing and interpreting semantic priming tasks, it is therefore important to consider whether the priming (facilitation) effect is caused by semantic category relationships between words (e.g. *furniture-table*), by associative relationships (e.g. *tiger-stripes*), or by a combination of seman-tic and associative relationships, as in Meyer and Schvaneveldt's experi-ment (e.g. *nurse-doctor, salt-pepper*). Unless otherwise indicated, the term *semantic priming* refers in this chapter to facilitation due to any of these types of semantic relationships (see box 3.2).

Box 3.2 Types of semantic priming

Depending on particular semantic relationships between prime and target words, semantic priming phenomena can be broken down into several more specific categories. These include associative priming, category priming, and mediated priming.

Associative priming is a form of semantic priming for prime and target words that are close semantic associates of each other but are not members of the same semantic category. For example, associatively related pairs of words are *sugar-sweet* and *grass-green*.

Category priming is a form of semantic priming for prime and target words that are members of the same semantic category. For example, *bird-robin* and *furniture-table* are categorically related pairs of words.

Mediated priming, as opposed to direct semantic priming, refers to priming between words that are not related directly. Examples of such words are *stripes-lion*. The semantic relationship between these two words is mediated by the word *tiger*.

Since early demonstrations of semantic priming (Meyer & Schvaneveldt, 1971; Meyer & Schvaneveldt, 1976; Neely, 1976), this phenomenon has been observed in a variety of tasks, using different types of stimuli (for reviews, see Lucas, 2000; McNamara, 2005; Neely, 1991). For example, McNamara and Altarriba (1988) investigated whether native speakers of English would demonstrate mediated semantic priming (see box 3.2). McNamara and Altarriba set out to determine if native speakers of English would demonstrate semantic priming for pairs of words, such as *stripes* and *lion*, that are related to each other via another (mediating) word, such as *tiger*. In one of their experiments, for example, these researchers showed that their participants were 22 milliseconds faster at deciding whether *stripes* was a real word when it was preceded by *lion* than when it was preceded by an entirely unrelated word (e.g. *beach*). More importantly, a mediated priming effect was found to be smaller than a direct priming effect (e.g. between *tiger* and *lion*), suggesting that semantic priming effects are sensitive to the semantic distance between words and that directly related words may have stronger or more direct links in human memory than indirectly related words.

Another example of semantic priming effects demonstrated in a different task comes from studies conducted by Slowiaczek (1994). This researcher used a single-word naming task to investigate semantic priming effects in native English speakers. The goal of this study was to test whether speakers access semantic information in simple word naming. Slowiaczek asked her participants to listen to semantically related word pairs (*fingers-hand*) and semantically unrelated word pairs (*wall-hand*) and then to repeat aloud the second word in each pair. The participants were found to be 62 milliseconds faster at initiating the production of words (e.g. *hand*) when these words followed a semantically related word (e.g. *fingers*) as opposed to when they followed an unrelated word (e.g. *wall*). This finding suggests that in single-word naming, speakers access the meanings of words and that, as a result, this task is sensitive to semantic relationships among words in memory.

Properties of Semantic Priming

Nearly 40 years of research on semantic priming have yielded interesting insights into the nature of this phenomenon. One of these insights concerns the extent to which semantic priming is automatic and to which it is governed by intentional, strategic processes. Automatic processing is typically defined as one that is fast, ballistic (unstoppable) and that proceeds without conscious intention or awareness. On the other hand, strategic (controlled) processing is slower; it requires conscious intention and awareness, and it is driven by specific, often conscious, processing strategies (see Schneider & Chein, 2003, and Segalowitz & Hulstijn, 2005, for discussion of automatic and controlled processing in L1 and L2).

At least in part, semantic priming represents an automatic process. For example, semantic priming is found when prime and target words are separated by a fraction of a second, at stimulus-onset-asynchrony (SOA) intervals of merely 200 milliseconds or much less (Neely, 1991). Because strategic processes require substantial amounts of time to develop, brief delays between the prime and the target thus ensure that the obtained priming effects are due to automatic processes alone (Neely, 1977, 1991). Semantic priming is found in situations when participants do not anticipate the possibility of encountering a related word pair (Fischler, 1977), when participants are instructed to ignore prime words (Fuentes & Tudela, 1992), and even when participants are explicitly trained not to expect a target that is semantically related to the prime (Favreau & Segalowitz, 1983; Neely, 1977). These demonstrations show that, at least in its early stages (when measured at prime–target intervals shorter than 200 milliseconds), semantic priming represents an automatic process of activating mental representations of words, a process largely unaffected by task instructions or expectations.

Semantic priming, however, is also subject to effects of controlled processing, particularly in its later stages (when measured at prime–target intervals longer than 200 milliseconds). In semantic priming experiments, controlled processing may take the form of several strategies. One such strategy is an expectancy strategy (for more details, see McNamara, 2005, chapter 9, and Neely, 1991). This strategy refers to the situation when participants, after seeing a given prime word, create mental lists of possible words that can appear as targets (Keefe & Neely, 1990; Neely, Keefe, & Ross, 1989). For example, if participants see *lion* as a prime, they may anticipate seeing the semantically related *tiger, zebra*, or *leopard* as a target. If one of these anticipated words indeed happens to be the target, this target will be processed more rapidly and accurately than an unrelated target, giving rise to facilitation (priming) effects. In this case, priming effects arise as a consequence of building mental expectations between the prime and the target word (a strategic process) rather than as a consequence of activating mental links between them (an automatic process). Because semantic priming is produced by both automatic and strategic processes, researchers need to be careful in designing semantic priming tasks. We revisit this point below.

A closely related aspect of semantic priming is the extent to which it is a conscious phenomenon. Put differently, the question here is whether participants who demonstrate semantic priming effects do so with or without awareness of the prime. As is the case with the automatic versus strategic processing distinction, the issue here is far from being settled (Greenwald, Klinger, & Schuh, 1995; Holender, 1986). On the one hand, there is a relatively large body of evidence that semantic priming occurs even when participants cannot identify the prime or cannot detect its presence. This evidence comes from studies using masking (see pp. 83–84), a procedure that greatly minimizes the likelihood that a prime is detected by participants (Fischler & Goodman, 1978; Marcel, 1983). This evidence also comes from studies using other procedures (e.g. word discrimination) to estimate participants' levels of prime awareness (Dagenbach, Carr, & Wilhelmsen, 1989; Hirshman & Durante, 1992). On the other hand, there is some evidence that semantic priming does not occur for primes that are not attended and therefore not noticed consciously, at least under certain testing conditions (Lachter, Forster, & Ruthruff, 2004; Naccahe, Blandin, & Dehaene, 2002). This aspect of semantic priming needs to be clarified in future research.

Semantic priming effects are generally short-lived. Facilitation effects of a semantically related prime are typically detectable only if the target word immediately follows the prime. Given that the delays between the prime and the target are often very brief (several hundred milliseconds), semantic priming effects rarely survive delays of longer than 1–2 seconds (Masson, 1995). In fact, it appears that a single intervening word presented between the prime and the target (e.g. *doctor-tree-nurse*) can greatly reduce priming effects (Joordens & Besner, 1992). With two or more intervening words, semantic priming effects are typically eliminated (Zeelenberg & Pecher, 2002; but see Joordens & Becker, 1997). These findings suggest that semantic priming, based on the evidence available to date, operates on a relatively short time course.

Similar to auditory and syntactic priming effects, semantic priming effects appear to display a relative constancy in language development. For example, semantic priming effects (often comparable to those shown by adults) have been documented in children (Nakamura, Ohta, Okita, Ozaki, & Matsushima, 2006; Plaut & Booth, 2000) and even in 19-month-old infants (Friedrich & Friederici, 2004, 2005). Several researchers, in fact, linked these priming benefits, which tend to increase with children's age (West & Stanovich, 1978), to children's developing semantic networks throughout childhood (Nakamura et al., 2006; Nation & Snowling, 1999). These results underscore the involvement of semantic priming in language processing by children and adults and suggest that semantic priming may provide a window into the development and organization of the lexicon throughout an individual's lifespan.

Relevance of Semantic Priming to L2 Processing and Learning

The preceding discussion suggests that semantic priming effects are robust and general, found in a variety of tasks and in different groups of individuals. These effects are largely automatic (yet susceptible to strategic influences). They often proceed without conscious attention or awareness. They ebb and flow on a relatively short timescale in response to encountered semantic information. These properties of semantic priming have led many researchers to hypothesize that semantic priming reflects some fundamental properties of the way individuals organize their knowledge of the lexicon and the way they retrieve and use this knowledge (Neely, 1991; Ratcliff & McKoon, 1988).

Over the years, more than a dozen different theoretical models have been proposed to explain semantic priming (for an excellent discussion of semantic priming models, see McNamara, 2005). According to one influential model, termed *the spreading activation theory of semantic priming* (Collins & Loftus, 1975), semantic priming effects arise as a consequence of spreading activation among semantic concepts in memory. Semantic concepts are represented in memory as interconnected nodes, with more similar concepts—those that share common properties—being stored closer together and having more links than less similar concepts. According to this theory, when a semantic concept is activated, activation from this concept spreads to all interconnected conceptual nodes. The amount of this activation depends on the distance between nodes. More similar concepts receive larger amounts of activation than more dissimilar, distant ones. Thus, for example, when the meaning of a word like *table* is accessed, the meanings of related words like *chair* or *stool* get activated too. By virtue of this activation, responses to these latter words are speeded (primed) relative to responses to non-activated words like *road* or *cloud*.

As the spreading activation theory of semantic priming suggests, semantic priming effects might reflect the architecture of human memory, of particular ways in which individuals access and store meanings of words. It is not surprising, therefore, that semantic priming has emerged as a technique of choice for many researchers trying to investigate the development and use of semantic knowledge in different populations of individuals: from children (e.g. Nation & Snowling, 1999) to the elderly (e.g. Cameli & Phillips, 2000), to bilinguals, multilinguals, and L2 learners (e.g. Jiang & Forster, 2001). In the following section, we review some of the research carried out using the semantic priming paradigm, with a particular focus on bilingual and L2 semantic processing.

Questions Addressed in L2 Semantic Priming Research

Over the last several decades, research on semantic priming in bilinguals and L2 learners has proceeded along two paths (see box 3.3). The distinction between them is both methodological and conceptual. The first line of research has predominantly concerned itself with documenting semantic priming effects *within* bilinguals' or L2 learners' two languages, examining within-language priming. In within-language semantic priming experiments, participants typically first perform a task in one language (e.g. responding to a prime-target pair *lion-tiger* in English) and then do the same in the other language (e.g. responding to a prime-target pair *chat-chien* [*cat-dog*] in French). One goal of within-language priming research is to document whether bilinguals or L2 learners exhibit similar patterns of semantic priming in both their languages (e.g. Favreau & Segalowitz, 1983; Kirsner, Smith, Lockhart, King, & Jain, 1984; Phillips, Segalowitz, O'Brien, & Yamasaki, 2004). Another goal is to determine whether these patterns resemble those found in monolingual speakers of both languages (e.g. Altarriba & Canary, 2004; Devitto & Burgess, 2004; Frenck-Mestre & Prince, 1997; Mack, 1986).

The other line of research has focused on semantic priming effects *between* bilinguals' or L2 learners' two languages. In between-language (or cross-language) semantic priming studies, participants perform a task that contains words in both their languages. For example, they may see or hear L1–L2 or L2–L1 prime-target pairs that are related to each other semantically (e.g. *cat-chien* or *chien-cat*) or that are direct translations of each other (e.g. *dog-chien* or *chien-dog*). One goal of cross-language priming research is to determine how bilinguals and L2 learners organize their two languages: whether they store and access the meanings and forms of words in both their languages in an independent or interdependent manner (e.g. Altarriba, 1992; Basnight-Brown & Altarriba, 2007; Jiang, 1999; Keatley, Spinks, & de Gelder, 1994). In the remainder of this section, we review these two lines of research in greater detail.

<hr>

Box 3.3 Within-language and cross-language semantic priming

In within-language semantic priming experiments, participants respond to prime-target pairs with lexical items from the same language. For example, an English prime is always paired with an English target and a French prime is always paired with a French target.

In cross-language semantic priming experiments, participants respond to prime-target pairs with lexical items from both languages. For example, an English prime is paired with a French target, and/or a French prime is paired with an English target.

<hr>

Semantic Priming in a Speaker's L1 and L2

One question addressed in within-language semantic priming research concerns the extent to which bilinguals and L2 learners demonstrate similar semantic priming effects in both their languages. The logic of these studies is the following. Priming effects appear to be indicative of the strength and richness of semantic relationships among words in a language (Keatly et al., 1994; Kirsner et al., 1984). If this is indeed the case, then comparing priming effects in bilinguals' and L2 learners' two languages can reveal whether semantic links in the L2 are similar to those found in the L1. The studies that have addressed this question have typically yielded two findings. For bilinguals and L2 learners who are not as proficient in their L2 as they are in their L1, priming effects are often greater in the L1 than in the L2 (Favreau & Segalowitz, 1983; Frenck & Pynte, 1987; Phillips et al., 2004). However, for bilinguals and L2 learners who are equally proficient in both their languages, L1 and L2 priming effects appear to be equivalent (Kotz, 2001; Kotz & Elston-Güttler, 2004; Schwanenflugel & Rey, 1986).

One of the first comparisons of semantic priming effects in the L1 and the L2 was reported by Favreau and Segalowitz (1983). These researchers tested bilingual speakers of English and French who were classified into two groups: those who were equally fast readers in both languages and those who were faster in their L1 than in their L2. Despite these differences in reading speed, both groups achieved the same high threshold of comprehension (based on gist questions). The participants completed a lexical decision task, separately in English and French, in which they judged whether a letter string represented a real word. Among several experimental manipulations employed in this study, the following was the most critical. In one of the conditions, Favreau and Segalowitz explicitly instructed their participants that prime words would be a category name (e.g. *bird*) followed by a semantically *un*related target—an exemplar of another category (e.g. *carrot*). That is, the participants were trained to expect vegetable names after seeing the category name *bird*. On some occasions during the experiment, however, the researchers "surprised" their participants by showing them "unexpected" (albeit semantically related) target words, bird names in this case. In other words, contrary to their expectations, the participants would sometimes see a target word that was semantically related to the prime word (e.g. *bird-sparrow*).

Favreau and Segalowitz reasoned that if bilinguals activate semantic information in both their languages automatically (upon seeing prime words in each language) then they should demonstrate semantic priming effects even under such "surprising" conditions, when semantic related-ness conflicted with the participants' expectations. However, these facilitation effects were predicted to occur only when the interval between the onset of the prime and the target was very short (200 ms) so that there would be no time for expectations to override what is normal automatic response. Results revealed important differences in L1 and L2 semantic priming effects between the two bilingual groups in this 200 millisecond interval condition. Those bilinguals who were equally fast in both their languages, as predicted, showed comparable facilitation for semantically related target words in both their languages. Because these priming effects were found for semantically related target words (e.g. *bird-sparrow*) despite the participants' expectations of seeing unrelated targets (e.g. *bird-carrot*), these (balanced) bilinguals processed semantic information automatically in both L1 and L2. Put differently, these bilinguals were able to benefit from semantic information to a comparable degree in both languages. By contrast, those bilinguals who were faster at reading in their L1 than in their L2 showed facilitation effects only in their L1, not their L2. These bilinguals did not process semantic information automatically in their L2 and were therefore less likely to benefit from such information. Taken together, these findings suggest that language proficiency might determine the degree to which bilinguals activate and use semantic information in both their languages (see also Kotz, 2001; Kotz & Elston-Güttler, 2004).

Semantic Priming in Monolinguals versus Bilinguals and L2 Learners

A related yet conceptually separate question addressed in within-language semantic priming research concerns the extent to which semantic priming effects in bilinguals and L2 learners are comparable to those shown by monolinguals. Again, based on the premise that semantic priming effects reflect the interconnectedness and richness of semantic networks in memory, this line of research investigates whether the L1 and L2 semantic systems in bilinguals and L2 learners resemble those of monolingual speakers. In one of the first semantic processing studies addressing this issue, Mack (1986) discussed this research objective in terms of what she called an apparent paradox. Bilinguals (particularly those who acquire both languages early in life) and proficient L2 speakers, she reasoned, may often use their languages at near-native levels of fluency, often considering themselves completely "balanced" in both languages. Yet these individuals may often do so "without being able to function as monolinguals in either language" (p. 464). Since then, a number of studies have explored this issue, investigating whether the organization of semantic information is equivalent in bilinguals and L2 learners versus monolinguals (Altarriba & Canary, 2004; Devitto & Burgess, 2004; Elston-Güttler & Friederici, 2005; Frenck-Mestre & Prince, 1997; Scherlag, Demuth, Rösler, Neville, & Röder, 2004).

Frenck-Mestre and Prince (1997) were among the first to show that (proficient) L2 learners and native speakers of a language can access and use semantic information in a similar manner. These researchers tested a group of native English speakers and two groups of French L2 learners of English. One group of learners (the more proficient speakers of English) had trained to be English teachers and had resided in an English-speaking country. The other group (the less proficient speakers of English) had only received English instruction at secondary school in France. The participants performed a lexical decision task in which they judged whether the presented strings of letters were English words or nonwords. Frenck-Mestre and Prince used three types of prime-target semantic relationships. Some primes were antonyms of the target words (*wet-dry*), other primes were synonyms of the target words (*small-little*), while others formed collocations with the target words, that is, words that are frequently used together (*lock-door*).

The researchers reasoned that L2 learners would demonstrate semantic priming effects similar to those found in native English speakers if these learners had achieved what these researchers called "autonomy" of L2 semantic processing. In their view, autonomous semantic processing was characterized by automatic, unstoppable (ballistic) activation of links between semantically related word pairs. That is, the activation of semantic information in response to the prime word (e.g. *wet*) should spread to a semantically related target word (e.g. *dry*) and, as a result, should speed or prime the response to this word. The native English speakers and the more proficient L2 speakers appeared to process semantic information precisely in this manner. These two participant groups showed comparable semantic priming effects for all three types of semantic relationships among L2 words (antonyms, synonyms, collocations). In contrast, the less proficient L2 speakers did not show semantic priming effects for any semantic relationship. These findings support the view that L2 speakers, at least those who have reached a high level of L2 proficiency, may access and use the semantic information in their L2 as native speakers do.

The findings reported by Frenck-Mestre and Prince suggest that proficient L2 learners can attain a certain level of L2 "autonomy", being able to process semantic information in the L2 in a nativelike fashion. However, even the most proficient of L2 learners may not *always* function in their L2 as native speakers. Devitto and Burgess (2004) provided evidence for this claim (see also Altarriba & Canary, 2004; Elston-Güttler & Friederici, 2005). These researchers tested several groups of participants in a lexical decision task similar to those described earlier. One group comprised monolingual English speakers; two others included L2 learners of English who had learned it either before or after age five. What is interesting about this study is that the critical prime-target pairs seen by the participants were only weakly associated (*city-grass*), unlike pairs that bear strong associative relationships (*green-grass*).

Devitto and Burgess hypothesized that the monolinguals would show priming effects for these weak semantic associations but that the L2 learners might not do so. The researchers argued that these learners' L2 learning experience may not have been sufficiently rich for them to create semantic links for weakly associated words. As predicted, the monolinguals indeed showed a reliable semantic priming effect, responding faster to target words like *grass* after seeing weakly associated prime words like *city*. However, the L2 learners (those who learned English before age five and those who acquired it thereafter) showed no such priming benefits. It appears that, despite an early exposure to the L2 and an extensive amount of experience with it, at least some learners may be unable to create the semantic links that are as elaborate as those found in monolinguals. This and similar findings (e.g. Altarriba & Canary, 2004) also highlight the important role of language experience in shaping L2 semantic networks.

Organization of L1–L2 Lexicons

One question that has sparked considerable interest in semantic priming research over a number of years relates to how bilinguals and L2 learners store their languages in memory. The issue here is whether users of two languages have shared or separate stores for their two languages. If semantic concepts are shared across the two languages, then presenting a word in one language should prime (facilitate) responses to semantically related words in the other language. For example, accessing the word *chat* in French should activate both its translation equivalent in English (*cat*) as well as semantically related words in this language (*dog, pet, bark*, etc.). Shared conceptual representations would imply that language comprehension and production in L1 and L2 have a common basis and that both languages form an interrelated system, at least at the conceptual level. Conversely, if semantic concepts are separate across the two languages, then presenting words in one language should not facilitate responses to semantically related words in the other language. In other words, accessing the word *chat* in French should not activate similar or related words in English. Separate conceptual representations of this sort would suggest that the two languages are organized in memory separately and that speaking and comprehending in L1 and L2 do not interfere with each other.

The shared-separate question of bilingual conceptual representations has been studied extensively using the between-language (or cross-language) priming paradigm. In a typical cross-language priming experiment, participants are presented with a prime in their L1 (e.g. *table*) and are asked to respond to a target in their L2 (e.g. *chaise* ["chair" in French]), or vice versa. Researchers commonly use two types of semantically related words in these experiments: L1–L2 translation pairs (e.g. *cat-chat* in English and French) and L1–L2 semantically related pairs (e.g. *dog-chat* in English and French). Experiments with L1–L2 translation pairs are referred to as cross-language translation priming studies. In turn, experiments with L1–L2 semantically related pairs are termed cross-language semantic priming studies. Cross-language priming is established in studies of this kind if hearing or seeing a word in the L1 facilitates (speeds up) participants' responses to this word's translation equivalent or its semantic associate in the L2, and vice versa.

The evidence available to date regarding cross-language priming effects is somewhat mixed (for an excellent review, see Altarriba and Basnight-Brown, 2007). Some cross-language priming studies yielded robust priming effects in both L1–L2 and L2–L1 directions (Chen & Ng, 1989; Kirsner et al., 1984; Schwanenflugel & Rey, 1986). Others reported no significant cross-language priming effects in either direction (Frenck & Pynte, 1987; Grainger & Beauvillain, 1988; Keatley & De Gelder, 1992). Yet other studies revealed asymmetrical cross-language priming effects: larger effects in the L1–L2 direction and smaller effects in the L2–L1 direction (Altarriba, 1992; Gollan, Forster, & Frost, 1997; Jiang, 1999; Jin, 1990). There are several methodological reasons for these discrepancies (see Altarriba & Basnight-Brown, 2007), including the composition of experimental materials (de Groot & Nas, 1991; Jin, 1990; Keatley et al., 1994), participants' language proficiency (Chen & Ng, 1989; Grainger & Beauvillain, 1988), and the time interval between the presentation of the prime and target words (Altarriba, 1992). To illustrate cross-language priming techniques and to discuss some methodological concerns related to their implementation, we review one cross-language priming study below.

In a cross-language translation priming study with Spanish-English bilinguals, Altarriba (1992) set out to investigate whether translation equivalents in English and Spanish (e.g. *sweet-dulce*) share conceptual representations in bilingual memory. The participants were presented with English (or Spanish) prime words in a lexical decision task and asked to respond to Spanish (or English) target words that were translations of the primes. Altarriba's experiment had several interesting methodological aspects. One aspect related to the composition of the experimental materials; the other concerned the amount of time between the presentation of the prime and target words.

First, Altarriba carefully controlled the number of translation pairs and the number of nonwords in the experimental lists, keeping both of them low. These two factors (referred to in the priming literature as the *relatedness proportion* and the *nonword ratio*, respectively) are said to be important in controlling participants' use of conscious, controlled strategies to perform the task. If the number of translation pairs (i.e. related words) is high, then translation equivalents become salient in the experiment. As a result, participants create expectations about upcoming target words, anticipating possible targets and thereby improving their performance (de Groot, 1984). If, on the other hand, the number of nonwords is high, then participants may be biased to make nonword lexical decisions, which obscures their performance in the task (Neely & Keefe, 1989). By keeping both numbers low, Altarriba thus ensured that her participants were less likely to rely on strategies in performing the task.

Second, Altarriba varied the amount of time between the presentation of the prime and target words. She used two values: a short interval of 200 milliseconds and a long interval of 1,000 milliseconds. The reason for manipulating this variable was to determine if cross-language translation priming effects depend on the amount of time that participants have for processing the prime word. There is evidence that longer time intervals (particularly for primes presented in a less dominant language) encourage participants to translate prime words from their less dominant to their more dominant language and to rely on other explicit strategies. Brief time intervals (typically 200 milliseconds or less), in contrast, do not permit participants to employ such strategies and are said to tap into the automatic, unstoppable bases of semantic priming (McNamara, 2005; Neely, 1991).

The obtained translation priming effects appeared to depend both on the direction of priming (L1–L2 vs. L2–L1) and on the prime–target interval (200 ms vs. 1,000 ms). In the 1,000 millisecond time interval condition, the translation priming effects were statistically significant in both translation directions. Altarriba interpreted these priming effects as reflective of conscious, controlled processing. In the 200 millisecond condition, however, the translation priming effects were statistically significant in one direction only: from the bilinguals' more dominant to their less dominant language. This priming effect (likely reflective of automatic processing) suggested two conclusions. First, semantic concepts appeared to be shared across the bilinguals' two languages. The reason here is that a word like *sweet* could prime its translation equivalent *dulce* only if the bilinguals accessed the same semantic representation (the meaning of "sweet") for both words. Second, such semantic concepts appeared to be linked more strongly to words in the bilinguals' more dominant language than in their less dominant language. This is because semantic priming was found only in one direction: when *sweet* preceded *dulce*, not in the opposite way. Overall, this pattern of results indicates that bilinguals and L2 learners organize semantic information in their two languages in a complex manner and that this organization may depend on the degree of dominance or the level of proficiency in a language.

In summary, semantic priming research has investigated several issues in L2 processing, including how the L1 and L2 lexicons are organized and how the semantic networks of bilingual speakers compare with monolingual and L2 speakers. And, as with any research, asking and answering interesting questions about semantic priming depends on using appropriate methods and carefully constructed materials. In the following section, we introduce the three primary tasks that are typically used in semantic priming research.

Tasks Used in Semantic Priming Research

Logic of Semantic Priming Experiments

The premise of semantic priming experiments is that semantic priming effects largely arise at the conceptual processing level (Lupiker, 1984). Put differently, semantic priming effects arise largely because of overlap in meaning between prime and target words, not overlap in their form, such as orthography, morphology, or phonology (Finkbeiner, Forster, Nicol, & Nakamura, 2004; but see Duyck, 2005). Semantic priming experiments, therefore, are designed to encourage language users to access the conceptual, meaning-related information of presented prime and target words. A larger meaning overlap or stronger semantic links between prime and target words should therefore result in larger semantic priming effects. For example, a researcher may find evidence of a semantic priming effect if a presentation of a word (e.g. *furniture*) facilitates a response to a semantically related word (e.g. *desk*). One goal of semantic priming experiments is to measure the extent of this facilitation for semantically related words relative to semantically unrelated words.

Suppose, for example, that in a lexical decision task, participants took on average 679 milliseconds to respond to target words preceded by semantically related prime words, but required 749 milliseconds on average to respond to target words preceded by unrelated words (baseline control words). In this case, a researcher may conclude that these participants' prior experience with semantically related prime words somehow facilitated their responses to target words. A researcher may then estimate the extent of this facilitation, or the magnitude of the semantic priming effect, at 70 milliseconds (749–679). Of course, there is a lot of theoretical debate about what exactly is facilitated in terms of processing due to semantic overlap between prime and target words (see McNamara, 2005, chapters 2–7, for an overview of semantic priming models). Nevertheless, as was discussed earlier, semantic priming reflects some fundamental properties of how individuals organize their knowledge of the lexicon and how they retrieve and use this knowledge. As such, semantic priming has proven to be an extremely valuable paradigm for investigating these issues. In the next sections, we discuss the three tasks used in semantic priming research.

Lexical Decision Task

Materials and procedure. Lexical decision tasks have been used in numerous investigations of semantic priming, both in the L1 (see McNamara, 2005) and in the L2 (see Altarriba & Basnight-Brown, 2007). Although the majority of lexical decision tasks have been conducted in the visual modality (using written words and nonwords), auditory lexical decision tasks (using spoken words and nonwords) have been employed in a number of investigations (e.g. Radeau, 1983). For a description of auditory lexical decision tasks, see Goldinger (1996b). Examples of auditory lexical decision tasks in the L2 can be found in Woutersen et al. (1994, 1995).

In a lexical decision task, participants typically see (or hear) one or two letter strings and are asked to decide whether the second letter string (target) constitutes a real word in a given language. On some occasions, letter strings represent real words (e.g. *vase*). On other occasions, letter strings form nonwords (e.g. *metch*). When administering lexical decision tasks, researchers are interested in measuring the speed and accuracy of participants' responses to word targets as a function of the preceding word (prime). Some of these targets are preceded by a semantically related word (or its translation equivalent), forming semantically related prime-target pairs (e.g. *grass-green, stove-hot*). Other targets are preceded by semantically unrelated words, forming semantically unrelated pairs (e.g. *road-key, mouse-pillow*). The remainder of task materials usually includes nonword targets preceded by word primes (e.g. *watch-sakt, flower-tagres*). The three types of materials (related word-word pairs, unrelated word-word pairs, and word-nonword pairs) are randomized and presented to participants with a certain interval (known as the *stimulus onset asynchrony* or *SOA*) between the first and the second item of the pair. Participants are instructed to make a word/nonword decision to the second word in each pair by pressing either a *yes* or a *no* response key as quickly and as accurately as possible. As was discussed earlier, evidence of semantic priming is obtained in this task if participants' responses to targets preceded by semantically related primes are facilitated in comparison to their responses to targets preceded by semantically unrelated primes. A schematic illustration of a lexical decision task appears in figure 3.1.

Dependent variables. The dependent variables used in a lexical decision task are response accuracy and response latency. Response accuracy is measured as the proportion (or percentage) of correct lexical decisions to each type of target (related, unrelated, or nonword) to the total number of each type of target presented. For example, if a participant saw 64 related word-word pairs overall and correctly identified 60 of the targets in these pairs as real words, then this participant's response accuracy for this type of target (real words preceded by semantically related words) is .94. Response latency or reaction time is defined as the amount of time between the onset of the target word and the participant's response to it. In lexical decision experiments, response latencies are typically recorded by stimulus presentation software running the experimental procedure (e.g. *DMDX, E-Prime, PsyScope*). In the calculation of response latencies, researchers typically consider only response latencies for correct lexical

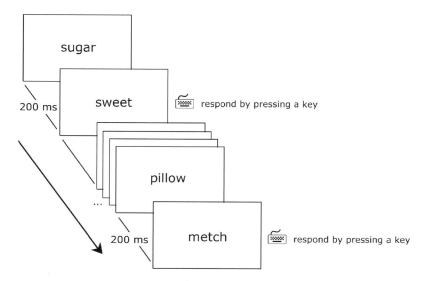

Figure 3.1 A schematic illustration of a (within-language) primed lexical decision task (modeled after Altarriba, 1992) This illustration depicts the following sequence of events for each trial: (1) the first letter string is presented for 200 ms, (2) this letter string is then replaced by the second letter string, (3) participant makes a lexical decision to the second letter string by pressing a response key, (4) if participant makes a mistake, the word "ERROR" appears on the screen. Words *sugar* and *sweet* represent a semantically related prime-target pair. Words *pillow* and *metch* represent a word-nonword pair.

decisions. A sample semantic priming study using a lexical decision task is presented in box 3.7.

Independent variables. Researchers often manipulate several independent variables in lexical decision tasks (and other tasks described in this section). One such set of variables includes the various semantic relationships between prime and target words. For example, semantic priming effects have been investigated for prime-target word pairs that are synonyms or near-synonyms of each other (e.g. *small-little*), that are antonyms of each other (*e.g. young-old*), that are semantic associates (e.g. *sugar-sweet*), that collocate (co-occur) with each other (e.g. *waste-time*), that are more or less typical members of a semantic category (e.g. *body-hand* vs. *body-hair*), that are cognates (translations with similar spellings) across L1 and L2 (e.g. *house-huis* [house in Dutch]), or that are translation equivalents (e.g. *hand-mano* in English and Spanish). By manipulating these types of semantic relationships, researchers attempt to determine how individuals represent and use various kinds of semantic information in their memory. Table 3.1 summarizes the various semantic relationships

Table 3.1 Semantic relationship variables used in semantic priming studies

Within-language designs	*L2 Studies*
Semantically related words	Devitto & Burgess (2004); Dong, Gui, & MacWhinney (2005): Ex. 1; Kotz & Elston-Güttler (2004); Fox (1996): Ex. 1, 2; Ibrahim & Aharon-Peretz (2005); Kiran & Tuchtenhagen (2005); Kotz (2001); Schwanenflugel & Rey (1986): Ex. 1, 2; Favreau & Segalowitz (1983)
Synonyms, antonyms	Dong et al. (2005): Ex. 1; Frenck-Mestre & Prince (1997): Ex. 1
Collocations	Frenck-Mestre & Prince (1997): Ex. 1
Homographs (words with multiple meanings)	Elston-Güttler & Friederici (2005); Finkbeiner et al. (2004): Ex. 4–6; Frenck-Mestre & Prince (1997): Ex. 2

Cross-language designs	*L2 Studies*
Semantically related words	de Groot & Nas (1991): Ex. 3, 4; Dong et al. (2005): Ex. 1; Fox (1996): Ex. 1; Ibrahim & Aharon-Peretz (2005); Schwanenflugel & Rey (1986): Ex. 1, 2; Silverberg & Samuel (2004); Tzelgov & Eben-Ezra (1992); Keatley et al. (1994): Ex. 1, 2; Basnight-Brown & Altarriba (2007)
Translation equivalents	Altarriba (1992); Alvarez, Holcomb, & Grainger (2003); Fox (1996): Ex. 2; Gollan et al. (1997); Grainger & Frenck-Mestre (1998); Jiang & Forster (2001): Ex. 1–4; Jiang (1999); Keatley et al. (1994): Ex. 3; Basnight-Brown & Altarriba (2007)

Cognates	de Groot & Nas (1991): Ex. 1, 2; Gollan et al. (1997); Sanchez-Casas, Davis, & Garcia-Albea (1992)
Interlingual homographs (false cognates)	de Bruijn, Dijkstra, Chwilla, & Schriefers (2001); Elston-Güttler, Gunter, & Kotz (2005); Kerkhofs, Dijkstra, Chwilla, & de Bruijn (2006)
Synonyms, antonyms	Dong et al. (2005): Ex. 1

Note: Ex. = Experiment.

Box 3.4 Sample results from a lexical decision task

The results of a lexical decision task can be reported in a tabular format. The following table (adapted from Experiment 1 in de Groot & Nas, 1991) shows lexical decision latencies and error rates for native Dutch speakers of English in Dutch and English within-language priming conditions.

Mean reaction times (RT) and error rates (ER) as a function of prime-target relationship and language

Prime-target relationship	English prime-English target		Dutch prime-Dutch target	
	RT	*ER*	*RT*	*ER*
Semantically related	559	.01	504	.01
Unrelated	610	.04	574	.05
Semantic priming	51		70	

Overall, native Dutch speakers of English showed statistically equivalent priming effects for semantically related words in English (e.g. *calf-cow*) and in Dutch (e.g. *kalf-koe*).

---

investigated in a selection of published semantic priming studies. Because the literature on L1 semantic priming is vast (see McNamara, 2005) and the focus of this chapter is on L2 processing and learning, this summary is restricted to L2 semantic priming research. Sample results from a lexical decision task are provided in box 3.4.

Pronunciation (Naming) Task

Materials and procedure. Pronunciation (also known as shadowing or naming) tasks have been used in several investigations of semantic priming in both L1 (Balota, Black, & Cheney, 1992; Slowiaczek, 1994) and L2 (Larsen, Fritsch, & Grava, 1994; Tzelgov & Eben-Ezra, 1992), albeit to a much lesser extent than have lexical decision tasks. Although most pronunciation tasks have relied on visual presentation of prime and target words, spoken prime and target words have also been used in investigations of semantic priming (Slowiaczek, 1994). For an interesting version of the pronunciation task, see Bates and Liu (1996) and Liu, Bates, Powell, and Wulfeck (1997).

In a pronunciation task, participants typically see (or hear) one or two words on a computer screen and are asked to pronounce the second word (target). Here, researchers are interested in the amount of time that participants require to initiate the production of the target word. Some of the targets are preceded by a semantically related word (or its translation equivalent), forming semantically related prime-target pairs (e.g. *blue-sky*). Other targets are preceded by semantically unrelated words, forming semantically unrelated pairs (e.g. *forest-wrench*). As in the lexical decision task, the experimental materials (related word pairs and unrelated word pairs) are randomized and presented to participants with a certain delay (known as the *stimulus onset asynchrony* or SOA) between the first and the second item of the pair. Participants are instructed to pronounce the second word in each pair as quickly and as accurately as possible. Participants usually speak into a microphone connected to a voice-activated timer, which is controlled by the software running the experimental procedure. This timer, activated by participants' voices, records the amount of time that elapses between the presentation of the prime and participants' production of the target. Evidence of semantic priming is obtained in this task if participants' production of targets preceded by semantically related primes requires less time to initiate than their production of targets preceded by unrelated primes. A schematic illustration of a pronunciation task appears in figure 3.2.

Dependent variables. The dependent variables commonly used in the pronunciation task are similar to those used in repetition tasks found in auditory priming research (see chapter 2, pp. 41–43). These include measures of response latency. In pronunciation tasks, response latency is often defined as the length of time (in milliseconds) between the onset of the target word (i.e. its appearance on the screen or its auditory presentation) and the onset of its repetition. Response latencies are typically calculated only for correct pronunciations of target words.

Independent variables. One independent variable that researchers manipulate in pronunciation tasks (and in other semantic priming tasks described in this section) involves the amount of time between the presentation of each prime word and target word, that is, the stimulus onset asynchrony (SOA). It is generally acknowledged that a longer SOA results in a "deeper", more elaborate processing of the prime and likely encourages participants to use certain strategies to perform the task. In contrast, a shorter SOA is believed to ensure that participants' performance on the

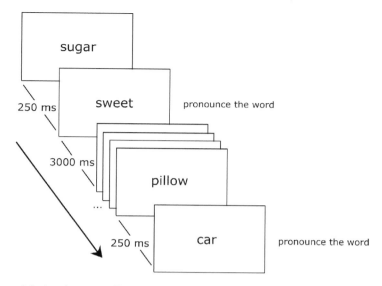

Figure 3.2 A schematic illustration of a (within-language) primed pronunciation task (modeled after Larsen et al., 1994). This illustration depicts the following sequence of events for each trial: (1) the prime word is presented for 250 ms, (2) the prime word is replaced by the target word, which stays on the screen for 3000 ms, (3) participant pronounces the target word. Words *sugar* and *sweet* represent a semantically related prime-target pair. Words *pillow* and *car* represent a semantically unrelated prime-target pair.

task is influenced by an automatic, unstoppable activation of semantic information available in the prime and target words (McNamara, 2005, chapter 9). By manipulating SOA, researchers thus attempt to determine whether participants activate semantic information automatically or by means of strategies (e.g. translation). The different ranges of SOA values (shown separately for within- and cross-language designs) used in a selection of published L2 semantic priming studies are summarized in table 3.2, and the results of a pronunciation (naming) task are illustrated in box 3.5

Semantic Categorization Task

Materials and procedure. Like lexical decision and pronunciation tasks, semantic categorization tasks have also been used in semantic priming research in both L1 (Bueno & Frenck-Mestre, 2002; Forster & Hector, 2002; Frenck-Mestre & Bueno, 1999) and L2 (Alvarez et al., 2003; Finkbeiner et al., 2004; Grainger & Frenck-Mestre, 1998; Phillips et al., 2004; Sanchez-Casas et al., 1992). In semantic categorization tasks,

Table 3.2 Stimulus-onset-asynchrony (SOA) values used in published semantic priming studies

Within-language designs	L2 Studies
70 ms or less	Frenck-Mestre & Prince (1997): Ex. 1
100 ms	Frenck-Mestre & Prince (1997): Ex. 2; Schwanenflugel & Rey (1986): Ex. 2
200–250 ms	Elston-Güttler & Friederici (2005); Dong et al. (2005): Ex. 1; Favreau & Segalowitz (1983)
300–350 ms	Frenck-Mestre & Prince (1997): Ex. 2; Schwanenflugel & Rey (1986): Ex. 1
400–500 ms	Elston-Güttler & Friederici (2005)
600–950 ms	Fox (1996): Ex. 1, 2; Kiran & Tuchtenhagen (2005)
1000–2000 ms	Ibrahim & Aharon-Peretz (2005); Kotz & Elston-Güttler (2004); Kotz (2001); Favreau & Segalowitz (1983)

Between-language designs	L2 Studies
60 ms or less	de Groot & Nas (1991): Ex. 3; Gollan et al. (1997); Grainger & Frenck-Mestre (1998); Jiang & Forster (2001): Ex. 3, 4; Jiang (1999): Ex. 1, 2
100 ms	Jiang (1999): Ex. 3; Schwanenflugel & Rey (1986): Ex. 2; Basnight-Brown & Altarriba (2007)
200–250 ms	Altarriba (1992); de Groot & Nas (1991): Ex. 3; Dong et al. (2005): Ex. 1; Jiang & Forster (2001): Ex. 1; Jiang (1999): Ex. 4, 5; Keatley et al. (1994): Ex. 1–3; Tzelgov & Eben-Ezra (1992)
300–350 ms	Schwanenflugel & Rey (1986): Ex. 1; Silverberg & Samuel (2004)
400–500 ms	de Bruijn et al. (2001); Elston-Güttler et al. (2005); Kerkhofs et al. (2006); Silverberg & Samuel (2004)
600–950 ms	Fox (1996): Ex. 1, 2; Silverberg & Samuel (2004); Tzelgov & Eben-Ezra (1992)
1000–2000 ms	Ibrahim & Aharon-Peretz (2005); Keatley et al. (1994): Ex. 1
over 2000 ms	Alvarez et al. (2003)

Note: Ex. = Experiment.

participants typically see one or two words on a computer screen and are asked to decide if the second word (target) is a member of a specific semantic category. Here, researchers are interested in participants' accuracy and response latency with which they are able to categorize each target word (e.g. *hammer, apple*) correctly as a member of a given category (e.g. *tool, fruit*).

Box 3.5 Sample results from a pronunciation task

The results of a pronunciation task can be reported in a tabular format. The following table (adapted from Larsen et al., 1994) shows pronunciation latencies for Latvian-English bilinguals in a cross-language semantic priming condition (Latvian primes followed by English targets).

Means (*M*) and standard deviations (*SD*) of response latencies for primed and unprimed words in the cross-language condition

Prime-target relationship	M	SD
Semantically related	786	151
Unrelated	782	123
Semantic priming	−4	

Overall, Latvian-English bilinguals showed no statistically significant semantic priming effect for English (L2) targets preceded by Latvian (L1) primes.

As in lexical decision and pronunciation tasks, prime-target word pairs are used in semantic categorization tasks as well. Some targets are preceded by semantically related words (or their translation equivalents), forming semantically related prime-target pairs (e.g. *pomme* [French for "apple"]-*apple*). Other targets are preceded by semantically unrelated words, forming semantically unrelated pairs (e.g. *voiture* [French for "car"]-*apple*). Both these targets are "exemplar" targets, requiring a *yes* response when presented in the "fruit" category. The remainder of task materials usually includes "non-exemplar" targets (e.g. *watch*), which require a *no* response when presented in the "fruit" category. Like exemplar targets, these targets are also paired with related (*montre* [French for "watch"]-*watch*) and unrelated (*père* [French for "father"]-*watch*) primes.

All exemplar and non-exemplar prime-target pairs are randomized and then presented to participants blocked by semantic category (e.g. "fruits", "tools") with a certain stimulus onset asynchrony (SOA) between the first and the second item of the pair. As discussed earlier, the SOA may be very brief, and the prime may be preceded and/or followed by a mask (e.g. XXXXX), so participants may not be aware of its presence. Participants are told that they will see the name of a semantic category followed by several pairs of words. They are then instructed to indicate, by pressing a response key as quickly and as accurately as possible, whether the second word in each pair is a member of the given semantic category. Evidence of semantic priming is obtained in this task if participants' responses to exemplar targets preceded by semantically related primes are facilitated in comparison to their responses to exemplar targets preceded by unrelated primes. A schematic illustration of this task appears in figure 3.3.

Dependent variables. The dependent variables used in a semantic categorization task are similar to those used in a lexical decision task: response accuracy and response latency. Response accuracy is measured as the proportion (or percentage) of correct semantic categorization decisions (*yes* responses) to each type of exemplar target (related and unrelated) to the total number of each type of target presented. For example, if a participant saw 24 related prime-target pairs (exemplar targets) overall and identified 18 of the targets correctly as belonging to a particular semantic category, then this participant's response accuracy for this type of target is .75. Response latency or reaction time is defined as the amount of time between the onset of the target word and the participant's response to it. As in lexical decision tasks, response latencies are recorded by stimulus presentation software running the experimental procedure (e.g. *DMDX*, *E-Prime*, *PsyScope*). In calculation of error rates

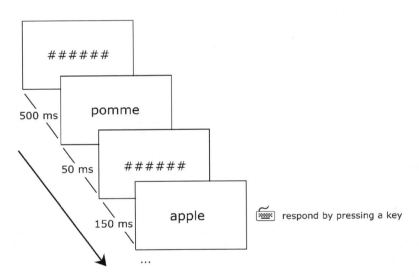

Figure 3.3 A schematic illustration of a (cross-language) primed semantic categorization task (modeled after Finkbeiner et al., 2004). This illustration depicts the following sequence of events for each trial: (1) a forward mask (# # # # # #) is presented for 500 ms, (2) the mask is replaced by the prime word (e.g. *pomme*) which stays on the screen for 50 ms, (3) a backward mask (# # # # # #) is presented for 150 ms, (4) this mask is replaced by the target word (e.g. *apple*), (5) participant makes a categorization decision to the target word. Words *pomme* (French for "apple") and *apple* represent a semantically related (cross-language translation) prime-target pair.

and response latencies, researchers typically consider only responses to exemplar targets (i.e. those requiring a *yes* decision).

Independent variables. Yet another independent variable often manipulated in semantic categorization tasks (and in other semantic priming tasks described in this section) involves the visibility of the prime word. Researchers manipulate the visibility of the prime word for similar reasons they employ shorter SOAs separating prime and target words— to minimize the extent to which participants rely on controlled, strategic processing in completing the task. The goal here is to make the presentation of the prime word so "invisible" to participants so that they would process the prime but would not be aware of its presence. If semantic priming still occurs under such conditions—when participants are not aware of the prime and cannot detect its presence—then it is argued that semantic priming effects are largely automatic and are unaffected by strategic influences (McNamara, 2005, chapter 14).

To minimize the visibility of prime words, researchers typically employ masking techniques. These include forward masking, backward masking, and both forward and backward masking. In backward masking, for example, a prime is presented very briefly (often for about 50 ms) and is followed by a pattern mask (e.g. XXXXXX or XWXWXW) and then the target word to which participants respond. Other masking procedures involve forward masking (when a pattern mask precedes the prime) and both forward and backward masking (when the prime is preceded and followed by a pattern mask). The masking techniques (again, presented separately for within- and cross-language designs) used in a selection of published L2 semantic priming studies can be found in table 3.3, and the results of a semantic categorization task can be found in box 3.6. We conclude this section with a summary of an L2 semantic priming study, which is highlighted in box 3.7.

Table 3.3 Masking techniques used in published semantic priming studies

Within-language designs	*L2 Studies*
Forward masking	Frenck-Mestre & Prince (1997): Ex. 1, 2
Both forward and backward masking	Fox (1996): Ex. 1, 2
Unmasked	Dong et al. (2005): Ex. 1; Elston-Güttler & Friederici (2005); Elston-Güttler et al. (2005); Kotz & Elston-Güttler (2004); Favreau & Segalowitz (1983); Ibrahim & Aharon-Peretz (2005); Kotz (2001)
Between-language designs	*L2 Studies*
Forward masking	Gollan et al. (1997); Jiang & Forster (2001): Ex. 3, 4; Jiang (1999): Ex. 1–3; Basnight-Brown & Altarriba (2007): Ex. 2

(*Continued Overleaf*)

Table 3.3 Continued

Between-language designs	L2 Studies
Both forward and backward masking	Grainger & Frenck-Mestre (1998); Jiang & Forster (2001): Ex. 1; Finkbeiner et al. (2004): Ex. 1–3; de Groot & Nas (1991): Ex. 2–4; Fox (1996): Ex. 1, 2; Jiang (1999): Ex. 4, 5
Unmasked	Altarriba (1992); Alvarez et al. (2003); de Groot & Nas (1991): Ex. 1; Dong et al. (2005): Ex. 1; Ibrahim & Aharon-Peretz (2005); Keatley et al. (1994); Schwanenflugel & Rey (1986): Ex. 1; Silverberg & Samuel (2004); Tzelgov & Eben-Ezra (1992); Basnight-Brown & Altarriba (2007): Ex. 1

Note: Ex. = Experiment.

Box 3.6 Sample results from a semantic categorization task

The results of semantic priming tasks (including semantic categorization tasks) can also be reported in a graphical format. The following figure (based on data from Experiments 1 and 2 in Finkbeiner et al., 2004) depicts mean response latencies for native Japanese speakers of English in semantic categorization and lexical decision tasks. Response latencies represent data only from *yes* trials in both tasks. This graph shows a significant semantic priming effect in the semantic categorization task but not in the lexical decision task.

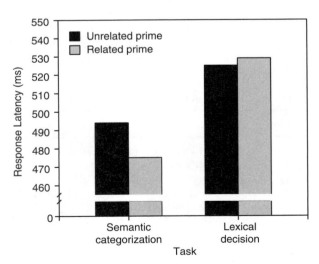

Response latencies for Japanese (L1) targets preceded by related and unrelated English (L2) primes in semantic categorization and lexical decision tasks.

Sample L2 Semantic Priming Study

Box 3.7 Sample L2 semantic priming study

Silverberg, S., & Samuel, A. G. (2004). The effect of age of second language acquisition on the representation and processing of second language words. *Journal of Memory and Language*, *51*, 381–398.

Background: Previous research has demonstrated that age of L2 learning may determine how learners represent and use their L2. The goal of this study is to investigate whether early and late learners of an L2 differ in their organization and use of conceptual (semantic) information in their two languages.

Research questions: Do early and late learners of an L2 show semantic priming effects, which would suggest that their L1 and L2 share a single conceptual representation? Do early and late learners show equivalent semantic priming effects?

Participants: 72 L2 learners of English, all L1 speakers of Spanish. Of these, 24 were early learners (mean age of L2 learning = 4.7) while 48 were late learners (mean age of L2 learning = 12.1). Half of the late learners had high L2 proficiency (comparable to early learners' proficiency), half had low L2 proficiency.

Materials: The materials included 72 English (L2) primes, 72 Spanish (L1) targets, and 96 Spanish nonwords. In one of the three priming conditions, L2 primes were matched either with semantically related L1 targets (*nail-tornillo* ["screw" in Spanish]) or with unrelated L1 targets (*bark-tornillo*).

Procedure: The participants completed a lexical decision task, with targets following primes at three different SOAs: 350, 500, and 650 ms. A methodological innovation of this task was that primes and targets were presented in adjacent trials (not in pairs), which made it less likely for participants to detect prime–target relatedness and minimized their reliance on strategic processing. Semantic priming is established in this task if participants respond faster to the targets preceded by semantically related primes than to the targets preceded by semantically unrelated primes.

Analysis: The dependent variable was a priming effect score, calculated by subtracting (for each participant) the reaction time for semantically related targets from the reaction time for semantically unrelated targets.

Results: Because SOA did not systematically affect the pattern of results, the data were collapsed across this variable. Results revealed a statistically significant semantic priming effect for the early learners (49 ms) but not for the high proficiency (−4 ms) or the low proficiency (16 ms) late learners.

(Box 3.7 Continued)

Box 3.7 Continued

Discussion: Because L2 primes (e.g. *nail*) facilitated the processing of L1 targets (e.g. *tornillo*) for the early learners, these learners appear to have shared conceptual representations for words in their two languages. Because no such facilitation was found for the late learners, including those who were matched to the early learners in L2 proficiency, late learners appear to have separate conceptual representations for words in their two languages.

Implications: In the same study, evidence was found for shared and for separate conceptual representations for L1 and L2 words. Implications of these findings are twofold. First, age of L2 learning appears to be an important factor determining the L1–L2 language architecture. Second, future semantic priming studies need to consider age of L2 learning, as this variable may explain often disparate findings available to date in cross-language semantic priming research (see Altarriba & Basnight-Brown, 2007).

Issues to Consider in Semantic Priming Research

Selecting an Appropriate Task

As with any psycholinguistic tasks, the semantic priming tasks discussed in this chapter are based on certain assumptions. One assumption common to all tasks is that they encourage language users to access conceptual information about words. The idea here is that language users cannot perform the task (e.g. pronounce a word or decide whether or not a letter string is a real word) without accessing the meaning of the presented word. Although all of the tasks described in this chapter require retrieval of semantic information (e.g. Slowiaczek, 1994), it appears that some tasks may do so to a greater extent than others. For example, there is evidence that semantic categorization tasks necessarily require access to semantic information whereas lexical decision tasks might not (e.g. Balota & Chumbley, 1984). Some researchers in fact attribute the existence of contradictory findings in cross-language semantic priming research precisely to this purported difference between tasks (Finkbeiner et al., 2004; Grainger & Frenck-Mestre, 1998).

Other researchers have pointed out that the extent to which semantic priming tasks involve semantic, conceptual processing also depends on the nature of the materials used (Lupiker, 1984). For example, participants may be more likely to access conceptual-level representations for words that are related semantically as members of the same category (e.g. *lion-tiger*) than for words that share associative links (e.g. *tiger-stripes*). These two types of relationships between words are discussed in box 3.2.

In designing semantic priming tasks, it is important to consider issues such as these because valid interpretations of task results (e.g. that bilinguals represent L1–L2 conceptual information in a shared or a separate manner) clearly depend on the extent to which participants access conceptual information in performing a task. One way to address this issue in L2 semantic priming studies is to test participants in several tasks within a single study, using similar (preferably identical) materials that span a range of semantic relationships. Such designs may help understand whether and to what degree semantic processing in bilinguals and L2 learners is specific to particular tasks (e.g. Finkbeiner et al., 2004) and particular materials (e.g. Frenck-Mestre & Prince, 1997).

The semantic priming tasks described in this chapter also differ in a number of other ways. For example, the tasks differ in terms of the processing operations involved in performing each task. Lexical decision and semantic categorization tasks involve comprehension processes. In contrast, pronunciation tasks ostensibly include both comprehension and production components. In interpreting task results, it is important to consider how semantic priming effects depend on access to semantic information in speaking versus comprehending a language.

Semantic priming tasks also differ in terms of the types of materials used in each and the data that these materials yield. Some researchers have argued that pronunciation tasks are superior to lexical decision tasks because the former include more materials that yield usable data points than the latter (Larsen et al., 1994). The argument here is that between a third and a half of the items in a lexical decision task are nonwords whereas all items in a pronunciation task are real words. (Recall that nonwords are included in a lexical decision task as distractors or fillers.) Moreover, pronunciation tasks may seem to be slightly more "naturalistic" from the participant's point of view than lexical decision tasks, as pronouncing words is ostensibly a simpler, more common task than deciding whether a letter string is a word or a nonword.

Last but not least, semantic priming tasks may differ in the extent to which they are susceptible to strategic, controlled processing. Some researchers have argued that lexical decision tasks, because they require participants to distinguish between words and nonwords, are particularly prone to effects of strategic processing (Balota & Chumbley, 1984). Participants may, for example, "search" for a relationship between primes and targets, engaging in a strategy that may inflate their word or nonword response rate (see McNamara, 2005, chapter 9). In contrast, pronunciation tasks, and perhaps semantic categorization tasks, are ostensibly less influenced by participant strategies. As a result, they might yield a "cleaner" semantic priming effect. Despite these concerns, lexical decision tasks have been used successfully in semantic priming research, and researchers have developed certain procedures to minimize strategic and other

Table 3.4 Factors to consider when deciding among semantic priming tasks

Consideration	Appropriate task(s)
Both comprehension and production processes involved	Pronunciation
Comprehension processes involved	Lexical decision, semantic categorization
Less "natural" tasks	Lexical decision
More "natural" tasks	Pronunciation, semantic categorization
Most commonly used task	Lexical decision
Nonwords needed	Lexical decision
Participant strategies play an important role	Lexical decision
Tape recorder or voice-activated millisecond timer required	Pronunciation

unwanted effects in such tasks. In the following section, we discuss several of these procedures and outline other issues to be considered in designing semantic priming experiments. Some of the factors to consider when deciding among the three semantic priming tasks are listed in table 3.4.

Selecting Materials

Researchers typically begin creating a semantic priming study by selecting appropriate materials to use. This step is crucial because the quality of the study depends on the quality of the materials used. As was discussed earlier, all semantic priming tasks include at least two types of words: word pairs that are related in meaning and those that are not. Researchers therefore need to make sure that the word pairs they identify as related are indeed related in meaning and, conversely, that the word pairs they identify as unrelated are indeed unrelated. There are several sources researchers can consult. For example, researchers can first examine published semantic priming studies. The majority of published reports include an appendix that lists the entire set of study materials. Researchers can also consult word norms databases, for example, the University of South Florida Word Norms database (Nelson, McEvoy, & Schreiber, 1998) or the WordNet database (Fellbaum, 1998). Such databases are called norms databases because they often not only include extensive lists of words but also provide important information about each word's properties. For instance, these properties include indices of how concrete or imageable words are or how strongly these words are associated semantically to other words (e.g. Altarriba, Bauer, & Benvenuto, 1999). In creating materials for lexical decision and pronunciation tasks, researchers can thus consult such databases to select word pairs that are strongly associated semantically as related prime-target pairs and, conversely, those that are not strongly associated semantically as unrelated prime-target pairs. Similar norms databases are also available for words grouped into particular semantic categories (e.g. Battig & Montague, 1969; Ueda & Mandler, 1980). In creating materials for semantic categorization tasks, researchers can consult these sources to choose words that are clear exemplars of a given semantic category.

In the absence of suitable word databases and norms, researchers often carry out their own word-norming study prior to conducting their experiment. For example, prior to conducting a lexical decision task, Silverberg and Samuel (2004) asked 50 native speakers of English to go through a list of potential target words and to write down a number of words that participants would associate with each. Upon seeing the word *salt*, a participant could, for example, respond by writing down *pepper* or *white*. These researchers then tallied all the responses and selected the most frequent one given for each target word. For example, if 45 of 50 participants listed *pepper* as their first response to the word *salt* and only 5 listed *white*, then *pepper* was paired with *salt* as a semantically associated prime-target pair. In cross-language translation-priming studies, researchers often conduct similar word-norming studies. Such studies are important because some words in one language may have more than one translation in another (e.g. *divan* in Russian can be translated as *sofa* or *couch* in English). Researchers thus need to ensure that the prime-target translation pairs they intend to use are indeed the most common translation equivalents across languages.

Matching Task Materials

As in auditory priming tasks, researchers need to pay particular attention to lexical characteristics of words in creating semantic priming tasks. Such lexical characteristics, among others, include word frequency, word length, and word cognate status (translation equivalents that are similar in spelling and pronunciation, e.g. *musicien-musician* in French and English). It is important to control for these word characteristics in creating materials for semantic priming tasks because these characteristics are known to affect the magnitude of priming effects (e.g. Balota & Chumbley, 1984; de Groot & Nas, 1991). For example, more frequent words may be accessed in memory more rapidly than less frequent words. Such differences in access speed may thus influence the extent of semantic activation for more and less frequent words. Similarly, shorter words may have a speed advantage over longer words because they are processed faster (in reading and listening). In addition, shorter words may be higher in frequency than longer words. Last but not least, cognate words across languages enjoy a special status because of phonological and orthographic similarity between them (e.g. de Groot & Nas, 1991; Sanchez-Casas et al., 1992). Such phonological and orthographic overlap between cognates may influence the extent of semantic priming effects and may bias the results of an experiment. Researchers, therefore, need to control for these variables in creating experimental and control word lists, matching words across these lists on word frequency, number of letters or syllables per word, and using only non-cognate words across the participants' languages (unless, of course, cognate status is a variable of interest). Finally, as is the case with any psycholinguistic study, all the materials need to be counterbalanced to minimize potential idiosyncratic (negative) effects of task materials on task outcomes (see chapter 2, pp. 47–50). McNamara (2005, chapter 8) provides an excellent example of how to counterbalance materials for a semantic priming study.

Nonwords and their Properties

An important design issue specific to a lexical decision task involves creating nonwords. Nonwords are needed because this task requires participants to decide whether or not the presented sequence of letters is a real word in a language. Nonwords are often created manually by changing one letter in real words. For example, nonwords *foltow, cose, rable* were created by substituting one letter in the following English words: *follow, case,* and *table,* respectively. Researchers can also use special programs to create large numbers of nonwords with specific properties, for example, nonwords of a certain length, a particular syllable structure, nonwords in various languages, or nonwords containing certain vowels or consonants. *WordGenerator* (current version 1.7) and *WordGen* (Duyck, Desmet, Verbeke, & Brysbaert, 2004) are examples of such programs available free of charge on the Web (type *WordGenerator* in Google to locate *WordGenerator* download sites; *WordGen* is available at http:// users.ugent.be/~wduyck/Wouter%20Duyck/wordgen.html).

In a lexical decision task, it is important that nonwords be pronounceable (i.e. phonologically possible) in a given language. All of the above nonwords are phonologically possible in English. In contrast, *ngo* (created by substituting one letter in the word *ago*) is not pronounceable, as no English word starts with an *ng* sequence. Unpronounceable nonwords (those that do not resemble any possible words in a language) may introduce a certain bias in an experimental procedure. Such nonwords may "stand out" as being unlike any other items in an experiment. As a result, participants might be fast at making a *no* judgment on these nonwords, influencing the extent to which semantic priming effects are shown. For cross-language lexical decision tasks, Altarriba and Basnight-Brown (2007) recommend that researchers also include nonwords that are pronounceable in the L2 in addition to those that are pronounceable in the L1. Such a design, they argue, will result in task materials that are equivalent in both languages, free of bias toward either language.

In addition to carefully controlling the type of nonwords used in a lexical decision task, researchers should also consider how *many* nonwords to include. If the number of nonwords is larger than the number of real words, then participants may be biased to make nonword responses. On the contrary, if the number of nonwords is smaller than the number of real words, then participants may be biased to make word responses (McNamara, 2005; Neely et al., 1989). These biases are based on strategic processes whereby participants "search" for a relationship between the presented targets and primes. The prevalence of nonwords over words (or vice versa) might encourage such strategic processes, influencing participants' decisions at the response selection stage (i.e. when they make a word or a nonword response). In order to minimize such biases, it is suggested that researchers keep the nonword ratio (or the proportion of nonwords to the total number of nonword and unrelated word trials) at about .5. Another important number to keep in mind in designing lexical decision and pronunciation tasks is the relatedness proportion, which is the total number of related word pairs to the total number of word pairs. It is suggested that researchers keep this proportion as low as possible to minimize other kinds of strategic processes, capable of affecting semantic priming effects (for details, see an excellent discussion in Altarriba & Basnight-Brown, 2007).

Presentation Format

A researcher wishing to use lexical decision and pronunciation tasks to study semantic priming should carefully consider the presentation format of task materials. In previous research, prime and target pairs have been presented in several ways. Some researchers presented both primes and targets simultaneously in a single format, effectively with an interval (SOA) of 0 milliseconds (e.g. Kirsner et al., 1984). Other researchers presented primes and targets in a double format, asking participants first to read the prime and then, after it had been replaced by the target, to respond to the target (e.g. Altarriba, 1992). Yet other researchers presented primes and targets sequentially on separate trials, requiring participants to respond to each (e.g. Silverberg & Samuel, 2004). In a comprehensive review of cross-language semantic priming research, Altarriba and Basnight-Brown (2007) argued that this last presentation format—when primes and targets are presented sequentially on separate trials requiring participants to make a response first to the prime and then to the target—appears to be most suited for this kind of research. By presenting primes and targets sequentially, researchers minimize the likelihood that participants would somehow "link" primes and targets in their minds and would develop a certain strategy for processing them.

Silverberg and Samuel (2004) successfully implemented this kind of presentation format in a cross-language lexical decision task (see also Basnight-Brown & Altarriba, 2007). In their version of this task, adapted from McNamara and Altarriba (1988), the researchers embedded target words in sequences that varied randomly in length between two and five items. More importantly, these researchers required their participants to respond to each item presented, making either a word or a nonword decision. From the researchers' perspective, one item in each sequence (trial *n*) was designated as a prime for the next item in the sequence (trial *n* + *1*). From the participants' perspective, however, any two adjacent items were not different from any other items, as the participants were required to make a decision about each and every one of them. By presenting items in this format, Silverberg and Samuel thus ensured that the relationship between primes and targets was not apparent to their participants and, as a result, discouraged them from relying on strategic processing in completing the task.

Additional Uses of Semantic Priming Methods

Over the last several decades, semantic priming (whether in L1 or L2) has attracted a great deal of attention in language processing research. Therefore, the factors that contribute to the ecological validity of semantic priming methods (see chapter 1, pp. 4–6, for more details) are relatively well understood (Altarriba & Basnight-Brown, 2007). This is because semantic priming studies (especially in the L1) have focused on a relatively wide variety of languages, targeted different populations of language users, and made use of diverse tasks including neuroimaging techniques such as fMRI. Rigorous research of this kind needs to be carried out in the L2, testing different populations of L2 users (stable bilinguals, learners of different ages, multilinguals) and using several priming tasks within the same study (for an example, see Basnight-Brown & Altarriba, 2007). In the following sections, we describe areas of future research that are not only interesting from a theoretical standpoint but could also bolster the ecological validity of semantic priming research.

Studying Semantic Priming in Sentential Contexts

There are several avenues of research to be explored using semantic priming methods. One of these is studying semantic priming in contexts that are larger than individual words. Although the processing of individual words is revealing of basic psycholinguistic mechanisms of accessing word meaning and retrieving word forms from memory, such processing is not fully representative of the different ways speakers use language on a daily basis. For example, when listening or speaking, language users activate semantic information for several words simultaneously or near-simultaneously. This information is used in real time for encoding and decoding sentences in production and comprehension. It is therefore important to investigate how language users access and use this information in comprehending and speaking utterances that are longer than individual words—phrases, sentences, or longer units of discourse. For example, do L2 learners and bilinguals activate multiple sources of semantic information simultaneously when comprehending and producing sentences? Do they activate semantic information for words in both their languages, even if one of the languages is irrelevant to the task at hand? How does the activation of semantic information unfold as bilinguals and L2 learners comprehend or produce sentences in their two languages? There are some preliminary answers to these questions from a handful of studies that have investigated L2 semantic priming in sentential contexts (Elston-Güttler & Friederici, 2005; Elston-Güttler et al., 2005; Love, Maas, & Swinney, 2003). More research of this kind is needed to determine exactly how bilinguals, multilinguals, and L2 learners use semantic information in their languages and how this information interacts with other types of information available, including syntactic, morphological, and phonological.

Individual Differences and Semantic Priming

Another line of research to be explored concerns the study of bilinguals' and L2 learners' individual differences in the activation and use of semantic information in both their languages. It is well known that individual differences in attention, memory, and language aptitude (among others) underlie the processing of many different aspects of an L2 in bilinguals and L2 learners (e.g. Trofimovich, Ammar, & Gatbonton, 2007; see Robinson, 2002, for review). It is therefore likely that such individual differences may also determine how bilinguals and L2 learners access and use semantic information in their L2. That is, individual difference factors—for example, the size of working memory or ability to efficiently allocate attention between processing tasks—might influence precisely the kind of processing involved in semantic priming. For example, do individual differences in cognitive abilities (memory, attention, or language aptitude, for example) determine how bilinguals and L2 learners activate semantic information in their L2? Do such individual differences determine whether bilinguals and L2 learners create and use shared (or separate) conceptual representations in both their languages? Answers to these questions may not only clarify why some bilinguals and L2 learners do not reach "autonomy" in their L2 processing but may also suggest what experiences may be beneficial for them in developing such autonomy.

To date, there have been a handful of studies that have looked at individual differences in L2 semantic processing. For example, Segalowitz and his colleagues have investigated individual differences in bilinguals' and L2 learners' automaticity (efficiency) of L1 and L2 semantic processing (e.g. Phillips et al., 2004; Taube-Schiff & Segalowitz, 2005; for review, see Segalowitz & Hulstijn, 2005). More research is needed to investigate the role of other individual difference factors in L2 semantic processing. The overall objective of this research would be to understand the role of individual differences from a perspective that views L2 learning as the development of flexible and fluent cognitive processing skills (see Segalowitz, 1997, for more details on this view of individual differences).

Summary

In this chapter, we introduced semantic priming and the topics that have been explored in L1, bilingual and L2 research using semantic priming methods. We described the three experimental tasks used in semantic priming research (lexical decision, pronunciation, and semantic categorization) and pointed out some issues that researchers might consider when designing such tasks. Finally, we suggested some additional ways in which semantic priming can be used in L2 research. In the next chapter, we focus in more detail on syntactic priming.

Follow-up Questions and Activities

1. Locate a published empirical study that investigates semantic priming in L1, bilingual, or L2 processing or acquisition and answer the following questions:

   a) What question(s) does the study attempt to address by using a semantic priming task?

   b) What specific task is used in this study? Is that task appropriate for the stated question(s)?

   c) How do the researchers select and present their materials in their semantic priming task? What kinds of semantic relationships do they study?

   d) Do the researchers consider that some of their findings might be caused by strategic (controlled), as opposed to automatic, processing?

   e) How do they ensure that the reported semantic priming effects can be interpreted as meaningful?

2. For the following research questions, explain what semantic priming tasks and what materials would be most appropriate.

a) How do bilinguals and L2 learners access and use semantic information in both their languages?

b) How elaborate are semantic networks in bilinguals' and L2 learners' L1 and L2?

c) How do bilinguals and L2 learners represent and use conceptual information for cognate and noncognate words in their two languages? How do they represent and use conceptual information for concrete and abstract words, and for words that have multiple meanings (e.g. *bank*: financial institution and river side)?

d) Devitto and Burgess (2004) found that L2 learners, unlike monolingual speakers, do not show semantic priming effects for weakly associated L2 word pairs (e.g. *city-grass*). What kinds of L2 learning experiences might enable L2 learners to demonstrate semantic priming effects for such types of words?

e) Frenck-Mestre and Prince (1997) argue that advanced L2 learners achieve what they call autonomous semantic processing in the L2. What factors might influence whether L2 learners do or not achieve this type of processing?

f) Does L2 learners' working memory (their ability to simultaneously process and store verbal information relevant to the processing task at hand) influence the extent to which they access and use semantic information in their L1 and L2?

3. List at least two methodological issues that are important to consider in designing and implementing semantic priming tasks. Explain why these issues are important.

4. In an excellent review of cross-language semantic priming research, Altarriba and Basnight-Brown (2007) offered 12 methodological recommendations for future priming research. Locate and read Altarriba and Basnight-Brown's article. In your opinion, which recommendations do you think are the most critical and which are the least critical?

5. Besides those mentioned in this chapter, what other topics might L2 researchers use semantic priming tasks to investigate?

6. In terms of their materials development, procedure, and analysis, which of the tasks used in semantic priming research seems to be the easiest to implement? Which ones seem more difficult?

7. Imagine that you are planning to conduct a semantic priming study using a pronunciation task with learners of a language you know. For this task, you will need a list of materials. Your assignment is to create such a list by carrying out a word-

norming study of your own. First, identify a list of a minimum of 15 possible target words (use common, concrete words). Second, ask at least 10 native speakers of the language you are targeting to write down the first several words that come to mind when reading each target word. Third, tally your respondents' answers and select, for each target word, the most frequent response (i.e. the most frequent semantic associate of each word). Finally, based on these results, organize your materials into two sets: (a) semantically associated prime-target pairs and (b) semantically unassociated prime-target pairs. An example for Russian words is shown in table 3.5.

Table 3.5 Sample word-norming results

Associated prime-target pairs	Unassociated prime-target pairs
sol-sahar (salt-sugar)	*kniga-vilka* (book-fork)
. . .	. . .

4

SYNTACTIC PRIMING

In this chapter, we define syntactic priming and describe how syntactic priming methods have been used in L1 and L2 processing and acquisition research. We introduce the four experimental tasks used in syntactic priming research and describe in detail the materials, procedure and analysis of each task. We highlight an example study that used syntactic priming to investigate L2 acquisition, and we point out issues to consider when designing syntactic priming studies. We conclude the chapter with suggestions for additional uses of syntactic priming methods in L2 research.

What is Syntactic Priming?

Syntactic priming refers to a general tendency for language users to produce a syntactic structure following previous experience with that structure. Like auditory and semantic priming, syntactic priming also fits well with Gladwell's description of priming as mental operations, which in this case, keep tabs on the syntactic structure of the language occurring around us. Similar to auditory priming, syntactic priming involves the priming of language form, as opposed to the priming of language meaning associated with semantic priming. For example, if a person hears an interlocutor produce a double-object dative (e.g. *Susie baked her friends a cake*) she is more likely to produce another double-object dative later in the conversation than to produce an equally acceptable prepositional dative (e.g. *John bought a bicycle for his mother*). Speakers tend to produce the recently encountered syntactic structure even if the initial and subsequent utterances do not have any of the same lexical items, metrical properties, or thematic roles (see box 4.1).

Box 4.1 Syntactic priming

Syntactic priming (also referred to as *structural priming*) is the tendency for speakers to produce a particular syntactic structure (as opposed to an equally acceptable structure) after recent exposure to that structure. The initial exposure through production or comprehension (the prime) is believed to activate linguistic information, combinatorial nodes, and/or other aspects of sentence structure, with residual activation facilitating subsequent production (the response or target).

However, the term syntactic priming has also been used to refer to a different phenomenon, which is the facilitation of word processing due to the word's compatibility with a prior syntactic structure. In this paradigm, the focus is on how the syntactic structure of an initial stimulus affects subsequent processing of a lexical item that is either compatible or incompatible with that structure. For more information on this type of syntactic priming, see Nicol (1996).

Why would language users produce a syntactic structure they have recently encountered as opposed to an equally acceptable alternative? The process of comprehending or producing a syntactic structure is believed to activate the structural information stored with individual lexical items (like subcategorization information stored with verbs) and/or phrase structure frames. Once this activation occurs, residual activation remains and facilitates the subsequent use of that same structure. Put simply, it is easier for speakers to access a syntactic structure that has been recently activated than to access a completely new structure. The activation believed to underlie syntactic priming can occur if a speaker hears and repeats a syntactic structure (e.g. Bock, 1986, 1989; Bock et al., 1992), or if a speaker only hears a syntactic structure (e.g. Branigan, Pickering, & Cleland, 2000; Branigan, Pickering, Liversedge, Stewart, & Urbach, 1995; Pickering, Branigan, Cleland, & Stewart, 2000). Comparison studies have shown that there is no apparent difference in the strength or persistence of syntactic priming in the two contexts for adults and older children (Bock, Dell, Chang & Onishi, 2007; Huttenlocher, Vasilyeva, & Shimpi, 2004; McDonough, 2006; Savage et al., 2003). Although some recent studies have investigated whether hearing and/or producing a prime structure facilitates subsequent comprehension, rather than production, of a target structure (Arai, van Gompel, & Scheepers, 2007; Ledoux, Traxler, & Swaab, 2007), the majority of syntactic priming research examines its occurrence in language production.

As described in box 4.1, syntactic priming is defined as the tendency to produce a syntactic structure following previous experience with that structure. To clarify our terminology, what we refer to as syntactic priming is the general tendency for speakers to produce a syntactic structure that was recently encountered. It is measured by calculating how frequently speakers produce a particular structure following exposure to that structure, compared to their use of that structure following exposure to an alternate structure. Unlike auditory and semantic priming research, which typically measure speed and/or accuracy of processing, syntactic priming research typically elicits language production data, which is then analyzed in terms of its syntactic form. And unlike auditory and semantic priming, which can include a wide variety of lexical items in the experimental materials, syntactic priming is limited to those syntactic structures that have at least two alternate forms.

Because syntactic priming involves the production of a recently encountered structure as opposed to an alternate structure that expresses the same meaning, the syntactic structures tested in priming research must allow alternate forms. As an example of a syntactic structure typically targeted in syntactic priming research, consider dative constructions. Some dative verbs can occur as a prepositional dative (e.g. *she gave the present to her mother*), or as a double-object dative (e.g. *she gave her mother the present*). Datives have been widely tested in syntactic priming research because the availability of these two syntactic structures to express the same meaning allows researchers to determine whether prior exposure to a specific dative form (the prime) influences a speaker's subsequent production (the response or target). In addition to datives, other structures that have been widely tested in syntactic priming research include active/passive transitives, spray-load constructions, verbs that take NP and/or clausal complements, and relative clauses.

The data in table 4.1 (adapted from table 3 in Bock, 1989) illustrates syntactic priming involving prepositional and double-object datives. The participants produced more prepositional dative responses after prepositional dative primes (400) than after double-object dative primes (272). Similarly, they produced more double-object dative responses after double-object dative primes (705) than after prepositional dative primes (563). Their production of dative responses indicates syntactic priming because there was an association between the structure they were exposed to and the structure of their responses.

Syntactic priming generally is not concerned with the overall frequency of the two alternate structures. For example, the data in table 4.1 shows that in general the participants produced more double-object datives (1268) than prepositional datives (672), and even produced more double-object datives (563) than prepositional datives (400) after prepositional dative primes. The important relationship tested in syntactic priming research is whether participants produce a particular structure more

Table 4.1 Dative responses by prime

Prime	Reponses	
	Prepositional dative	Double-object dative
Prepositional dative	400	563
Double-object dative	272	705
Total	672	1268

often after they have just been exposed to it, as opposed to when they have been exposed to the alternative.

An additional measure occasionally reported in syntactic priming studies involves the analysis of the participants' responses in a baseline phase before they were exposed to primes in the experimental trials (Hartsuiker & Kolk, 1998a; Hartsuiker & Westenberg, 2000). A *baseline phase*, is when researchers first elicit the target structures from the participants without providing any models of the structure (see box 4.2). They then expose the participants to the two (or more) alternate forms of the target structure in the experimental materials and calculate the proportions of responses after each form. There is an additional comparison between the participants' production of the target structures during the baseline and experimental tasks to determine whether their tendency to produce the alternate structures changed. In this approach, the focus is not only the relationship between a previously encountered structure and the participant's immediate production, but also changes in the participants' overall tendency to produce each structure.

Box 4.2 Baseline

The term *baseline* has been used in syntactic priming research to refer to the initial trials of an experiment in which the participants' production of the target structures is elicited without exposing them to any primes (e.g. Hartsuiker & Kolk, 1998a). Their initial production of the structures in the absence of primes is then compared to their subsequent production of those structures following the primes.

In some studies, the term *baseline prime* refers to a prime that does not induce a participant to use one of the alternating syntactic forms (Hartsuiker, Kolk, & Huiskamp, 1999). For example, sentence completion studies that investigated relative clause attachment (e.g. Desmet & Declercq, 2006) used three prime fragments: a prime that would lead the participant to produce a high-attachment relative clause, a prime that would lead them to produce a low-attachment relative clause, and a prime that could be completed without a relative clause. The third prime was referred to as the baseline prime, as it did not encourage speakers to use either type of relative clause. Their response to the baseline primes was used as an indication of their preference for high or low attachment relative clauses in the absence of a relative clause prime.

The inclusion of a baseline phase is illustrated in the data in table 4.2 (adapted from table 3 in Hartsuiker & Kolk, 1998a). In terms of syntactic priming, the participants produced more prepositional datives after prepositional dative primes (53) than after double-object dative primes (42).

Table 4.2 Comparison of production during baseline and experimental trials

Trial	Reponses	
	Prepositional datives	*Double-object datives*
Baseline phase	22	17
Prepositional dative primes	53	40
Double-object dative primes	42	47

Similarly, they produced more double-object datives after double-object dative primes (47) than after prepositional dative primes (40).

In terms of their baseline production, the participants produced more prepositional datives than double-object datives, and their production of both dative forms increased in the priming trials. By including a baseline phase, researchers can determine the initial frequency with which participants produce particular linguistic structures, and then to assess how exposure to those structures in the priming trials affects their production.

In summary, syntactic priming has been defined as the tendency for speakers to produce a syntactic structure following previous experience with that structure as compared to previous experience with the alternate structure (see box 4.1). While some researchers have begun to explore whether exposure to prime structures facilitates the subsequent comprehension of target structures, most syntactic priming research has investigated the facilitative effect of exposure to primes on subsequent language production. The goal of this chapter is to look at syntactic priming in more detail, focusing on the studies that have examined its role in language production. We first characterize the role of syntactic priming in L1 and L2 processing and learning, and discuss ways of eliciting it. We describe the four experimental tasks commonly used in syntactic priming research, and outline methodological considerations when designing syntactic priming studies. Prior to providing the details of each syntactic priming task, we present an overview of the topics investigated in L1, bilingual and L2 syntactic priming research.

Syntactic Priming in L1 Processing and Acquisition

Topics Explored in Syntactic Priming Research

One of the early topics explored in syntactic priming research was the relationship between meaning-oriented and structure-oriented speech production processing. Bock (1995) argued that structural features that are not crucial to understanding message content can be ignored during comprehension, but those structural features must be processed during production in order to formulate utterances that convey the speaker's intended meaning and conform to the relevant grammatical rules. She suggested that language production may involve distinct processing mechanisms that create either meaning or form. During speech production, errors are constrained by structural conditions that remain in place even when disruptions in meaning occur. For example, errors that involve substitution occur between members of the same grammatical form class, which preserves the structural integrity of the utterance even when the meaning becomes ill-formed. In a series of experiments, Bock and colleagues (1986, 1989; Bock & Loebell, 1990; Bock et al., 1992) investigated whether speakers' picture descriptions were influenced by prior exposure to sentences with similar syntactic structures. These experiments indicated that speakers are sensitive to the structural properties of previously produced sentences even when they have no semantic or discourse relationship.

Another topic investigated in early syntactic priming research was the mechanisms involved in sentence recall. Potter and Lombardi (1990) used syntactic priming to investigate whether immediate recall of sentences was due to regeneration from conceptual representations or verbatim memory of the sentence's surface features. They argued that the conceptual message of a sentence is represented in memory, but that the surface features of that sentence are not represented in short-term memory. As a result, in order to recall a comprehended sentence a speaker regenerates the surface syntax, drawing upon the conceptual message and active lexical representations. To test their claims, Potter and Lombardi used the sentence recall technique to determine whether speakers' recall of sentences would be affected by the presentation of an intervening word or sentence that called for an alternative syntactic structure. If recall was based on verbal memory, the participants' recall of the original sentence would not be affected by the intervening word or sentence. However, if recall was based on regeneration from conceptual representation, then participants' recall of the original sentences could be altered by switching to the alternative structure suggested by the intervening word or sentence. In a series of experiments (Potter & Lombardi, 1990, 1998; Lombardi & Potter, 1992), they demonstrated that sentence recall occurred as a result of regeneration from conceptual representations, rather than verbatim memory of a sentence's surface features.

A major focus of syntactic priming research has been to identify the mechanisms responsible for its occurrence. One of the earliest explanations for syntactic priming was offered by Bock (1990), who suggested that it may occur as the result of the activation and reuse of sentence assembly processes. These processes are responsible for combining different constituents at the phrase level within an utterance. Processing mechanisms relevant for the processing of an initial utterance become activated, and as a result of residual activation, the combination of constituent structures will be reused in subsequent utterances. In an alternate explanation for syntactic priming, Pickering and Branigan (1998, 1999) have argued that it occurs as a result of feature-based activation of linguistic information at the lemma level. For example, each individual verb has three types of syntactic information associated with it: a node representing its syntactic category, nodes for its syntactic features, and nodes for its combinatorial information (the syntactic structures that the verb can occur in). They suggested that syntactic priming occurs due to the activation of combinatorial nodes (such as NP PP or NP NP for some dative verbs). The activation of a combinatorial node does not immediately fade, and can influence the processing of subsequent utterances with lexical items that also allow the same combination. Recent studies have provided support for the feature-based activation account by demonstrating that syntactic priming is greater when the initial and subsequent utterances involve the same lexical item, and that it can occur in response to single word primes, which is not predicted by the procedural account.

Researchers working from the feature-based account have also investigated how the syntactic information stored with lexical items interacts with other aspects of lexical representation, such as phonological and semantic information. Most contemporary models of language production state that the information associated with individual lexical items consists of two levels: a) phonological and morphological information and b) syntactic and semantic information. However, as pointed out in chapter 1, models differ in terms of how they posit the direction of flow of information between the two levels. In *feedforward* accounts, conceptual information activates forward to the word level, where it then moves forward to the word-form node and the relevant phonemes. In contrast, *interactive* accounts posit that feedback can occur in both directions. In other words, activation of phonemes can feed "backwards" to influence semantic and syntactic levels. While both accounts predict the occurrence of activation from the lexical item to the related syntactic structure, only the interactive account predicts that activation of phonological information could also affect syntactic structure. While syntactic priming studies have yet to support an interactive approach in which phonological information influences syntactic structure (Cleland & Pickering, 2003), research continues to investigate this possibility.

Some researchers have questioned the feature-based account because syntactic priming has been shown to occur with relative clause attachment, which is not feature-based syntactic information that is stored with individual lexical items (Desmet & Declercq, 2006; Scheepers, 2003). These findings can be accounted for if the feature-based account includes the possibility that the sequence of phrasal units generated by the application of syntactic rules remains activated and facilitates subsequent production of that same sequence. Finally, some researchers have argued that syntactic priming may be attributable to the activations of constructions (form and meaning) and thematic roles, rather than phrase structure representations alone (Chang et al., 2003; Hare & Goldberg, 1999).

Properties of Syntactic Priming

Compared to auditory and semantic priming, syntactic priming has a shorter empirical tradition, with experimental syntactic priming research only gaining prominence in the 1980s through the work of Bock and colleagues. Much of the early syntactic priming research focused on defining the phenomenon and ensuring that syntactic priming could not be explained by similarities in the phonological, lexical or semantic features of the primes and targets. Subsequent research has focused on exploring the impact of intervening time and material, modality, and how tense/aspect/number features affect the strength or persistence of syntactic priming. A sampling of the factors tested in L1 syntactic priming studies are summarized in table 4.3.

Overall, the findings of these studies have shown that speakers tend to be unaware of the syntactic features of their speech that are susceptible to priming. Even when experimental conditions encourage participants to remember the sentences, they are not able to accurately identify which sentences they had seen before. Morphological features—such as number, tense, and agreement, functional words including prepositions, and phonological features—do not appear to affect syntactic priming. Although the magnitude of syntactic priming is greater when the same verb is used in both the prime and target prompts, it occurs in language production even when there are no shared lexical items between the prime and the target. However, recent studies suggest that this might not be the case with comprehension priming, as syntactic priming during comprehension appears to be limited to contexts where the prime and the target share lexical items (Arai et al., 2007).

Syntactic priming does not appear to be modality-specific, in that it occurs both within and between modalities. In other words, it does not matter whether the prime and the target are in the same modality (either both oral or both written) or are in different modalities. In addition, syntactic priming persists despite intervening material and time, which suggests that it, like auditory priming, is not a transient phenomenon. Finally, syntactic priming has been shown to occur in a variety of populations, including L1 adults, L1 children at various ages, L1 children with specific language impairment (Marinelle, 2006), bilingual adults, L2 learners, and Broca's aphasics (Hartsuiker & Kolk, 1998b), which suggests that it may be a basic component of language processing. By targeting

Table 4.3 Factors tested in L1 syntactic priming studies

Variables	Studies
Semantic overlap between prime and target	Cleland & Pickering (2003)
Lexical overlap between prime and target	Arai et al. (2007); Bock (1989); Cleland & Pickering (2003); Ledoux et al. (2007); Pickering & Branigan (1998)
Modality	Cleland & Pickering (2006); Hartsuiker & Westenberg (2000)
Thematic/event roles	Bock & Loebell (1990): Ex. 1, 2; Chang et al. (2003); Griffin & Weinstein-Tull (2003); Hare & Goldberg (1999)
Complexity of prime noun phrases	Fox Tree & Meijer (1999): Ex. 2
Repetition of function words	Bock (1989); Fox Tree & Meijer (1999): Ex. 1
Valency of events	Potter & Lombardi (1998)
Intervening time or material between prime and target	Bock & Griffin (2000); Bock et al. (2007); Boyland & Anderson (1998); Branigan, Pickering & Cleland (1999); Branigan, Pickering, Stewart, & McLean (2000); Hartsuiker & Kolk (1998a)
Metrical similarity	Bock & Loebell (1990); Bock et al. (1992)
Animacy	Bock et al. (1992)
Single word primes	Melinger & Dobel (2005)
Tense, aspect & number of verb	Pickering & Branigan (1998)

Note: Ex. = Experiment.

such diverse language users, syntactic priming studies can positively contribute to the ecological validity of priming research.

Relevance of Syntactic Priming to L2 Processing and Learning

Recently, L1 acquisition researchers have adopted syntactic priming techniques to explore the nature of children's linguistic representations. In a series of studies, Tomasello and colleagues (e.g. Lieven, Behrens, Speares, & Tomasello, 2003; Matthews, Lieven, Theakston, & Tomasello, 2005; Tomasello & Brooks, 1998) have investigated whether children have abstract linguistic representations or whether their initial language development is characterized by lexically-based word patterns. They argued that in an early stage of linguistic development (about 2 to 2.5 years) children have only weak syntactic representations, which are associated primarily with specific lexical items. Over time based on exposure to the frequency with which certain linguistics structures appear in the input, their linguistic representations gradually grow in strength and abstractness. Syntactic priming studies (Savage et al., 2003, 2006) have supported this developmental trajectory by showing that young children produce developmentally-advanced structures only when their utterances share lexical items (such as verbs and pronouns) with the utterances produced by the researcher. However, older children (4 years and up), much like adults, can produce the syntactic structures produced by the researcher even when their utterances consist of entirely new lexical items. Additional syntactic priming studies have shown that syntactic priming occurs with older children (4- and 5-year-olds) in the absence of shared lexical items, but it does not occur with younger children (3-year olds) unless the children orally repeat the primes before producing responses (Huttenlocher et al., 2004; Shimpi, Gámez, Huttenlocher, & Vasilyeva, 2007).

L2 acquisition researchers have also begun to investigate the relationship between syntactic priming and L2 development. While L1 speech production studies have investigated alternation between two equally appropriate and fully-acquired syntactic structures, L1 and L2 acquisition studies focus on alternation between developmentally simple and complex structures, grammatical and ungrammatical structures, or appropriate versus inappropriate structures. For example, English L2 learners often demonstrate variation in their production of *wh*-questions with auxiliary verbs. Before they have fully acquired this form, they often alternate between two forms, the first of which is a *wh*-question with *wh*-fronting and the auxiliary in second position, such as *where is the man going?* which is a developmentally-advanced from. The second structure is a *wh*-question with *wh*-fronting without any auxiliary verb, such as *where the man going?*, or with the auxiliary verb placed between the subject and verb rather than before the subject, such as *where the man is going?* While this developmentally-simple form is not grammatically accurate, L2 learners who have yet to fully acquire *wh*-questions often alternate between the developmentally advanced and simple question forms.

Questions Addressed in L2 Syntactic Priming Research

Although syntactic priming tasks have been used extensively in L1 speech processing research, they have not been widely adopted in bilingual and L2 research. The primary question addressed in bilingual research concerns the organization of syntactic information in the L1 and L2. For L2 research, the initial question was whether syntactic priming occurs in L2 speech production, while currently researchers are investigating whether syntactic priming facilitates L2 development. We review these questions in the following sections.

Organization of L1–L2 Syntactic Information

As described in chapter 3, cross-language semantic priming studies have investigated how bilinguals organize their L1 and L2 lexicons, particularly whether exposure to a word in the L1 facilitates responses to a word's translation equivalent or semantic associate in the L2. Similarly, bilingual syntactic priming research has investigated how syntactic information is represented. One possibility is that bilinguals store syntactic information separately, which is referred to as the *separate-syntax account*. In this model, speakers have separate representations for each language, which means that linguistic information that is relevant for both languages would be stored twice. This could be useful if the syntactic structures that occur in both languages are superficially similar but actually have separate constructions. Having separate language stores could also be more efficient if a bilingual primarily uses one language at a time. The other account states that at least some syntactic information used in both languages is shared, which is referred to as the *shared-syntax account*. Any linguistic information that is shared by the two languages would only be represented once, which reduces redundancy. It also would be efficient if a bilingual frequently switched between languages during conversation.

Syntactic priming has been used to test whether syntactic representations are stored separately or shared for bilinguals. The shared-syntax account predicts that cross-language priming would occur, as activation of the syntactic structure in one language would facilitate production of the related structure in the second language. However, the separate-syntax account predicts that cross-language priming would not occur, since activation of linguistic information in one language would not affect the linguistic information of the second language.

The findings of cross-linguistic priming studies have demonstrated that syntactic priming occurs cross-linguistically, which supports the shared-syntax account (Bernolet et al., 2007; Desmet & Declercq, 2006; Hartsuiker et al., 2004; Loebell & Bock, 2003; Meijer & Fox Tree, 2003; Salamoura & Williams, 2006, 2007; Schoonbaert et al., 2007). However, there is disagreement regarding whether priming is due to activation of the syntactic information associated with individual lexical items, or whether it is due to activation of phrase structure configuration rules that are independent of specific lexical items.

Syntactic Priming in L2 Speech Production

Unlike bilingual speech processing studies, which have investigated the occurrence of syntactic priming between languages, L2 priming research investigates within-language priming, similar to L1 studies. The participants are exposed to sentences in the L2 and asked to produce sentences in the L2. Another difference between bilingual and L2 priming research is that the participants in L2 studies typically have not attained as high a rate of ultimate achievement in their second language. They may still be in the process of acquiring their L2 either though formal instruction or through recent arrival in second language environments where they have considerably more exposure to the L2 than they previously had. The initial question asked in L2 syntactic priming research was simply whether it occurred, as the previous research had been carried out with L1 and bilingual speakers exclusively. Consequently, researchers first explored whether priming occurred in L2 speech production, and studies indicated that it did occur for dative constructions (Gries, 2005; McDonough, 2006; Schoonbaert et al., 2007, Experiment 1) and alternation in word order between adjective + noun phrases and relative clauses (Bernolet et al., 2007, Experiment 2).

A more interesting question for L2 acquisition research, however, is whether syntactic priming can facilitate the production of the developmentally-advanced structure and discourage the production of the interlanguage alternative. The following example illustrates the potential role of syntactic priming in such scenarios (from McDonough & Mackey, 2008). In this task, a Thai EFL learner who alternated between developmentally simple and complex *wh*-question forms was carrying out an information gap task with a scripted interlocutor. Unbeknown to the learner, the interlocutor had been scripted with a series of developmentally-advanced questions. In turn 26, the scripted interlocutor asked the question *Where do you play volleyball?* The participant answered the question, and in turn 29 when it was her turn to ask a question, she similarly produced a developmentally-advanced question *What do you like to do?* Although several surface features differed, the learner's question shared the same syntactic structure as the question produced by the scripted interlocutor in turn 26.

[26] Scripted interlocutor: Where do you play volleyball?
[27] Learner: Uh in the stadium in Chiang Mai University.
[28] Scripted interlocutor: Mhm.
[29] Learner: In your free time what do you like to do?
[30] Scripted interlocutor: Uh I always play with my dogs.

In this case, syntactic priming may encourage the L2 learner to produce the developmentally-advanced structure as opposed to the less advanced form. More information about this study is provided in box 4.3.

Sample L2 Syntactic Priming Study

Box 4.3 Sample L2 syntactic priming study

McDonough, K., & Mackey, A. (2008). Syntactic priming and ESL question development. *Studies in Second Language Acquisition*, *30*, 31–47.

Background: Previous interaction studies have demonstrated a positive relationship between learners' responses to interactional feedback and L2 development. Most studies focused on learners' immediate responses that either incorporated the form modeled in the feedback move or involved a reformulation of a previous utterance. Some studies examined responses in the form of primed production, which occurred when learners produced the modeled or reformulated structure in subsequent turns using different lexical items. However, because primed production occurred in an interactive context where learners also received interactional feedback, it was unclear whether primed production alone also facilitated development.

Research question: Is there a relationship between syntactic priming and ESL question development?

Participants: 46 Thai EFL learners enrolled in undergraduate degree programs and 6 Thai English major students who acted as scripted interlocutors

Target structure: Questions. Development operationalized as a learner's progression in Pienemann and Johnston's (1987) developmental sequence.

Design: Pretest-posttest design carried out over a 7-week period. Tests (administered in weeks 1, 3, & 7) consisted of communicative activities that the learners carried out in pairs. The learners assigned to the priming group participated in two 20-minute treatment sessions (week 2) in which they carried out communicative activities with the scripted interlocutors, who had scripts containing developmentally-advanced question forms (stage four and five questions). The learners assigned to the control group carried out the tests only.

Analysis: Questions in the test and treatment data were coded for stages in the developmental sequence and stage assignment. The occurrence of syntactic priming was determined by calculating the number of developmentally-advanced questions produced by the learners after the scripted interlocutors' developmentally-advanced questions and same/lower-level questions.

Results: Syntactic priming occurred with the learners producing more developmentally-advanced questions after the scripted interlocutor's developmentally-advanced questions than after the interlocutor's same or lower-level questions. Learners who had higher levels of syntactic priming were more likely to advance to the next stage of question formation.

Discussion: Not all learners with high levels of syntactic priming advanced to a higher stage of question formation. Learners whose primed questions contained a wide variety of question words and main verbs were more likely to develop than learners whose primed questions repeated the same question words and main verbs used by the scripted interlocutors.

Implications: Syntactic priming involving the productive use of developmentally-advanced questions with a wide variety of lexical items may be more beneficial for question development than syntactic priming that involves simple repetition of question forms with the same lexical items provided by an interlocutor.

Tasks Used in Syntactic Priming Research

Logic of Syntactic Priming Experiments

The basic logic of syntactic priming experiments is that language users will produce a specific syntactic structure more often when they have just been exposed to that structure, as opposed to when they have been exposed to an alternative structure. As a result, all syntactic priming studies investigate syntactic structures for which a minimum of two equally acceptable alternatives exist. In acquisition studies, however, the alternating structures may be equally acceptable in a learner's interlanguage but not equally acceptable according to the target language norms. In order to determine whether syntactic priming has occurred, researchers expose language users to both of the alternating structures through primes, and calculate how frequently they produce (or recall) them through targets (or responses).

In order to minimize the likelihood that the participants might figure out the purpose of the experiment, researchers create a cover task for the experiment. For example, for picture description and sentence recall tasks, researchers often explain that the purpose of the experiment is a recognition-memory task in which participants will be tested in terms of how well they can remember sentences and/or pictures. Alternatively, they may explain that the goal of the experiment is to determine how well people can communicate when they can not see each other, such as in a scripted interaction task, or to find out how people complete sentence fragments, which is often used with a sentence completion task. By including a cover task that masks the true objective of the experiment, researchers hope to minimize the participants' attention to language form.

In addition to the cover task, filler sentences unrelated to the target structure are used to help reduce the likelihood that the participants will recognize the targeted linguistic structure. While the number of fillers varies, typically at least one filler intervenes between prime-target pairs.

Due to the need to insert fillers between prime-target pairs, the lists of items in syntactic priming studies are generally not randomized. Instead pseudo-random lists are created in order to ensure that prime-target pairs do not occur consecutively. The types of structures that have been used as fillers for the most frequently targeted structures in syntactic priming research are summarized in table 4.4.

Although the basic logic of syntactic priming experiments is the same, the four tasks commonly used in syntactic priming research (picture description, sentence recall, sentence completion, and scripted interaction) differ slightly in terms of their materials and procedures. We describe each task in more detail in the following sections.

Picture Description Task

One of the earliest methods used in syntactic priming research was the picture description task developed by Bock (1986). At that time, Bock speculated that the process of assembling syntactic structures created activation

Table 4.4 Sample fillers used in syntactic priming studies

Target structure	Filler structures	Study
Datives	Reflexives, locatives, existentials, clefts, pseudo clefts, predicate adjectives, complement constructions	Bock (1986)
Transitives	Intransitives, datives, predicate adjectives, predicate locatives, clausal subject and object complements, reflexives	Bock et al. (1992)
Object-raising verbs	Prepositional datives, simple transitives, bare intransitives, intransitives with prepositional phrases of location	Griffin & Weinstein-Tull (2003)
Spray-load constructions	Unaccusatives, unergatives, *there*-constructions, truncated passives, clefts, copulas, tough movement structures, locative inversions structures, *that*-complements, and infinitival complements	Chang et al. (2003)
Word order in subordinate clauses (Dutch)	Datives, transitives, locatives, and *wh*-questions	Hartsuiker & Westenberg (2000)
Locative expressions (Dutch)	*Wh*-questions, imperatives, intransitives, transitives with preposed objects	Hartsuiker et al. (1999)

in production mechanisms, with residual activation of those mechanisms remaining and facilitating the subsequent production of identical structures. Consequently, the task first elicits production of a linguistic structure through repetition of the prime sentence, which is then followed by spontaneous production through description of the target picture.

Materials and procedure. Participants are informed that the picture description task is a running recognition memory experiment and that the primary goal is to decide whether they have seen a picture or heard a sentence before. They are instructed to orally repeat each sentence and describe each picture with a single grammatically correct sentence, which are explained as techniques that will help them remember the sentences and pictures. Since the primary task is explained as a recognition decision, some pictures and sentences differ in relatively subtle ways, such as the age or gender of an agent, or the role of a person in an event, so that the participants are engaged in the cover task. By presenting the recognition decisions as the primary task goal, the degree to which the participants consciously attend to their picture descriptions is minimized.

The participants are tested individually, with the sentences typically presented by computer using *E-Prime*, *PsyScope* or similar software (see Appendix for more information about these programs), and their prime repetitions and target picture descriptions are audio-recorded. The presentation of each sentence and picture is typically self-paced. The participant presses a key on a computer keyboard or a button on a response box and an item appears on the computer screen. For sentences, the instructions *listen and repeat* appear and then the sentence is presented auditorily. At the end of the sentence, the instruction *repeat* appears. For pictures, the instruction *describe* appears. When participants have finished repeating the sentence or describing the picture, they press a button and recognition questions appear and remain on the screen until they have pressed the appropriate button (*yes* or *no*). A typical sequencing of events in the picture description task is illustrated in figure 4.1 (adapted from Bock & Griffin, 2000).

Since the task was devised when researchers were interested in the grammatical encoding associated with language production, it involved the participant's repetition of the prime before producing a target. However, since some researchers now suggest that syntactic priming is due to the activation of linguistic information that can occur through comprehension only, repetition of the prime is sometimes eliminated. Comparative studies have shown that eliminating repetition of the prime does not affect the occurrence of syntactic priming for adults, but studies with young children (3-year olds) suggest that priming may occur only if the prime is repeated before the target is produced (Shimpi et al., 2007). Researchers have also modified the picture description task by providing single word primes, instead of sentence primes, which the participants read silently before describing a target picture (Melinger & Dobel, 2005),

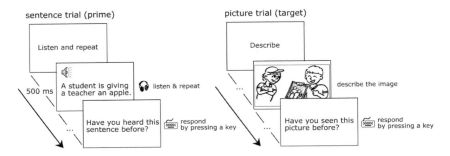

Figure 4.1 A schematic illustration of a picture description task (based on Bock & Griffin, 2000). This illustration depicts both sentence and picture trials in this task. For sentence trials, the sequence of events is the following: (1) the message *Listen and repeat* is displayed for 500 ms, (2) a sentence is played back to participant, (3) participant repeats the sentence, (4) participant pushes a button causing the prompt *Have you heard this sentence before?* to appear, (5) participants responds by pressing a key. For picture trials, the sequence of events is the following: (1) the message *Describe* is displayed, (2) participant pushes a button causing an image to appear, (3) participant describes the image, (4) participant pushes a button causing the prompt *Have you seen this picture before?* to appear, (5) participants responds by pressing a key.

as well as by presenting the prime sentences visually instead of auditorily (Hartsuiker & Kolk, 1998a). Representative studies that have used a picture description task are listed in box 4.4.

Analyzing and reporting results. If repetition of the prime sentences has been included in the procedure, the sentence repetitions are analyzed for accuracy. Minor deviations from the original sentence are typically ignored, such as changes in inflection, closed-class words, hesitations, articles, and individual lexical items that do not affect the overall syntactic structure of the prime sentence. Only the target picture descriptions that occur after accurate prime repetitions are analyzed. In terms of coding the target picture descriptions, the main coding categories represent the two syntactic structures that alternate and are the focus of the study. For example, transitive picture descriptions are typically coded as active or passive. Whereas actives contain an agent in subject position and a patient in object position, passives contain a main verb preceded by a form of *be* or *get*, followed by a *by*-phrase with the agent. Actives must have an acceptable passive counterpart, and passives must have an acceptable active counterpart. A third coding category generally referred to as "other" is often included and is used to classify responses that cannot be coded as either of the two syntactic structures. Ungrammatical features or surface-level changes unrelated to the syntactic structures being studied, such as minor changes in tense, number, or articles, are typically ignored, as are pauses.

Box 4.4 Picture description task studies

Study	Language	Topic	Participants	Structure	Findings
Bock (1986)	English L1	Effect of conceptual representations on syntactic priming	144 university students (across 3 experiments)	Datives & transitives	Priming was not based on shared conceptual features
Bock (1989)	English L1	Effect of closed-class elements on syntactic priming	288 university students (across 2 experiments)	Datives	Prepositions (*to* or *for*) in dative constructions did not influence the occurrence of priming
Bock & Loebell (1990)	English L1	Effect of event structure, metrical similarities, & closed-class similarities on syntactic priming	192 university students (across 3 experiments)	Datives & transitives	Event roles, prepositions, and metrical similarities did not influence the occurrence of priming
Bock et al. (1992)	English L1	Effect of animacy on syntactic priming	192 university students	Transitives	Animacy of subject NPs did not influence the occurrence of priming
Bock & Griffin (2000)	English L1	Occurrence of priming across intervening material	216 university students (across 2 experiments)	Datives & transitives	Priming occurred even when as many as 10 unrelated sentences intervened between the prime and the target
Bock et al. (2007)	English L1	Occurrence of priming from comprehension to production across intervening material	384 university students (across 2 experiments)	Datives & transitives	Priming from comprehension to production persisted when as many as 10 unrelated sentences intervened between the prime and the target

(Box 4.4 Continued)

Box 4.4 Continued

Study	Language	Topic	Participants	Structure	Findings
Hartsuiker & Kolk (1998a)	Dutch L1	Occurrence of syntactic priming with previously untested languages & structures	210 university students (across 3 experiments)	Datives & transitives	Priming occurred with dative constructions, but not transitives. Production of the target structures was greater during the priming task than the baseline.
Hartsuiker et al. (1999)	Dutch L1	Occurrence of syntactic priming involving word order	84 university students	Locatives	Priming occurred, which was attributed to priming of constituent structure linearization
Loebell & Bock (2003)	German-English bilinguals	Occurrence of cross-linguistic syntactic priming	48 German-English bilinguals	Datives & transitives	Cross-linguistic priming occurred for datives only
Melinger & Dobel (2005)	German & Dutch L1	Lexical activation of cross-linguistic syntactic priming	40 native speakers of German & 82 native speakers of Dutch	Datives	Single words were sufficient to prime dative constructions

The results are typically presented as a proportion score. The proportion is calculated as the number of target picture descriptions for one (or both) of the alternating syntactic forms divided by the total number of picture descriptions. This is calculated separately for each prime type, and the scores can be reported in tables or through figures. For an example of the results from a picture description task that examined the participants' production of prepositional datives following prepositional dative primes and double-object dative primes, see box 4.5.

Box 4.5 Sample results from a picture description task

The results of a picture description task can be reported graphically. The following figure (adapted from Experiment 3 in Bock & Loebell, 1990) shows the proportion of picture descriptions with prepositional datives that were produced after prepositional dative primes and double-object dative primes.

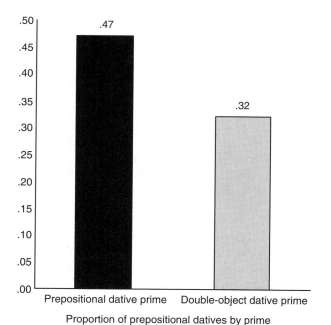

Proportion of prepositional datives by prime

Overall, these L1 English speakers produced more prepositional dative picture descriptions following prepositional dative primes (.47) than following double-object dative primes (.32).

Sentence Recall Task

The sentence recall task was developed by Potter and Lombardi (1990), who investigated whether immediate recall of sentences was due to regeneration from conceptual representations or verbatim memory of the sentence's surface features. Because native speakers' short-term recall of sentences is highly accurate, simply asking them to recall sentences would provide little information about the memory representations being used. Consequently, they developed a sentence recall task to induce representation-dependent errors during short-term recall.

Materials and procedure. In the sentence recall task, participants are informed that the experiment is a memory task and that the primary goal is to determine whether words appeared on a previous list. By engaging the participants in a distractor task after the presentation of the sentence to be recalled, the likelihood that they can simply memorize the sentence is minimized, thereby forcing regeneration from conceptual memory. The participants are tested individually and silently read a sentence from a computer screen that shows only one word at a time at a fast rate, which is referred to as *rapid serial visual presentation*. Then, either a number or word identification task is presented as the distractor task. For the number identification task, the participants are shown a horizontal array of five single-digit numbers, after which a number written as a word appears and the participants decide whether that number appeared in the horizontal array and click the appropriate key on the keyboard. For the word identification task, the participants are shown a list of words that either appeared or did not appear in the sentences. After seeing the word list, they are asked the question *Did the word X appear in the previous sentence?* and they make a recognition decision. After the number or word distractor task, the participants are prompted to say the original sentence out loud, and their sentence recall is audio-recorded.

Disruptions in the recall of the original sentence are induced by including a word in the distractor list that has the same meaning as a word used in the sentence to be recalled (usually a verb), but requires a different syntactic form. For example, the participants might read a sentence with a double-object dative, such as *The woman gave the library several new books.* The list of words used for the distractor task would include *donate*, which does not allow the double-object form and must occur in the prepositional dative form. In the recall task, the participants may modify the original sentence by using *donate* instead of *give*, which requires that they change the original double-object dative form to the prepositional dative form, i.e. *The woman donated several new books to the library.* The sequencing of events in the sentence recall technique is illustrated in figure 4.2 (adapted from figure 1 in Chang et al., 2003).

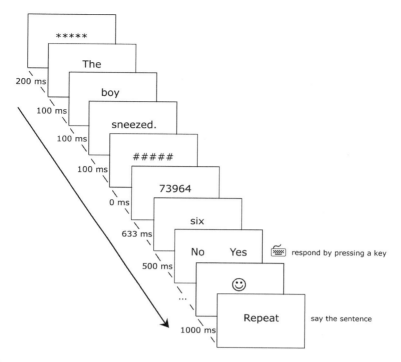

Figure 4.2 A schematic illustration of a sentence recall task (modeled after Chang et al., 2003). This illustration depicts the following sequence of events for each trial: (1) a fixation prompt (*****) is presented for 200 ms, (2) a sentence is presented one word at a time with a 100 ms interval, (3) a pattern mask (# # # # #) is presented and immediately replaced by a five-digit number (e.g. 73964), which stays on the screen for 533 ms, (4) after a 100 ms delay, a probe number is presented written out as a word; this number stays on the screen for 500 ms, (5) the probe number is replaced by a prompt for a *yes* or *no* response, (6) participant indicates whether the probe number was part of the five-digit sequence, (7) feedback about the response (☺ or ☹) appears for 500 ms screen, (8) after a 500 ms delay, participant is prompted to recall the sentence.

In a modification of the sentence recall task, sentences are ordered so that a prime sentence can influence the participant's recall of a target sentence. Chang and colleagues (Chang et al. 2003) used this modification of the sentence recall task to test spray-load alternation, which refers to variation in the order of the theme (the object that moves) and the location (the place that the object is moved to). For example, verbs such as *spray* can express the location NP before the object NP (*I spray the lawn with fertilizer*) or the object NP before the location NP (*I spray fertilizer on the lawn*). In the modified task, the participants see a sentence, perform a number distraction task, and then recall the sentence. The sentences are ordered so that a target sentence is preceded by a prime or an unrelated sentence. When the prime mismatches the target sentence but suggests an alternative structure to express the same meaning, the participants often produce the structure of the prime rather than the target. For example, if participants first read and recall an NP location + NP object prime such as *The maid rubbed the table with polish* and then see an NP object + NP location target, such as *The farmer heaped straw onto the wagon*, they often reverse the order of the NPs in the second sentence when they recall it.

Subsequent modifications of the sentence recall task include presenting multiple sentences before eliciting recall (Fox Tree & Meijer, 1999; Griffin & Weinstein-Tull, 2003; Meijer & Fox Tree, 2003). The target sentence is generally presented first, and is the sentence to be recalled by the participant. After presenting the target, a prime sentence that either matches or mismatches the syntactic structure of the target structure is presented. After silently reading the prime and target sentences, the participants do a distractor task that involves a simple word identification decision (Fox Tree & Meijer, 1999; Meijer & Fox Tree, 2003). After the distractor task, the participants recall the target sentence, and disruptions to the target's syntactic structure often occur when the prime sentence has a conflicting syntactic structure.

In some studies, the participants recall the prime sentence, rather than simply read it silently, before they recall the target sentence (Griffin & Weinstein-Tull, 2003). In this modification, a cue for the sentence to be recalled is provided, which is typically the initial words of a sentence up to its main verb. Despite variations in the technique, the purpose of the sentence recall task is to determine whether the syntactic structure of a distractor item or a prime lead the participants to alter the syntactic structure of the target during recall. Sample studies that used the sentence recall task are provided in box 4.6.

Analyzing and reporting results. If the task includes recall of both prime and target sentences, first the participants' prime sentence recalls are checked for accuracy. The accuracy rate is typically expressed as a percentage by dividing the number of correctly recalled primes by the total number of prime sentences. Based on the percentage scores, an inclusion criterion is set and only participants who achieve the minimum accuracy level are considered in the analysis. The inclusion criterion reported in previous studies has ranged from 67% to 95% accuracy. Next, the participants' recall of each target sentence is coded according to its syntactic structure. Three coding categories are typically used, one for each alternating structure and *other*. For example, dative sentence recalls are generally coded as prepositional datives if they have a main verb plus the patient expressed as the direct object and a prepositional phrase expressing the beneficiary. They are coded as double-object datives if they have a main verb followed by the beneficiary in the indirect object position and

Box 4.6 Sentence recall task studies

Study	Language	Topic	Participants	Structure	Findings
Chang et al. (2003)	English L1	Effect of thematic roles on syntactic priming	83 university students	Datives & spray-load constructions	Semantic features may contribute to priming
Fox Tree & Meijer (1999)	English L1	Effect of complexity of NPs on syntactic priming	107 university students (in 2 experiments)	Datives	Priming occurred when dative constructions had either simple or complex NPs
Griffin & Weinstein-Tull (2003)	English L1	Relationship between conceptual representations and syntactic priming	116 university students (across 2 experiments)	Clausal complement constructions	Priming may be based on both constituents in syntactic structures and elements in conceptual structures
Lombardi & Potter (1992)	English L1	Regeneration of syntax in short-term memory	68 university students (across 2 experiments)	Datives	Recall of datives was affected by the intrusion of another verb that supported the alternate form
Meijer & Fox Tree (2003)	Spanish-English bilinguals	Occurrence of between-language syntactic priming	76 university students (in 3 experiments)	Datives, double negation, direct object pronoun word order	Priming occurred between languages for datives and direct object pronoun word order. No priming occurred for double negation
Potter & Lombardi (1990)	English L1	Regeneration of syntax during sentence recall	100 university students (across 4 experiments)	Datives	Recall of datives was affected by the intrusion of another verb that supported the alternate form
Potter & Lombardi (1998)	English L1	Occurrence of syntactic priming during sentence recall	66 university students (across 3 experiments)	Datives	Priming occurred even when the prime was read without being recalled before the target was produced

then the patient in the direct object position. Prepositional datives without a double-object dative counterpart, such as *donate*, are typically scored as *other*. In other words, the dative recalls must be acceptable in both the prepositional dative and double-object dative forms or they are coded as *other*.

The results are typically presented as a percentage score based on the number of recalls in which the participants switched the syntactic structure of the target sentence following each type of prime sentence. For example, Fox Tree and Meijer (1999, Experiment 1), investigated whether prime sentences interfered with the recall of double-object dative target sentences. Participants first read a target double-object dative sentence, and then read a prime sentence that was either a double-object dative or a prepositional dative. After performing a word distractor test, they were asked to recall the target double-object dative sentence. The number of times the participants changed the double-object dative targets to prepositional datives during recall (referred to as a "switch"), was calculated as a percentage for each prime type. For a summary of the results, see box 4.7.

Sentence Completion Task

The sentence completion task was created by Pickering, Branigan and colleagues (Pickering & Branigan, 1998) to elicit written production data. At that time, only the picture description and sentence recall tasks had been used to test syntactic priming and both of these tasks involved oral language production. Although the sentence completion task was initially designed to elicit written data, it has since been modified to elicit oral sentence completions.

Materials and procedure. In the sentence completion task, participants are informed that the purpose of the experiment is to determine what kind of sentences people produce. They are instructed to complete each fragment as quickly as possible with the first completion that they think of. The fragments have been manipulated so that the participants produce a particular target structure in a prime fragment. For example, Hartsuiker and Westenberg (2000) investigated syntactic priming involving word order in Dutch subordinate clauses, which can end with either *aux* + past particle, or past participle + *aux*. The prime fragments either ended with the *aux*, which elicited the *aux* + past participle word order, or ended with the participle, which elicited the past particle + *aux* word order. The prime fragments were followed by target fragments that ended with a direct object noun, which could be followed by either *aux* + participle or participle + *aux*.

Box 4.7 Sample results from a sentence recall task

The results of a sentence recall task can be reported in a simple figure. The following figure (created from Experiment 1 data in Fox Tree & Meijer, 1999) shows the percentage of "switches" that occurred when the participants recalled double-object dative target sentences after they had read either double-object dative primes or prepositional dative primes.

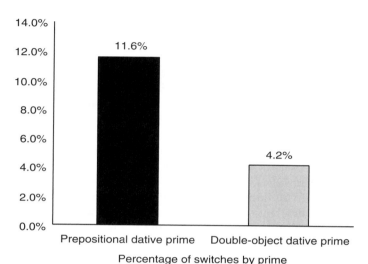

Percentage of switches by prime

Overall, when the participants recalled the double-object dative targets, they were more likely to switch them to prepositional datives when the prime sentence had been a prepositional dative (11.6%) instead of a double-object dative (4.2%).

In studies that elicit written sentence completion, the participants are given test booklets with the fragments. They are instructed to complete each fragment with a grammatical sentence and are typically given as much time as needed to complete all the fragments. For studies that elicit oral completions, the fragments are usually presented on a computer screen. The participants are asked to read the fragments aloud and then complete them, and their oral responses are audio-recorded. In studies that elicit both written and oral sentence completions, the participants are usually provided with a blank test booklet where they can write their completions after reading the fragments on the computer screen. When instructed to complete a fragment orally, they say the completion out loud and their responses are audio-recorded. An example of the procedure for eliciting both oral and written sentence completions is provided in figure 4.3 (based on Cleland & Pickering, 2006).

Although the task initially elicited written sentence completions, subsequent studies have modified it to elicit oral sentence completions or both oral and written sentence completions. Representative studies that used the sentence completion task to elicit oral and written data are listed in box 4.8.

Analysis and reporting. The participants' prime completions are analyzed to determine whether the participants have completed the primes as intended. For example, Scheepers (2003) classified prime completions as correct if the participants supplied the form targeted by the researcher and incorrect if they supplied another form. In other cases, the prime completions may be classified according to the syntactic structure, such as prepositional dative, double-object dative or other. The target completions are typically coded in terms of the two alternating syntactic structures and *other*. Scheepers (2003) classified target completions as subject relative clauses if the relative pronoun was in the subject position of the relative clause, and object relative clauses if the relative pronoun was in object position. All other completions were coded as *other*, which included ambiguous relative clauses or responses that did not imply a relative clause. In addition, the relative clauses were further classified in terms of their attachment, depending on whether they modified a noun phrase that occurred "high" or "low" in the hierarchical tree structure.

The results of the sentence completion task are typically presented as raw scores that indicate how many target completions occur after each prime type. The inferential statistics however, are generally calculated based on proportion scores. In the study by Scheepers (2003) mentioned previously, the participants completed target sentences in which the relative clause could be high attachment (refer to a noun phrase high in the tree structure), low attachment (refer to a noun phrase low in the tree structure), or unclassifiable. The participants' target sentences following high attachment and low attachment prime sentences are summarized in box 4.9.

Scripted Interaction Task

The scripted interaction task (also referred to as *confederate scripting*), was created by Branigan and colleagues (Branigan et al., 2000) to explore the occurrence of syntactic priming during conversation. They were investigating whether speakers aligned in their use of syntactic structures during conversation, and required a syntactic priming task that could be carried out during dyadic interaction. The picture description, sentence recall, and sentence completion tasks were not appropriate since they all involve individual speakers.

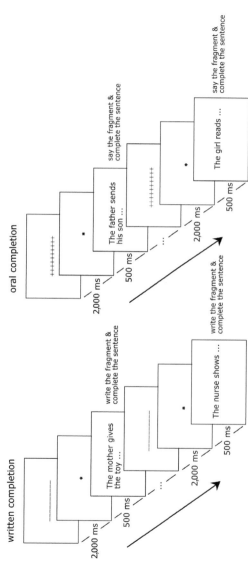

Figure 4.3 A schematic illustration of a sentence completion task (based on Cleland & Pickering, 2006). This illustration depicts the following sequence of events for each trial: (1) a prompt (————) or (+++++++++++) is presented for 2,000 ms, with the dashes indicating a written completion is required and the plus signs indicating an oral completion is required, (2) a fixation point (*) is presented for 500 ms, after which a sentence fragment appears, (3) participants produce the fragment and complete the sentence out loud or in writing, (4) when finished, they press the space bar and the sequence repeats.

Box 4.8 Sentence completion task studies

Study	Language	Topic	Participants	Structure	Findings
Branigan et al. (1999)	English L1	Persistence of syntactic priming across intervening stimuli	54 university community members	Datives (written)	Priming occurred but only when there was no intervening material
Branigan, Pickering, McLean, & Stewart (2006)	English L1	Role of local and global structure in the occurrence of syntactic priming	172 university community members (across 8 experiments)	Datives (oral)	Syntactic priming makes reference to local structure rather than global structure
Branigan et al. (2000)	English L1	Persistence of syntactic priming across intervening material and temporal delay	60 university community members	Datives (oral)	Priming was not affected by intervening material or temporal delay
Cleland & Pickering (2006)	English L1	Effect of modality on syntactic priming	64 university students (3 experiments)	Datives (oral & written)	Priming was greater when the verb was repeated, but was not affected by modality
Desmet & Declercq (2006)	Dutch L1, Dutch-English bilinguals	Occurrence of syntactic priming related to hierarchical tree configuration	84 university students (across 3 experiments)	Relative clause attachment (written)	Priming occurred independent of subcategorization frames or individual syntactic rules
Gries & Wulff (2005)	German L1, English L2	Occurrence of syntactic priming in L2 speech production	64 university students	Datives (written)	Priming occurred for both double-object and prepositional datives

Study	Language	Focus	Participants	Structure	Findings
Hartsuiker & Westenberg (2000)	Dutch L1	Dissociation between the construction of syntactic structure and word order generation	64 university students	Word order in subordinate clauses (oral & written)	Priming of word order occurred
Kaschak et al. (2006)	English L1	Cumulative effect of priming across trials	360 university students (2 experiments)	Datives (written)	Recent, equivalent exposure to both dative forms strengthened priming
Pickering & Branigan (1998)	English L1	Effect of individual verbs on syntactic priming	188 university community members (5 experiments)	Datives (written)	Priming was greater when the verb was the same
Pickering, Branigan, & McLean (2002)	English L1	Single-stage versus dominance-only levels of syntactic representation	149 university community members (across 4 experiments)	Datives (written & oral)	Production involves mapping pre-syntactic messages to fully-specific syntactic representations
Salamoura & Williams (2006)	Dutch L1, English L2	Lexical activation of cross-linguistic syntactic priming	26 university students or staff	Datives (oral)	Cross-linguistic priming occurred in response to single-verb primes
Salamoura & Williams (2007)	Greek L1, English L2	Effect of constituent order and thematic roles on cross-linguistic priming	108 university students (across 3 experiments)	Datives (oral)	Cross-linguistic priming was dependent on an overlap between constituent order and thematic roles
Scheepers (2003)	German L1	Occurrence of syntactic priming related to hierarchical tree configuration	90 university community members (across 3 experiments)	Relative clause attachment (written)	Priming occurred independent of subcategorization frames or individual syntactic rules

---

Box 4.9 Sample results from a sentence completion task

The results of a sentence completion task can be reported in a simple table. The following table (based on Experiment 1 data in Scheepers, 2003) shows the number of target completions (high attachment or low attachment) produced by the participants after high attachment and low attachment relative clause primes.

High and Low Attachment Target Completions by Prime

Prime completions	Target completions	
	High attachment	*Low attachment*
High attachment	104	116
Low attachment	62	149

Overall, the results indicate that the participants produced more high attachment target completions after high attachment primes (104) than after low attachment primes (62). In addition, they produced more low attachment target completions after low attachment primes (149) than after high attachment primes (116).

Materials and procedure. In the scripted interaction task, the researcher typically explains the cover story for the experiment, which may involve an explanation that the purpose of the study is to determine how well people communicate when they are unable to see each other, how the position of objects in pictures affects oral descriptions, how L2 learners use language during interactive tasks or simply that they are playing a game. The cover task is designed to provide a purpose for the task and minimize the likelihood that the participants will pay attention to the linguistic features of the picture descriptions, similar to the distractor tasks used in picture description and sentence recall tasks.

The participants schedule an individual session with the researcher. Either the researcher or a research assistant serves as the scripted interlocutor, who carries out a picture description activity with the participant. They take turns describing a set of pictures to each other. Whereas the participant has pictures with a verb written under each one, the scripted interlocutor has been given complete sentences. While listening to their partner's descriptions, they search for matching pictures from a group of related pictures displayed on the table in front of them (a barrier prevents them from seeing their partner's cards). The order of the pictures has been manipulated so that the scripted interlocutor provides a prime immediately before the participant describes a target picture. The experimental set up is shown in figure 4.4 (based on Pickering et al., 2000). In some recent L1 studies, the procedure has been modified so that the participant and the scripted interlocutor describe pictures that are presented on individual computer screens and press keys when responding to their partner's picture descriptions (e.g. Bernolet et al., 2007; Schoonbaert et al., 2007).

The scripted interaction task has also been modified when used in L1 acquisition research (Huttenlocher et al., 2004; Savage et al., 2003, 2006; Shimpi et al., 2007) in order to make it more appropriate for young children. In this version of the task, the researcher and children take turns describing pictures that are presented by computer or in picture card sets. The researcher often repeats the primes multiple times, and there are few or no fillers separating the prime-target pairs. In addition, there is no cover task other than telling children that they are playing a game. Some L2 studies have modified the task by using a wider-variety of communicative activities that do not require a picture selection set or boxes where interlocutors place the cards they have selected (McDonough & Mackey, 2008). Instead, the tasks have involved jigsaw tasks, picture differences tasks, or other communicative tasks that do not involve picture card

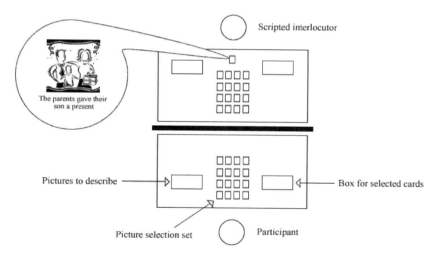

Figure 4.4 Experimental set up in a scripted interlocutor task (based on Pickering et al., 2000). The participant and scripted interlocutor are seated across from each other and a barrier prevents them from seeing each other's cards. They take turns describing pictures, and search for a picture in the selection set that matches their partner's description. Once identified, the card from the selection set is placed in a box. The pictures to be described are manipulated so that the scripted interlocutor describes a prime picture immediately before the participant describes a target picture.

placement, but similarly have a communicative goal and require a two-way flow of information. A list of sample studies that used the scripted interaction task is provided in box 4.10

Analysis and results. Once the audio-recordings are transcribed, the participants' picture descriptions following the scripted interlocutor's primes are classified according to their form. For example, Hartsuiker et al. (2004) classified the participant's transitive constructions as active, passive, or other, with the *other* category including code switches and sentences with passive morphology without the by-phrase. However, L1 and L2 acquisition studies have classified sentences with passive morphology as passives regardless of the occurrence of the by-phrase (Savage et al., 2006; Kim & McDonough, 2008). In general, morpho-syntactic features that are not directly relevant to the target structure are ignored in coding decisions, especially in L1 and L2 acquisition studies where the participants are unlikely to have fully acquired the language.

The results of the scripted interaction task are typically presented as raw scores or proportions that indicate how many target picture descriptions occurred after each prime type. In the study by Savage et al. (2003) mentioned previously, the children talked about pictures that could be described using a passive or an active sentence. The number of passives and actives they produced after the researcher's passive and active primes were totaled. The children's production of passives and actives are summarized in box 4.11. An example L2 syntactic priming study using the scripted interaction task was previously highlighted in box 4.3.

Issues to Consider in Syntactic Priming Research

Selecting an Appropriate Task

When deciding among the syntactic priming tasks described in the previous section, the most obvious consideration is the researcher's objective (see Gass & Mackey, 2007, for a general overview of data elicitation methods). If syntactic priming is being used to test L2 acquisition theory, the experimental task should approximate the conditions under which learning is believed to occur. For example, McDonough and Mackey (2008) were testing the Interaction Hypothesis (Gass, 2003; Gass & Mackey, 2007; Long, 1996), which states that interaction facilitates L2 learning by bringing together input, output and learner internal capacities such as attention. They hypothesized that syntactic priming might also account for the facilitative effect of interaction on L2 development by encouraging production of developmentally advanced forms. Since they were testing this hypothesis, the most appropriate task was scripted interaction, as it is the only syntactic priming task based in conversation. However, as the scripted interaction method originally devised by Pickering and

Box 4.10 Scripted interlocutor task studies

Study	Language	Topic	Participants	Structure	Findings
Bernolet et al. (2007)	Dutch L1, English L2, German L2	Effect of word-order repetition on cross-linguistic priming	156 university students (across 5 experiments)	Relative clauses and adjective-noun phrases	Within-language priming occurred in the L1 and L2, but cross-linguistic priming occurred only when the L1 and L2 had similar word order
Haywood, Pickering, & Branigan (2005)	English L1	Avoiding ambiguities during conversation	32 university students	Prepositional phrases and relative clauses	Priming occurred for both ambiguous and disambiguous sentences
Hartsuiker et al. (2004)	Spanish-English bilinguals	Bilinguals: shared or separate syntax between languages	24 Spanish L1, English L2 speakers	Passives	Priming of passives occurred between languages
Huttenlocher et al. (2004)	English L1	Occurrence & persistence of syntactic priming in young children	90 children ranging from 4;1 to 5;8	Datives & transitives	Priming occurred for both structures even when their sentences did not share lexical items with the primes
Kim & McDonough (2008)	Korean L1, English L2	Effect of shared lexical items on occurrence of syntactic priming	76 university students	Passives	More passives occurred when the learners' prompts had the same verbs produced by the scripted interlocutor
McDonough (2006)	Various L1s, English L2	Occurrence of syntactic priming in L2 speech production	104 university students (across 2 experiments)	Datives	Priming occurred for prepositional datives only

(Box 4.10 Continued)

Box 4.10 Continued

Study	Language	Topic	Participants	Structure	Findings
McDonough & Mackey (2008)	Thai L1, English L2	Relationship between syntactic priming and ESL question development	46 university students	Questions	Priming was associated with question development
Savage et al. (2003)	English L1	Occurrence of syntactic priming in young children	104 children ranging from 2;11 to 7;1 (across 2 experiments)	Actives & passives	Priming occurred with young children only when they could use pronouns in both NP slots
Savage et al. (2006)	English L1	Effect of type/token frequency on the persistence of syntactic priming in young children	66 children ranging from 4;0 to 5;6	Passives	Lexical variety in primes and repeated priming activities facilitated longer-term persistence of syntactic priming
Schoonbaert et al. (2007)	Dutch L1, English L2	Occurrence of within-language (L1 and L2) and cross-linguistic priming	150 university students	Datives	Priming occurred in the L1, L2, and between languages. Shared lexical items did not increase priming in the L2 to L1 condition
Shimpi et al. (2007)	English L1	Occurrence of syntactic priming with young children	128 children aged 2;3 to 4;6 (across 3 experiments)	Datives & transitives	Priming occurred for younger children only if they repeated primes before producing targets

Box 4.11 Sample results from a scripted interaction task

The data in the following table (from Savage et al., 2003) illustrate syntactic priming involving active and passive transitives with young children. The table shows the mean number of passive and active picture descriptions that the children produced after the researcher's active and passive primes.

Active and Passive Responses by Prime

	Active responses	Passive responses
Active primes	3.00	0.35
Passive primes	2.25	1.00

Overall, the results show that the children produce more actives after active primes (3.00) than after passive primes (2.25). Similarly, they produced more passives after passive primes (1.00) than after active primes (.35).

colleagues (Pickering et al., 2000) involves tightly controlled turn-taking during a picture description activity, they modified the procedure by including a variety of communicative tasks that had been used in previous interaction research. As a result, they had to provide the scripted interlocutor with numerous questions that could be used depending on each learner's performance on each task. Since the goal was to test this particular hypothesis, they selected the syntactic priming method most compatible with conversation and further adapted it to increase the authenticity of the interaction.

However, if L2 researchers are working from a different theoretical framework, then another priming task might be more appropriate. For example, if researchers are using syntactic priming to test whether L2 speech production supports a feedforward or feedbackward model, then the picture description task or the sentence completion task would be more appropriate. Since the objective is to determine how L2 message content becomes mapped onto words, grammatical forms, and sounds, researchers can investigate this topic with individual speakers rather than through conversation. Similarly, an L2 researcher investigating the impact of practice on the automatization of L2 morpho-syntactic rules might select the sentence completion task due to the ease of eliciting repeated written or oral production of specific morpho-syntactic structures that may be difficult to elicit through more spontaneous production. If researchers are more interested in the impact of language input on

L2 acquisition, then the sentence recall, sentence completion, and picture description tasks can be modified so that the prime is followed by a comprehension or recognition activity rather than recall or production.

Another factor that researchers might consider when deciding among tasks is the level of control they wish to impose on participants' production. The picture description, sentence recall, and sentence completion tasks limit participants to sentence-level production based on tightly controlled prompts. While the scripted interaction method also involves carefully designed prompts delivered by a scripted interlocutor, conversation involves greater interactivity and may result in unexpected language. For example, during the scripted interaction task intervening dialogue often occurs between the researcher's prime and the participants' responses. This intervening dialogue generally involves clarification requests and responses, or comments and responses to something an interlocutor had said, which is typical in conversation. The occurrence of intervening dialogue could be problematic, however, if the researcher was investigating the persistence of syntactic priming across trials as more tightly controlled turn taking would be necessary.

Finally, another important factor that may affect the choice of a syntactic priming task is the ease of eliciting the target structure. Similar to universal grammar research, syntactic priming studies frequently target linguistic structures that rarely occur in conversation or are difficult to elicit during spontaneous production tasks, such as *spray-load* constructions. In order to test such structures, the sentence recall technique might be the most appropriate method as the participants are not asked to produce new sentences, but simply recall sentences that have been created in advance by the researcher. Some of the factors to consider when deciding among the four syntactic priming tasks are listed in table 4.5.

Creating Materials

An important issue to consider when creating the lists of prime and target sentences is the selection of the individual lexical items that allow the alternate structures. Since many studies have targeted datives and transitives, researchers may simply select the same verbs that were used in previous studies. Other researchers have consulted linguistic corpora to identify whether individual verbs are more strongly associated with one of the alternative structures. Gries and colleagues (Gries, 2005; Gries & Wulff, 2005) have identified the distributional biases associated with prepositional datives and double-object datives, reporting that some verbs, such as *give* and *show*, are more likely to occur as double-object datives, while verbs such as *post* and *sell* are more likely to occur in the prepositional dative. Corpus data have also been used to identify the subcategorization frequencies associated with individual verbs that can occur

Table 4.5 Factors to consider when deciding among syntactic priming tasks

Consideration	Appropriate task(s)
Individual speaker	Picture description, sentence recall, sentence completion
Face to face conversation	Scripted interaction
Linguistic structures difficult to elicit	Sentence recall
Tightly controlled production	Picture description or sentence completion
Computer software required	Sentence recall, picture description, oral sentence completion
Low-tech data collection	Written sentence completion, scripted interaction
Production data	Picture description, sentence completion, scripted interaction
Recall rather than production	Sentence recall
No illustrations needed	Sentence recall, sentence completion

with either a noun-phrase or clausal complement (Gahl, Jurafsky, & Roland, 2004). The association between a verb and a specific syntactic structure may influence the "readiness" with which the verb undergoes priming, which researchers can control by selecting verbs based on their distributional patterns. For example, Kim and McDonough (2008) investigated the occurrence of syntactic priming with passive constructions and selected the target verbs based on their frequency in the passive form in the Longman Spoken and Written English Corpus (Biber, Johansson, Leech, Conrad, & Finegan, 1999). They included verbs that represented three categories: (a) verbs that occurred in the passive form 26 or more times per million words, (b) verbs that appeared in the passive between 2 to 18 times per million words, and (c) verbs that occurred in the passive no more than one time per million words. By carefully considering any distributional biases associated with individual lexical items, researchers can be more confident that priming is not due to a speaker's pre-existing tendency to associate certain verbs with particular syntactic structures.

For acquisition researchers, a crucial consideration in the selection of verbs is whether the participants are likely to know their meaning or to have used them in spontaneous production. For L1 acquisition studies, researchers should select verbs that children aged five and under are likely to know and be able to produce at that age. Savage and colleagues (Savage et al., 2003, 2006) selected verbs to occur in the passive based on the findings of studies that elicited spontaneous production from young children (such as Israel, Johnson & Brooks, 2000). They selected passive verbs that had been shown to occur in the spontaneous production of 4-year olds and that could be elicited through illustrations. For L2 acquisition researchers, high frequency verbs may be an appropriate choice as L2 speakers may be more likely to know and use these lexical items.

Another important consideration in the selection of verbs is how easily they can be elicited through illustrations, which is relevant for the picture description and the scripted interaction tasks only, since the sentence recall and sentence completion methods do not use pictures to elicit spontaneous speech. Once appropriate verbs have been selected, researchers may not be able to elicit those verbs through illustrations. For example, many of the verbs most strongly associated with the passive form in the Longman Spoken and Written English Corpus (Biber et al., 1999) occur in written discourse, especially academic prose. Those verbs strongly associated with the passive in conversation, such as *done, born*, and *called*, may be difficult to elicit in the full passive form through illustrations since the agent is generally unnecessary with these verbs.

In studies where the same verbs are used in both the primes and targets, the researchers need to create or locate multiple illustrations that elicit the same verb. Pictures that elicit various verbs may be located through on-line clip art collections, such as Microsoft Office clip art (http://office.microsoft.com/en-us/clipart/default.aspx), image search engines, such as Google Images, or illustrated picture books. Picture books may be particularly appropriate for L1 acquisition researchers as they may include characters that children are likely to recognize. They may also be a good source of illustrations for L2 acquisition researchers because they often depict high frequency lexical items, such as *teacher, student, farmer, house*. However, since picture books are generally targeted at children, such illustrations may be perceived by some adult L2 speakers as age-inappropriate.

Once the verbs have been selected, sentences using those verbs in the alternate syntactic structures should be created. The total number of prime-target pairs to be used in the experiment will vary based upon factors such as the age of the participants and their proficiency level. These factors may also influence the number of filler sentences to be inserted between each prime-target pair. L1 acquisition researchers working with young children may use as few as five prime-target pairs and no filler sentences due to the more limited attention span and level of cognitive development of young children. L2 acquisition researchers working with beginner or low-intermediate learners may also use fewer prime-target pairs and filler sentences in an effort to reduce the linguistic and cognitive demands of the task.

Analyzing Participants' Responses

When analyzing syntactic priming data, researchers typically present the participants' responses as proportions that are calculated for each syntactic structure separately. In this approach, the total number of each response (e.g. prepositional datives and double-object datives) produced after each prime is totaled. Then the sum of each syntactic structure is divided by the total number of responses following each prime type separately. One issue when calculating proportions is whether to include *other* responses in the denominator. Pickering and colleagues initially calculated proportion scores based on the total of each syntactic structure divided by all responses. However, some prime types were more robustly associated with *other* responses, which complicated comparisons across conditions. Therefore, they introduced the target ratio score in which each response type is divided by the total number of analyzable responses, which excludes *other* responses (e.g. Cleland & Pickering, 2006; Pickering et al., 2002).

To illustrate the target ratio score, consider the hypothetical data in table 4.6. The participants produced 100 prepositional datives, 48 double-object datives and 2 *other* responses in response to prepositional dative primes. They produced 50 prepositional datives, 70 double-object datives and 30 *other* responses in response to double-object primes. In this scenario, *other* responses are more robustly associated with double-object datives, suggesting that target ratio scores may be more appropriate. Since the participants produced 100 prepositional targets and 48 double-object dative targets following prepositional dative primes, the denominator would be 148 and the 2 other responses would be excluded. The prepositional dative ratio would be calculated by dividing 100/148, resulting in a ratio score of .68. The double-object dative ratio after prepositional dative primes would be 48/148, or .32. The same process would be carried out for the dative responses following double-object dative primes. The prepositional dative ratio for double-object dative primes would be 50/120 or .42, while the double-object dative ratio would be 70/120 or .58. When calculated in this way, the unequal distribution of *other* response is neutralized.

Table 4.6 Hypothetical target ratio data

Prime Type	Total number of targets			Target ratios	
	PD	DOD	Other	PD ratio	DOD ratio
PD	100	48	2	.68	.32
DOD	50	70	30	.42	.58

Note: PD = prepositional dative, DOD = double-object dative.

When *other* responses are excluded, the resulting ratio scores for the two syntactic structures are complementary within each prime type. Consequently, only one ratio score is needed for the statistical analysis and this choice is typically arbitrary. When using target ratios, the resulting statistical analysis determines whether there is a main effect for prime on the participants' production. Syntactic priming would be confirmed if the selected target ratio is greater following the corresponding prime type rather than the alternate prime type. However, if *other* responses are not excluded, then the proportion scores for each syntactic structure are not complementary. In this case, both proportion scores can be included in the statistical test. Rather than expect a main effect for prime, researchers instead look for a significant interaction between prime and response. Prior to carrying out the statistical tests, some researchers first perform an arc-sine conversion (this helps minimize the possibility of Type I error that is introduced by using proportion scores), while other researchers simply use the proportion scores.

Reliability and Validity

Measures of reliability and validity have not been widely reported in syntactic priming research. In terms of reliability, an important consideration for several of the syntactic priming tasks is the extent to which pictures consistently elicit the target structures. Even though an illustration depicts an agent, and an action, a patient, and a beneficiary, speakers might not automatically include all these elements in their picture descriptions. An illustration depicting a human agent may be less likely to elicit a passive picture description since passives are often used when the agent is inanimate. Also, the location of agents, patients, and beneficiaries may impact speakers' choices of syntactic structures. Consequently, researchers should pilot test the pictures that illustrate the target structures in order to ensure that they consistently elicit the relevant forms. In terms of analyzing syntactic priming data, L1 researchers typically apply straightforward coding categories based on linguistic features of the participants' sentences, and have not reported inter-rater reliability for those coding decisions. L2 studies, however, may benefit from the inclusion of inter-rater reliability measures since the participants may not have fully acquired the target language and the presence of many interlanguage features in L2 participants' picture descriptions may require more subjective coding decisions.

Since syntactic priming research frequently targets datives and transitives in English, researchers often simply use the same verbs and sentences used in previous studies. However, it may be useful to explore whether particular lexical items are disproportionally associated with one of alternating structures, such as more frequent occurrence in the passive form as opposed to the active forms. By selecting lexical items that do not have any distributional biases or counterbalancing lexical items with different distributional patterns across conditions, researchers could enhance the internal validity of their studies. Including baseline production of the alternating structures may also be useful as researchers can determine if participants have individual preferences for one of the alternating structures, which can then be compared with their production of both forms during the priming tasks. This would allow researchers to rule out the possibility that syntactic priming could be attributable to the participants' existing stylistic preferences. Researchers working with L1 and L2 learners in an instructional context might consider the face validity of their studies by addressing the pedagogical value of the activities, their appropriateness for the learners' proficiency level, and relevance to course objectives.

As described in chapter 1 (see pp. 4–6), three factors can impact the ecological validity of priming research: language, population, and task. Although syntactic priming researchers have begun to investigate additional languages, primarily Dutch and German, the majority of syntactic priming studies have been carried out in English. Furthermore, the linguistic structures most commonly targeted in syntactic priming studies (in both English and other languages) are active/passive transitives and datives. Since syntactic priming is often used to investigate models of speech production, which presumably are universal, the ecological validity of the research tradition could be enhanced by expanding the target languages and structures. In terms of population, researchers have investigated the occurrence of syntactic priming among diverse language users, including non-impaired L1 speakers (adults and children of various ages), L1 adults with aphasia, L1 children with specific language impairment, bilinguals, and L2 learners. Despite this diversity, the vast majority of syntactic priming studies have targeted adult L1 speakers who are university students. By targeting other populations more frequently, researchers may gain greater insight into the mechanisms involved in syntactic priming as well as its role in language processing and acquisition.

Finally, in terms of the experimental task, the four syntactic priming tasks described in this chapter typically elicit sentence-level language production. Since language processing and acquisition generally occur through situated language use, incorporating more discourse-level elements into syntactic priming studies may be a more valid approximation of real-world conditions. Recent studies have used corpus-based analysis to examine whether syntactic priming occurs in spontaneous discourse (Gahl et al., 2004; Gries, 2005; Szmrecsanyi, 2005) and insights from these corpus studies can inform the design of experimental materials. Increasing the methodological diversity of syntactic priming research, such as using eye-tracking systems (Arai et al., 2007) or computing event-related potentials (Ledoux et al., 2007), might also positively impact its ecological validity.

Additional Uses of Syntactic Priming Methods

Interactive Oral Language Testing

With the increased use of interviews for oral language testing, researchers have called for additional studies that investigate the impact of the interlocutor on language learners' test performance (e.g. McNamara, 1996). Some proficiency tests include a speaking section in which learners interact individually with an examiner, such as IELTs, while others involve learners interacting with each other, such as the Cambridge Speaking Test. The use of interview tests, particularly those involving learners interacting with each other, has been widely debated with some researchers arguing in position papers that the format reduces anxiety and facilitates positive washback (Saville & Hargreaves, 1999), while others suggest that it may introduce considerable variation in learners' performance depending on the interlocutor (Foot, 1999). Empirical studies have explored how various characteristics of the interlocutor can impact learners' test performance during oral proficiency tests, including age, interaction style, language level, personality, gender, status, and acquaintanceship. Although linguistic features of learners' performance, such as accuracy, fluency, and complexity, have been widely studied in the task literature, holistic ratings and discourse structure have been the predominant focus of testing studies. Testing-oriented studies that examined linguistic features as well as holistic scores (e.g. O'Sullivan, 2002) considered the global measures of accuracy and complexity, but did not include a detailed analysis of specific syntactic structures. Norton (2005), however, provided an example of the discourse between learners carrying out a task in the Cambridge Speaking Test who appeared to appropriate conditional clauses from each other's discourse. Since syntactic priming research using the scripted interlocutor method has demonstrated that both L1 and L2 speakers converge in their use of syntactic structures during dialogue, future research in paired oral language testing might systematically investigate the extent to which convergence occurs during test performance and whether it impacts ratings.

Interaction Research

The interaction hypothesis of second language acquisition (Gass, 2003; Long, 1996; Mackey, 2007) states that interaction facilitates second language (L2) development by bringing together input features, internal learner capacities, and language production. Researchers have proposed various reasons for why interaction facilitates L2 development, such as it provides negative evidence, enhances the salience of positive evidence, raises learners' awareness of language form, and creates opportunities for learners to produce the target language and modify their inappropriate or ungrammatical utterances. Empirical studies that examined the relationship between language production during interaction and L2 development have predominantly explored learners' responses to interactional feedback, specifically responses that occur immediately following the feedback move. However, more recently interaction researchers have shown that learners' responses that occur beyond the third turn are also associated with L2 development (McDonough & Mackey, 2006). They argued that although learners may not have an opportunity to respond to recasts immediately or may simply acknowledge the recast, they may subsequently produce the syntactic structure modeled in the recast. This type of response, which they referred to as *primed production*, was positively associated with ESL question development, whereas learners' immediate responses to recasts were not. Subsequent follow-up studies, such as the one highlighted in box 4.3, have demonstrated that syntactic priming in the absence of interactional feedback is also associated with ESL question development. Future interaction research might investigate whether individual differences, such as working memory capacity and aptitudes, might predispose learners to benefit, or not, from the implicit learning processes associated with syntactic priming.

Researchers working in L2 classroom contexts have investigated the interactional feedback provided by L2 teachers in response to learners' non-targetlike forms (e.g. Havranek, 2002; Lyster & Ranta, 1997; Panova & Lyster, 2002; Sheen, 2004). The primary focus of this line of research is to discover how L2 teachers in a variety of instructional settings respond to learners' non-targetlike forms. These studies also investigate whether different types of interactional feedback are more likely to result in learner response, which is typically referred to as uptake. However, they have typically examined only those learner responses that occurred in the turn immediately following the teacher's feedback move. Future research might explore whether certain types of interactional feedback facilitate primed production of the syntactic structures targeted by the feedback, particularly types of feedback that encourage learners to produce that syntactic structure in new utterances or with new lexical items.

In addition to teacher feedback, L2 classroom research has also explored the effectiveness of different collaborative activities that create opportunities for learners to attend to form in the context of meaning. Previous classroom research has investigated how learners provide each other with interactional feedback (e.g. McDonough, 2004) and how learners use language to reflect on language form during collaborative tasks (e.g. Swain, 1998; Watanabe & Swain, 2007). Future research might target the design, implementation, and evaluation of classroom activities that create contexts for syntactic priming to occur, during teacher-learner interaction as well as learner-learner interaction. Many studies have already demonstrated the benefits of learner-learner interaction during pair and small group activities, such as the research into language-related episodes and interactional feedback, yet little research to date has explored whether syntactic priming occurs during pair and small group activities in L2 classrooms, or investigated what types of activities create contexts for priming to occur (McDonough, 2007).

L1 Influence

Another possible application of syntactic priming methods is to investigate the influence of the L1 in L2 acquisition. Most L1 influence studies have adopted a product orientation in which researchers elicit production data from L2 learners with different L1 backgrounds and then identify interlanguage features that may be related to structural features of their first languages (for an overview see Jarvis, 2000; Odlin, 2003). L1 influence researchers might adopt cross-linguistic priming methods to test syntactic structures that are formed differently in the L1 and L2. Previous cross-linguistic priming research has targeted structures that are formed similarly in both languages in order to determine whether primes delivered in one language would facilitate production of the same structure in the other language. For L1 influence studies, researchers could similarly provide primes in learners' L1 and elicit production in their L2. However, the target structure could be one that is grammatical in the L1 but not grammatical in the L2. L1 influence could be assessed according to the degree to which learners respond to L1 primes by producing L2 sentences with the L1 syntactic form rather than the more appropriate L2 structure.

Summary

In this chapter, we introduced syntactic priming and the topics that have been explored in L1, bilingual and L2 research using syntactic priming tasks. We described the four experimental tasks used in syntactic priming research—picture description, sentence recall, sentence completion, and scripted interaction—and pointed out some factors that researchers might consider when deciding among tasks to choose. Finally, we suggested some additional uses of syntactic priming for L2 research. In the next chapter, we highlight issues in the analysis of priming data and offer some suggestions for the reporting of priming research in applied linguistics and psychology journals.

Follow-up Questions and Activities

1. Locate a published empirical study that investigated syntactic priming in L1, bilingual, or L2 speech processing or acquisition and consider the following questions:

   a) What topic was syntactic priming used to investigate?

   b) What syntactic priming task was used? How appropriate was the task for the topic and the research question(s)?

   c) Did the study include baseline and/or post-priming production? Would the study have benefited from the inclusion of these phases?

   d) How were the validity and reliability of the materials and analysis checked?

2. For the following research questions and target structures, explain which syntactic priming task would be most appropriate.

   a) Subordinate clause attachment

   > *RQ*: Is syntactic information related to hierarchical tree configuration shared or separate between the languages of bilinguals?
   >
   > *Target structure*: Relative clause attachment—either high attachment or low attachment.
   >
   > *Example*: John met the boss of the employees who. . . .

   In many languages the relative clause may modify either *the boss* or *the employees*. A relative clause that modifies *the boss* is high attachment because that noun phrase occurs higher in the tree configuration. In contrast, a relative clause that modifies *the employees* is low attachment because that noun phrase occurs lower in the tree structure. Since the verb used in the relative clause must agree with either the singular *boss* or the plural *employees*, the agreement features can be used to help identify the intended attachment.

   b) Syntactic complexity

   > *RQ*: Does syntactic priming affect holistic ratings of complexity and accuracy?
   >
   > *Target structure*: Passives and ditransitive datives
   >
   > *Examples*: He went to the hospital in a helicopter (active) or He was taken to the hospital by helicopter (passive). Nancy poured the juice (monotransitive) versus Nancy poured her friends the juice (ditransitive).

c) Conceptual roles

> RQ: Does syntactic priming occur when sentences have identical constituent orders but different event roles?
> *Target structure:* Clausal complement constructions
> *Example: The police suspected that Joan was the criminal* (that-clause complement) versus *The police suspected Joan to be the criminal* (NP + infinitive complement).

3) Besides those mentioned in this chapter, what other topics might L2 researchers use syntactic priming methods to investigate?
4) In terms of their materials development, procedure, and analysis, which of the methods used in syntactic priming research seems to be the easiest to implement? Which ones seem more difficult?
5) Using the data in table 4.7 (from McDonough, 2006), code the datives that the L2 participant produced after the scripted interlocutor's dative primes (double-object datives and prepositional datives) and answer the following questions.

Table 4.7 Dative picture descriptions

Interlocutor	Participant 1	Participant 2	Participant 3	Participant 4
The farmer promised his wife the prettiest pig	A boy is pouring some coffee on a cup while a girl is holding a cup	A boy is pouring water for his friends	A boy is pouring some drinks for the girl	Jim was pouring some water for Mary
The seamstress is sewing the woman a new dress	A waiter is serving a woman	A man is serving the daughter the ice cream	The man is serving a lady	Man was serving an ice cream for the girl
The woman is painting a picture for her friend	A child on an apple tree handing an apple to his friends	The boy is handing an apple to his friend	The boy hand an apple to a lot of child	Jack handed a report to his friend
A mother is reading a book to her children	A boy is giving a pair of gloves to a girl	A girl is giving a pair of gloves to her friend	The mother gives a pair of gloves to her children	Mom gave the other glove to her kid
The boy saved his friend the best pumpkin	A group of girls are tossing a ball	Several children are tossing the ball	The childrens are tossing on the ground	The girls are tossing the ball to each other
The woman is lending the squirrels her arms	A father is cutting a birthday cake for her child	An old man is cutting a piece of cake for his granddaughter	The old man is cutting the cakes	Grandpa was cutting the cake for his grandchild

144

The girl is building her sister a tower of blocks	A chef is making a cake for two children	The cooker man had made a meal for his guests	A man makes a plate of food	Kids make something for other
The cows are singing a song to their animal friends	A father is buying a new bicycle to his daughter	The father bought a bicycle for his daughter and taught her to ride	The man buys a new bike for his daughter	They just bought a new bicycle for his kids
The girl is writing papers for her friends	A woman is bringing a glass of water to a mother and child	Mother brings a glass of water to her ill daughter	The mother brings a glass of water to a child	Mom brought a cup of tea for her kids
The sheep won the farmer the first prize	A girl is asking her teacher a question	The teacher is asking the little girl some questions	The girls asked her teacher a question	Teacher was asking the girl for something
The boy kicks the pillow to his mother	A woman is teaching some children on the beach	The old man is teaching her grandchildren the game in the sand	A woman is teaching her childrens a game	A teacher was teaching a game to a team
The man granted a wish to his friend	An old lady is cooking food for her husband	An old couple is cooking	The old woman cooked some food for his husband	Grandma cooked for grandpa

a) What coding categories did you create and why?

b) What interlanguage features, if any, did you ignore in your coding decisions?

c) To what extent do the participants' picture descriptions match the syntactic structure of the scripted interlocutor's primes?

5

ANALYZING AND REPORTING PRIMING DATA

In this chapter, we describe how to analyze priming data and how to carry out several statistical tests commonly used in priming research. Because our focus is on priming research, we do not provide the more general information about research design found in research design textbooks (such as Creswell, 2003; Dörnyei, 2007; Mackey & Gass, 2005). We also illustrate how to use SPSS to carry out statistical tests used in the analysis of priming data, but a more extensive introduction is available in texts by

Field (2005) and Salkind (2008). We conclude the chapter with an introduction to the journals in applied linguistics and psychology that publish priming studies.

Preliminary Considerations in Priming Research

Variable Types

As with other empirical studies, priming research involves various sets of data. Researchers think of such sets of data in terms of discrete categories, or variables. There are at least two types of variables in an experimental study—dependent and independent. *Dependent variables* (also known as *response variables*) are those variables that are being measured in the course of a task. For example, a researcher using a lexical decision task to investigate semantic priming in L2 learners will almost certainly measure response latency, or the amount of time that it takes for participants to make a word or a nonword decision. In this case, response latency is the primary measure of interest, and is the dependent variable. The number and type of dependent variables clearly depend on the nature of the task itself. For instance, an auditory identification task typically yields only one dependent variable, response accuracy. A lexical decision task, however, can yield two dependent variables, response latency and response accuracy.

In contrast, *independent variables* (also known as *manipulated variables*) are those variables that are selected by a researcher to determine their relationship to a dependent variable. Continuing with our example, the same researcher may also want to determine if semantic priming depends on learners' L2 proficiency, such that high proficiency learners show larger semantic priming effects than low proficiency learners. The researcher thus hypothesizes that there is a certain relationship between semantic priming and L2 proficiency and wishes to investigate this relationship in the lexical decision task. L2 proficiency is therefore an independent variable in this case. In priming tasks, researchers have used various independent variables. Some of them are specific to participant characteristics (e.g. participants' L2 proficiency, amount of L2 experience, language dominance). Others relate to the materials used (e.g. type of syntactic structure, word frequency, intonation in which words are spoken). Yet others are specific to the tasks themselves (e.g. amount of time between the presentation of primes and targets, reading vs. hearing words in a lexical decision task). Independent variables are often organized in terms of levels, or distinct groupings. For example, if the researcher chooses to test two groups of L2 learners (one group of high proficiency learners and one group of low proficiency learners), the independent variable of L2 proficiency is said to have two levels (high vs. low proficiency).

Experimental Designs

The notion of variable is closely tied to the notion of research design. When designing experiments, researchers purposefully create conditions of interest so that they can test hypotheses about how independent variables might influence the dependent variable. There are many different types of experimental designs available for the different kinds of questions researchers might ask (see Hatch & Lazaraton, 1991, and Keppel, 1982). A comprehensive discussion of all experimental research designs falls outside the scope of this book. Instead, we briefly describe the three most common research designs used in priming research.

One common research design used in priming research is a between-subjects design. The adjective *between-subjects* indicates that measurements of the dependent variable come from different groups of individuals or, in technical terms, from independent samples. For example, if researchers wish to compare response latencies in a semantic priming task among three different groups of learners (beginner, intermediate, advanced), they will use a between-subjects design to collect and analyze their data. In this case, the dependent variable is response latency. The independent variable —proficiency—is a between-subjects variable that has three levels: beginner, intermediate, and advanced. A schematic illustration of this design appears in figure 5.1. Researchers often analyze the data from designs like this using a one-way analysis of variance (ANOVA) or an independent samples *t*-test if there are only two groups. We describe this particular type of ANOVA in detail later in this chapter (see pp. 159–166).

Between-subjects designs can be more complicated, such as including more than one between-subjects variable. Suppose a researcher wishes to compare semantic priming effects among the three proficiency groups described previously, but also wants to investigate whether length of residence in a target-language country impacts priming. To answer this question, the researcher adds another between-subjects independent variable (length of residence) to the research design, which originally had proficiency as the only independent variable. The new independent variable—length of residence—has two levels: 3 years and 10 years. Both independent variables (proficiency, length of residence) are between-

Proficiency		
Beginner	Intermediate	Advanced
$n = 30$	$n = 30$	$n = 30$

Figure 5.1 A schematic illustration of a between-subjects design with one independent variable (proficiency). Separate groups of participants (30 in each cell) are designated by double lines.

subjects variables because the measurements of the dependent variable (response latency) come from six different groups of participants, defined by a combination of the two independent variables (see figure 5.2).

Researchers often analyze the data from this type of research design using two-way ANOVAs (also referred to as Factorial ANOVA), which is also described in detail later in this chapter (see pp. 166–168). The adjective *two-way* indicates that there are two independent variables in this design. When describing such research designs, researchers often use this wording: $x \times y$. For example, the design depicted in figure 5.2 can be described as 3×2 (proficiency × length of residence). The number of elements (x and y) in this description indicates how many independent variables there are: two in this case (proficiency and length of residence); hence this is a two-way design. The actual digit value for each element represents the number of levels of each independent variable. Thus, proficiency has three levels while length of residence has only two. Of course, it is possible to have more than two independent variables. In such cases, researchers would employ n-way ANOVAs. One, for example, can think of a three-way between-subjects design in which a researcher might have another between-subjects independent variable: gender (male vs. female). Such a design can be described as $3 \times 2 \times 2$ (proficiency × length of residence × gender).

Another common research design used in priming research is a within-subjects design. The adjective *within-subjects* indicates that measurements of the dependent variable come from the same individuals. Such measurements are also called repeated measurements because the same participants are tested at different points in time. The adjective *within-subjects* is therefore synonymous with the adjective *repeated-measures*. Both describe research designs in which measurements of the dependent variable come from non-independent or, in technical terms, correlated samples.

Within-subjects (or repeated-measures) designs are frequently employed in priming research. For example, a researcher might wish to determine if

		Proficiency		
		Beginner	Intermediate	Advanced
Length of residence	3 years	*n* = 15	*n* = 15	*n* = 15
	10 years	*n* = 15	*n* = 15	*n* = 15

Figure 5.2 A schematic illustration of a between-subjects design with two independent variables (proficiency, length of residence). Separate groups of participants (15 in each cell) are designated by double lines.

the extent of auditory priming effects varies as a function of time that elapses between the study phase of an experiment and the testing phase. This researcher can then test the same group of participants in a repetition (naming) task in which the test phase is separated from the study phase by 5 minutes, 1 day, and 1 week. In this case, the dependent variable is response latency. The independent variable—time—is a within-subjects variable that has three levels: 5 minutes, 1 day, and 1 week. A schematic illustration of this design appears in figure 5.3. Researchers often analyze the data from designs like this using a one-way repeated-measures ANOVA or a paired samples t-test if there are only two levels of the repeated variable. This type of ANOVA is discussed later in this chapter (see pp. 168–173).

Yet another design commonly used in priming research is a mixed design, one that includes *both* between- and within-subjects variables. In other words, such a design involves repeated measurements of the dependent variable (hence, within-subjects) that come from different groups of participants (hence, between-subjects). For example, a researcher might wish to change the within-subjects design depicted in figure 5.3 by adding another independent variable, a between-subjects variable in this case. Such a variable might be proficiency, as the researcher might hypothesize that learners of different proficiency levels show different auditory priming effects at various levels of the time variable (5 minutes, 1 day, and 1 week after the study task of the experiment). In this case, proficiency is a between-subjects independent variable with three levels (beginner, intermediate, advanced). Time is a within-subjects independent variable also with three levels (5 minutes, 1 day, 1 week). A schematic illustration of this design appears in figure 5.4.

Researchers often analyze the data from designs like this using two-way mixed repeated-measures ANOVAs, also described in detail later in this chapter (see pp. 168–173). The adjective *two-way* indicates that there are two independent variables in this design. The crucial difference between this design and a two-way fully between-subjects design discussed earlier is that at least one variable in this mixed design is a within-subjects independent variable. The design depicted in figure 5.4 can be described

Time		
5 minutes	1 day	1 week
$n = 30$	...	...

Figure 5.3 A schematic illustration of a within-subjects design with one independent variable (time). The same participants are tested at three points in time.

		Time		
		5 minutes	1 day	1 week
Proficiency	Beginner	$n = 30$	...	...
	Intermediate	$n = 30$	...	...
	Advanced	$n = 30$	...	...

Figure 5.4 A schematic illustration of a mixed (between-within) design with two independent variables: proficiency as a between-subjects variable and time as a within-subjects variable. Separate groups of participants (30 in each cell) are designated by double lines.

as 3×3 (proficiency × time) repeated measures design with proficiency (beginner, intermediate, advanced) as a between-subjects variable and time (5 minutes, 1 day, 1 week) as a within-subjects variable. Overall there are two variables. (Note that the between-subjects variable is always discussed first.) Each variable has three levels. Of course, as with fully between-subjects designs, it is possible to have more than two independent variables in a mixed design, as a long as there is at least one within-subjects variable. To analyze the data from such designs, researchers could employ n-way repeated-measures ANOVAs. One, for example, can think of a three-way mixed design in which a researcher might have another within-subjects independent variable: task type. In other words, the researcher might measure auditory priming effects for the beginner, intermediate, and advanced learners at three points in time using two tasks (e.g. naming and identification). Such a design can be described as $3 \times 3 \times 2$ repeated-measures design with proficiency (beginner, intermediate, advanced) as a between-subjects variable, and time (5 minutes, 1 day, 1 week) and task (naming, identification) as within-subjects variables.

Transforming Data

An important methodological assumption underlying analyses of priming data, particularly when researchers wish to use parametric statistics (see p. 158), is that the obtained data are normally distributed. Data are said to be normally distributed if they approximate the standard normal distribution (with a mean of 0 and variance of 1), resembling a bell-shaped standard normal curve. Meeting this assumption is especially important in the analysis of reaction time data, that is, measurements of response latency. The reason here is that reaction time data are frequently non-normally distributed or, in technical terms, they are usually positively skewed. This means that quite often there are a number of "outlier" data points that represent exceedingly long response latencies, spreading far along the x-axis. Such outlier response latencies can potentially bias the results of statistical analyses. Figure 5.5 (panel a) depicts a histogram of the distribution of response latencies collected from 60 L2 learners of Spanish in an auditory repetition task (based on Trofimovich, 2005). As this figure shows, the original response latencies measured in milliseconds are indeed somewhat skewed.

Although parametric statistical procedures are often robust to violations of the normality assumption (Glass, Peckham, & Sanders, 1972), researchers often apply a logarithmic (log) transformation to their reaction time data to correct for the positive (or negative) skew in data distributions. Data transformation can be carried out in any statistical software (SPSS users can select the *Compute* . . . option under the *Transform* menu and then choose the *LG10* function under the *Numeric Expression Choice* menu). Figure 5.5 (panel b) shows the distribution of the same response latency data depicted on the left after a *log* transformation has been applied. As this figure shows, a *log* transformation successfully "normalized" the distribution of the original data, such that the transformed distribution approximates the standard normal curve.

Researchers typically employ several other procedures to safeguard themselves from unwanted effects of outlier response latencies. One procedure involves removing outlier latencies. That is, researchers may choose to exclude from further data analyses those responses that are shorter and those that are longer than a particular value. For example, in analyzing data from a lexical decision task, de Groot and Nas (1991) excluded from further analyses all data points that were less than 100 milliseconds or more than 1,400 milliseconds. Researchers may also define the lower and upper bounds of "acceptable" response latencies in terms of the obtained distribution itself (in terms of its variability, to be exact). In analyzing

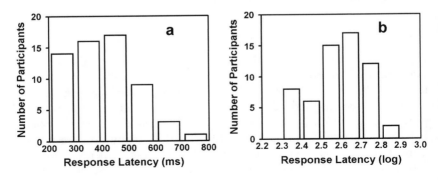

Figure 5.5 Sample distributions of raw (a) and *log*-transformed (b) response latency data.

similar data from a lexical decision task, Silverberg and Samuel (2004), for instance, considered only those response latencies that fell within the range of 3 standard deviations of the overall mean.

Instead of removing (or, in technical terms, trimming) outlier response latencies, and thus reducing the available dataset, researchers may choose to replace outlier response latencies. Some researchers replace outlier responses with a single score, usually defined in terms of the obtained distribution itself. For example, a researcher might decide to replace all response latencies that are shorter than 3 standard deviations of the mean with a single value (mean value − 3 standard deviation values, or $M - 3SD$), and all response latencies that are longer than 3 standard deviations of the mean with another single value ($M + 3SD$).

Other researchers prefer to use a procedure called *winsorizing* for replacing outlier responses in their dataset. Winsorizing involves trimming a certain number of data points and replacing those with a single value: the smallest and largest value that is not trimmed. Suppose a researcher has 80 response latencies in a distribution ($n = 80$) and chooses to trim outlier response latencies (extreme values) on each end of the distribution: for instance, the smallest 10% and the largest 10%. This number of to-be-replaced response latencies (g) on each end of the distribution will be 8 in this example. In order to winsorize this dataset, the researcher will then replace the 8 fastest response latencies with the next adjacent response latency $g + 1$ that is not trimmed (i.e. 9th response latency in a distribution ordered from fastest to slowest). Similarly, the researcher will replace the 8 slowest response latencies with the next adjacent response latency $n - g$ that is not trimmed (i.e. 72nd response latency in a distribution ordered from fastest to slowest). Researchers typically winsorize "raw" data for each individual participant, rather than winsorize data that are averaged across many participants. For example, in order to diminish the impact of outlier response latencies, Philips et al. (2004) winsorized all response latencies for each participant at the 10% level. In other words, these researchers replaced the fastest 10% and slowest 10% of response latencies for each participant (separately in each condition) with this participant's next fastest and slowest response latencies, respectively.

When reporting results of priming studies, it is important to clearly identify how outlier data have been treated and exactly how many outlier responses (in proportion to the entire dataset) have been removed or replaced (see Trofimovich, 2005, 2008, for examples of how to report this information). For more information on handling outlier data, see Wilcox (2005).

By-Subject and By-Item Analyses

In psycholinguistic studies, it is customary to carry out two sets of statistical analyses. These two sets of analyses are referred to as *by-subject* and *by-item analyses*. By-subject analyses are the standard analyses found in most empirical studies employing statistical procedures. These analyses treat participants as the unit of analysis. The goal is to determine if a given sample of participants demonstrates a pattern of responses that is similar or different from one to be found in another sample or in a population from which this sample is drawn. In order to calculate by-subject statistics, researchers average each participant's responses across a number of items. In the context of priming experiments, the term "items" refers to individual words that participants repeat or identify in an auditory priming experiment or, for example, to individual pictures that participants describe in a syntactic priming task. Table 5.1 presents a mini dataset of response latencies from an auditory repetition task (from Trofimovich, 2008). This dataset contains response latencies for five participants who repeated a set of five words. For subject-based analyses, researchers would average each participant's response latencies across the five words. Of course, this illustrative dataset is in actuality too small to use for any meaningful statistical analyses. The resulting set of means (presented in the final column in table 5.1) is subsequently used to calculate by-subject statistics.

The purpose of by-item analyses is to ensure that the results found in the standard by-subject analyses are not specific to a small set of "anomalous" items. Despite the utmost care that researchers often take in selecting, matching, and counterbalancing items for their experiments, it can happen that some items may appear somehow more difficult for participants than other items, for reasons that researchers may not anticipate. For example, some words used in a semantic priming task may be of lower frequency than the remaining words in the set, causing participants to show longer response latencies for these low-frequency words. Alternatively, some sentences used in a syntactic priming task may be slightly longer than the rest of the sentences, which makes it hard for participants

Table 5.1 Sample dataset used for calculating by-subject statistics

| Participant | Word | | | | | Mean |
	1	2	3	4	5	
1	490	490	462	464	597	501
2	310	310	262	278	695	371
3	745	745	642	722	539	679
4	959	959	971	954	809	930
5	351	351	351	374	441	374

to recall them. The goal of by-item analyses is thus to ensure that the effects found in by-subject analyses are not driven by such anomalous items. By calculating by-item statistics alongside by-subject statistics, researchers expect to find similar patterns of results in both sets of analyses.

In order to calculate by-item statistics, researchers re-organize their dataset so that they can calculate a mean of all participants' responses for each individual item. Table 5.2 shows the same dataset seen earlier. In this case, however, the dataset has been re-organized to compute by-item statistics. In this version of the dataset, items and subjects traded places such that now a researcher can calculate word-based averages across all five participants. The resulting set of means, presented in the final column, can subsequently be used to calculate by-item statistics.

Although separate subject- and item-based analyses are customary in cognitive psychology and psycholinguistic studies, computing by-item analyses alongside by-subject analyses is uncommon in applied linguistics research, particularly in L2 priming research. For reasons outlined earlier, by-item analyses should be a common feature of future L2 priming studies. Interested readers are referred to Clark (1973) and Raaijmakers, Schrijnemakers, and Gremmen (1999) for an in-depth discussion of both sets of analyses and of alternative statistical procedures.

Hypotheses

Although research hypotheses are rarely stated explicitly in applied linguistics and psychology articles, they still inform both the presentation and interpretation of the results. In particular, the null hypothesis, while rarely provided in a research article, is the basis for interpreting the findings. The *null hypothesis* is a statement that, within a given population, there is no difference among groups or no relationship among variables. Essentially, the null hypothesis is a statement about equality or lack of effect, assuming that in the absence of evidence to the contrary, there is no reason to presume that a relationship or difference exists. It serves as

Table 5.2 Sample dataset used for calculating by-item statistics

Word	Participant					Mean
	1	*2*	*3*	*4*	*5*	
1	490	310	745	959	351	571
2	490	310	745	959	351	571
3	462	262	642	971	351	538
4	464	278	722	954	374	558
5	597	695	539	809	441	616

the basis for comparing the results obtained from the sample (i.e. the actual participants in the experiment) with what is expected in the population. Furthermore, even if a difference or relationship were shown to exist, it may be due to chance rather than to a systematic reason. Therefore, the goal is to determine whether within a sample (that has been selected to represent a population), there is a relationship or difference that is greater than what could occur as a result of pure chance.

Whereas the null hypothesis is a statement of equality, the research hypothesis is a statement of inequality. In other words, it states that there is some relationship, difference or effect involving the variables under investigation. The research hypothesis may simply state that there is a relationship, difference, or effect without specifying the nature of the relationship, which is referred to as a *nondirectional research hypothesis*. Alternatively, there may be sufficient justification based on theory or empirical research to expect a particular type of relationship or effect, in which case a *directional research hypothesis* would be formulated. The choice of a directional or nondirectional research hypothesis has implications for the interpretation of inferential statistics. Because a directional hypothesis predicts a relationship in a particular direction, one-tailed tests of significance are used. In contrast, because a non-directional hypothesis does not predict in which direction a relationship will occur, two-tailed tests of significance are used. By directly testing the research hypothesis with the sample, the null hypothesis for the population is indirectly tested. As the null hypothesis is implied whereas the research hypothesis is explicit, researchers may include only the research hypothesis in an article. The various types of hypotheses are exemplified in table 5.3.

Describing Group Performance

Like most experimental research, priming studies typically report two types of statistics: descriptive and inferential. Descriptive statistics include measures of central tendency and dispersion. Measures of central tendency

Table 5.3 Different types of hypotheses used in priming research

Type of hypothesis	Wording
Null	L2 learners will show the same semantic priming effects in their L1 and L2.
Nondirectional	L2 learners will show different semantic priming effects in their L1 and L2.
Directional	L2 learners will show larger semantic priming effects in their L1 than in their L2.

indicate the average performance of a group, while measures of dispersion indicate the degree of variation within a group. The mean is the most commonly used measure of central tendency in priming research. The mean is defined as the sum of all scores divided by the total number of scores. However, the mean is the appropriate measure of central tendency only when the distribution is normal. If the distribution of scores is not normal, such as when there are extreme scores or outliers, then the median is more appropriate. The median is the score that is located at the middle of the distribution, with half of the scores falling above the midpoint and half of the scores falling below the midpoint. Because the distance to the middle of the distribution is irrelevant in the calculation of the median, this measure is less sensitive to extreme scores.

Each measure of central tendency has a corresponding measure of variance—standard deviation for the mean and interquartile range for the median. Both values, while calculated using different information, estimate the average distance of each score in a set from the average score. The standard deviation is the square root of the sum of each score's distance from the mean squared, which is then divided by the total number of scores minus one. The interquartile range is based on quartiles, and is calculated by subtracting the first quartile score from the third quartile score. The decision to report the mean/standard deviation or the median/interquartile range is based on the distribution. The mean/standard deviation are appropriate for normally distributed scores while the median/interquartile range are appropriate for non-normal distributions. The choice of descriptive statistics also impacts the use of inferential statistics, as some tests are based on the mean while others use the median.

Making Inferences about Populations

Whereas descriptive statistics provide the average performance and degree of variation within a set of scores, inferential statistics are used to make inferences about a population based on the performance of the sample. One way that researchers make inferences about a population is by determining if the results for the sample are statistically significant. The basic premise of statistical significance is that by comparing the results for a sample with a test distribution, researchers can determine whether those results are different than what could occur by chance. Probability plays an important role in significance testing, and it refers to the level of risk that a researcher is willing to take. In most psychology and applied linguistics studies, researchers are willing to accept a 5% risk that they may incorrectly conclude that the results are due to a systematic influence rather than chance. In other words, the possibility that the results are due to chance should be less than .05. In other fields, such as pharmacology or chemistry, researchers may be willing to take only a 1% risk, which is the level of risk associated with a probability level of .01. Through reference to the significance value associated with a test statistic, researchers can reject or accept the null hypothesis. When researchers determine that the results for the sample are due to a systematic influence instead of chance, then an inference from the sample to the population may be made. However, since many factors can influence the outcome of significance tests (such as distribution, sample size, and experimental procedure), researchers may want to weigh additional considerations before generalizing from the sample to the population. Some of these considerations include how well the sample represented the population, the theoretical or conceptual basis of the study, and the magnitude of any significant difference (referred to as the effect size).

Although all inferential statistics allow a researcher to determine whether the observed results are systematic or due to chance, there are two main types of statistics: parametric and nonparametric. Parametric statistics are generally considered more powerful because they are more likely to identify a difference or relationship that is not due to chance. However, they also assume that the data have certain characteristics, such as that the distribution of scores is normal and that the dependent variable has been measured using an interval scale. If the data do not have these characteristics, then nonparametric tests may be more appropriate since they are not based on such assumptions. In the following sections, the parametric tests commonly used to analyze priming data are introduced and illustrated through SPSS screenshots. When a parametric test has a nonparametric equivalent, the nonparametric test is also explained and illustrated through SPSS screenshots. However, in some cases there are no nonparametric alternatives, so researchers may wish to ensure that the data from their sample can meet the assumptions of the parametric tests.

If researchers use parametric statistics when it might not be appropriate (such as the data not meeting the assumptions), they may obtain a statistically significant finding and conclude that the results were not due to chance when in fact they were. This is referred to as a Type I error, and occurs when a null hypothesis is rejected (i.e. researchers conclude that the findings were due to something systematic rather than chance) when in fact the findings were due to chance. The opposite scenario is also possible, for example, if researchers use nonparametric (and less powerful) statistics and fail to reject the null hypothesis (i.e. they conclude that the findings were due to chance) when in fact there was a systematic influence in the data. This type of error is referred to as a Type II error. Having introduced the logic of inferential statistics, in the following section we describe some of the statistical tests, both parametric and nonparametric, that are often used in priming research.

Statistical Tests Used in Priming Research

Simple ANOVA

ANOVA, referred to as a simple analysis of variance or one-way analysis of variance, compares the variance due to differences between individuals within a single group to the variance due to differences between two or more groups. (Comparisons between two groups only are typically carried out using *t*-tests.) The ANOVA test statistic is the *F* test, which is calculated from the ratio of the variability between the groups to the variability within each group. Assumptions in the use of ANOVA include the following:

- there is only one numeric dependent variable that has a truly continuous interval or ordinal scale;
- there is only one independent variable with at least two levels;
- each observation is assigned to only one level of the independent variable (i.e. there are no repeated observations);
- the distribution of scores for each level of the independent variable is normal;
- the variance within each level of the independent variable is equal.

Because of space limitations, we do not elaborate on these assumptions further. Interested readers are referred to statistics manuals for further clarifications of certain terminology (e.g. *interval scale*) and for further explanations of assumptions (e.g. equal variance).

The probability value associated with the *F* value will indicate whether there is a significant difference among the scores for all of the groups, but it does not locate the significance between specific groups. In order to identify where the significant differences are located, post hoc tests are carried out. The post hoc tests commonly used with ANOVA include Bonferroni (when equal variance is assumed) and Tamhane's T2 (when equal variance is not assumed). These tests calculate all of the two-way comparisons among the groups, but adjust for multiple comparisons in order to avoid Type I error.

An example of the use of ANOVA in priming research is provided by Kim (2006), who investigated whether syntactic priming involving passives differed as a function of the participants' proficiency level. The scripted interlocutor method of syntactic priming was used, in which the researcher carried out a picture description activity with Korean EFL learners who represented three relative proficiency levels (high, mid, low), as determined by their performance on a cloze test. The scores in table 5.4 represent the proportion of passives produced by each participant immediately following the researcher's passive sentences. The learners' proportion score was

Table 5.4 Priming scores by proficiency level

Participant	Proficiency level	Passive priming score
1	Mid	.90
2	Low	.30
3	Mid	.80
4	High	.30
5	Low	.80
6	Mid	.10
7	Low	.00
8	High	.90
9	Low	.10
10	Mid	.20
11	High	.80
12	Mid	.30
13	Mid	.20
14	Mid	.10
15	Mid	.70
16	Mid	.80
17	Mid	.60
18	Low	.00
20	Low	.20
22	Low	.10
23	Mid	.50
24	Mid	.70
26	High	1.00
27	Mid	.40
28	High	.60
29	Mid	.60
30	Mid	.70
31	Low	.10
32	High	1.00
33	Low	.20
34	Low	.70
35	Low	.40
40	Low	.00
41	Low	.30
42	Low	.20
47	High	.50
51	High	.80
58	Low	.00
63	High	.40
68	High	1.00
72	High	.60
76	High	.60
78	High	.90
80	High	1.00
81	High	.70

based on the number of passive picture descriptions divided by the total picture descriptions that occurred immediately following the researcher's passive primes ($n = 10$). In this study, the independent variable was proficiency, which had three levels, while the dependent variable was the passive proportion score.

When calculating an ANOVA, the spreadsheet typically has one row per participant and columns that contain the participant identification number, the independent variable, and the dependent variable. As illustrated in figure 5.6, three columns were used for the data displayed in table 5.4, which were labeled *participant*, *proficiency*, and *score*. Notice that all three columns were set up as *numeric* variables in the *type* column, but only *score* has two decimal places since the participant identification and proficiency are whole numbers.

Although proficiency is listed in table 5.4 by categories (high, mid, low), it is entered into the spreadsheet with numeric values representing each category and the *type* column is set up as *numeric*. If it were entered as words with the type column set up as *string*, it might not be recognized by the statistical tests that are calculated using numeric variables. The categories of *low*, *mid*, and *high* used in table 5.4 can be converted to numeric variables, such as 1 for *low*, 2 for *mid*, and 3 for *high*. Once the column names, type, and decimal places have been entered, click on the *data view* tab to enter the data provided in table 5.4. The first 10 rows of data are illustrated in figure 5.7. Using figures 5.6 and 5.7 as a model, you can open a spreadsheet and enter all of the data provided in table 5.4.

Once you have entered all of the data into the spreadsheet, you can calculate an ANOVA. First, open the dialog box by clicking *Analyze*, *Compare Means*, and *One-Way ANOVA*. Then move the dependent variable *score* into the *Dependent List* box and the independent variable *proficiency* into the *Factor* box, as shown in figure 5.8.

Next, if you want to obtain descriptive statistics (such as means and standard deviations) and check the assumption about equal variance, click

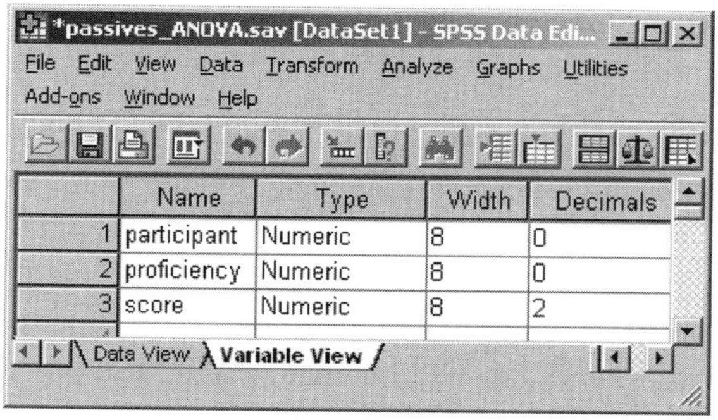

Figure 5.6 Setting up the spreadsheet for ANOVA.

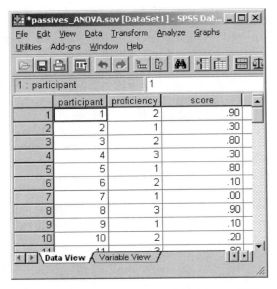

Figure 5.7 Entering data from table 5.4 into SPSS.

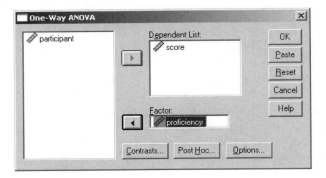

Figure 5.8 One-way ANOVA dialogue box.

on *Options* then *Descriptive* and *Homogeneity of Variance* and then *Continue*. Finally, to obtain post hoc tests, click on *Post Hoc* and select the desired test, such as *Bonferroni* or *Tamhane's T2* and *Continue*. Once all the options have been selected, click *OK* in the dialogue box shown in figure 5.8.

The resulting output consists of four main sections. The first section is a table that gives the descriptive statistics for each proficiency group, which are summarized in table 5.5. As indicated by the mean score, the high proficiency group had the highest score (.74), followed by the mid group (.51) and the low group scoring (.23).

Table 5.5 Descriptive statistics for passives scores by group

Proficiency group	N	Mean	SD	Minimum	Maximum
1 (low)	15	.23	.25	.00	.80
2 (mid)	15	.51	.27	.10	.90
3 (high)	15	.74	.23	.30	1.00

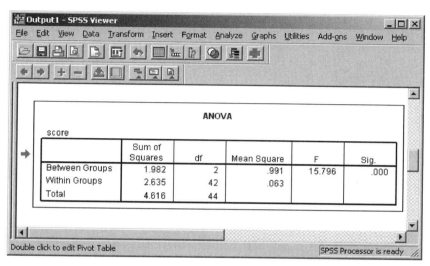

Figure 5.9 ANOVA output.

The second section of the output provides the results of the homogeneity of variances test, which is used to check whether the data meet the assumption that the variance is equal in each group. The output states that the Levene statistic was .577 with a probability value of .566, which indicates that the assumption of variance has been met (i.e. the null hypothesis should be accepted). Consequently, it is appropriate to use the Bonferroni post hoc test, since it assumes that the variance is equal. If you have selected *Descriptive* and *Homogeneity of Variance* under *Options*, the third section of the output is the results of the ANOVA, which are presented in tabular format as shown in figure 5.9. If you did not select *Descriptive* and *Homogeneity of Variance*, the output would begin with the ANOVA results table.

As described previously, ANOVA calculates an F statistic based on the ratio of variability between groups to the variability within groups. The first row of the table presents the information for the between-groups variability, which is expressed as the sum of squares. The sum of squares for between-groups variability is the difference between the mean of all groups and the mean of each group, which is then squared. The sum of squares for within-groups variability is the difference between each individual score in a group and the group mean, which is also squared. The degrees of freedom (*df*) are an approximation of the sample size, which is the number of groups minus one for the between-groups' *df* (3 – 1 = 2) and is the total sample size minus the number of groups for the within-groups' *df* (45 – 3 = 42). The mean square is the sum of squares divided by the degrees of freedom (1.982/2 = .991 and 2.635/42 = .063), and *F* is the between-groups mean square divided by the within-groups mean square (.991/.063 = 15.796). Finally, the significance value that is provided in the last column (.000) indicates that the null hypothesis (i.e. there is no difference in the scores of the three groups) can be rejected. The significance value reported in SPSS is generally rounded to three decimal places.

Although the results of the ANOVA indicate that there is a significant difference in the passive scores of the three proficiency groups, it does not indicate which groups differ significantly from each other. This information is available through the post-hoc test, which is the forth section of the ANOVA output, and is illustrated in figure 5.10. Each group is compared to each of the other two groups, with the mean difference in scores, standard error and significance level presented in the first three columns.

The output indicates that the mean difference between the low group (group 1) and the mid group (group 2) was significant [p = .011] as was the mean difference between the low group and the high group (group 3) [p = .000]. In addition, the mean difference between the mid group and the high group was also significant [p = .043].

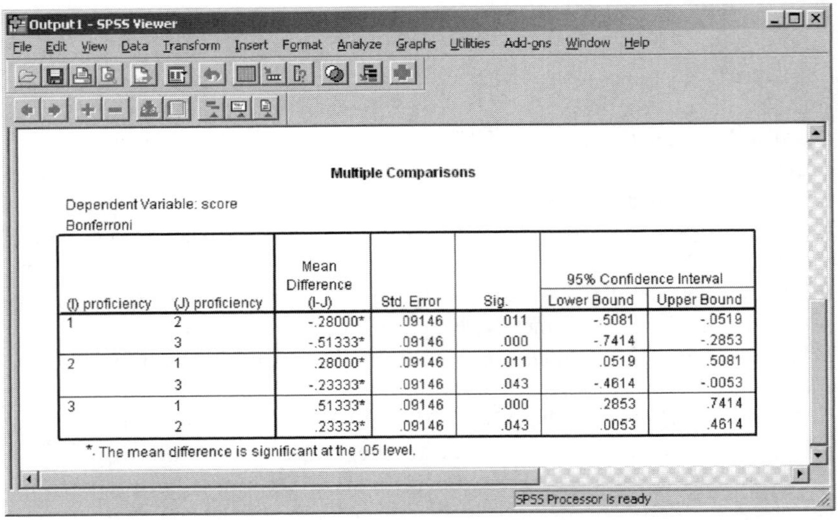

Multiple Comparisons

Dependent Variable: score
Bonferroni

(I) proficiency	(J) proficiency	Mean Difference (I-J)	Std. Error	Sig.	95% Confidence Interval Lower Bound	95% Confidence Interval Upper Bound
1	2	-.28000*	.09146	.011	-.5081	-.0519
	3	-.51333*	.09146	.000	-.7414	-.2853
2	1	.28000*	.09146	.011	.0519	.5081
	3	-.23333*	.09146	.043	-.4614	-.0053
3	1	.51333*	.09146	.000	.2853	.7414
	2	.23333*	.09146	.043	.0053	.4614

*. The mean difference is significant at the .05 level.

Figure 5.10 Post-hoc output.

When reporting ANOVA, researchers may include the ANOVA and post hoc tables in the results section, typically reproducing the information in a table generated in a word processing document rather than copying the table from the SPSS output. Alternatively, they may provide descriptive statistics in a table and report the relevant test output in the text. If reporting information in the text, the appropriate format for the current example would be $F(2, 42) = 15.80$, $p < .05$. The information in parenthesis is the df for the between-group estimate (2) and the df for the within-group estimate (42). For the post hoc tests, the p value and effect size are typically reported for each comparison.

If the data do not meet the assumptions of ANOVA (e.g. a non-normal distribution, a non-continuous scale, or a small sample size), it may be analyzed using a nonparametric test instead. The nonparametric equivalent of one-way ANOVA is a Kruskal-Wallis test, which can also be obtained through SPSS (*Analyze → Nonparametric Tests → K Independent Samples*). The dependent variable is entered in the *Test Variable List* and the independent variable is entered as the *Grouping Variable*, as shown in figure 5.11.

Once *proficiency* has been entered as the grouping variable, click on *Define Range* to indicate the group labels, for this example with 1 as the minimum and 3 as the maximum. The Kruskal-Wallis test does not include a post hoc test option, so if there is a significant difference among the groups, pairwise comparisons can be carried out to locate significance using individual Mann-Whitney tests (*Analyze → Nonparametric Tests → 2 Independent Samples*). To avoid Type I error, the initial alpha level should be divided by the number of comparisons. In the current example then, three Mann-Whitney tests would be carried out to compare groups 1 and 2, 1 and 3, and 2 and 3, with .05 divided by three, which results in an adjusted alpha level of .016.

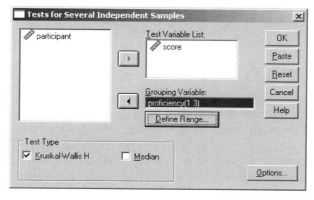

Figure 5.11 Dialog box for Kruskal-Wallis test.

ANOVA is a relatively simple test that is appropriate when an experiment involves a single dependent variable and a single independent variable that has at least two levels. For example, a researcher might use ANOVA to investigate whether variables such as proficiency, L1 background, modality, or priming task impact the occurrence of priming. However, many priming studies involve more complicated research designs that include multiple independent or dependent variables and repeated observations. In the following sections, factorial and repeated measures ANOVAs are introduced, and then linear mixed model is explained and illustrated through reference to auditory priming data.

Factorial ANOVA

Similar to a simple ANOVA, factorial or two-way ANOVA involves a between-groups design, has a single, numeric dependent variable, and is based on the same assumptions. However, whereas a one-way ANOVA is used when there is one independent variable with at least two levels, two-way or factorial ANOVA is appropriate when there are two (or more) independent variables that each have at least two levels. Factorial ANOVA considers each independent variable or factor separately, which are referred to as *main effects*, but also tests the interaction between factors, which is referred to as *interaction effects*. To illustrate the use of factorial ANOVA with priming data, consider a modification to the study described in the previous section (Kim, 2006). The study, as originally carried out, had one independent variable (proficiency level) and one dependent variable (production of passives), which made it appropriate for a one-way ANOVA. However, suppose the researcher had divided the learners into two groups. One group was given picture prompts that were labeled with the same verbs produced by the researcher, but the other group was given picture prompts that were labeled with different verbs. In other words, each of the two groups received different materials, and each group was therefore tested only once. In this modification, there would be two between-subjects independent variables: proficiency (high, mid, low) and prompt type (same verbs, different verbs). The learners' production of passives would then be considered in terms of both proficiency and prompt, as shown in table 5.6.

In this hypothetical data, the low proficiency learners' production of passives differed by prompt type, as they produced more passives in the same verb condition than in the different verb condition (.35 and .11 respectively). The mid proficiency learners also were affected by prompt type, producing more passives in the same verb condition (.62) than in the different verb condition (.39). While the high proficiency learners showed the same pattern, the difference in their production of passives in the same verb condition (.75) was only slightly higher than in the different

Table 5.6 Passive scores by proficiency group and prompt type

Proficiency group	Prompt type			
	Same verbs		Different verbs	
	Mean	SD	Mean	SD
1 (low)	.35	.23	.11	.30
2 (mid)	.62	.16	.39	.19
3 (high)	.75	.10	.71	.18

verb condition (.71). To determine whether proficiency and prompt type each impacted the learners' production of passives, a factorial ANOVA would be carried out, and this test would also indicate whether there was an interaction between the two factors. To calculate the factorial ANOVA, the variable *prompt* would be added to the spreadsheet previously illustrated in figure 5.7, converting the groups *same verbs* and *different verbs* into numeric values (such as same verbs = 1 and different verbs = 2).

Once the spreadsheet includes prompt type, the factorial ANOVA can be obtained by clicking *Analyze → General Linear Model → Univariate*. *Score* is entered in the *Dependent Variable* box, while *proficiency* and *prompt* are entered in the *Fixed Factor(s)* box. After clicking on *Options*, each variable and the interaction (indicated with an asterisk as proficiency*prompt) are moved to the *Display Means for* box and the *Compare Main Effects* box is ticked. The output of the factorial ANOVA is provided in a table, similar to the one-way ANOVA table (see figure 5.9), which lists the sum of squares, degrees of freedom, mean square, F statistic and probability for each variable and the interaction separately. The results are reported the same way as a one-way ANOVA, except that the relevant information (i.e. the F statistic, the degrees of freedom, and the p value) should be reported for each independent variable as well as the interaction.

The primary advantage of a factorial ANOVA is the inclusion of the interaction effect. Simply analyzing each factor separately may reveal that neither independent variable had a significant relationship with the dependent variable. However, it is possible that it is the combination of the two independent variables that impacts the dependent variable and this relationship can be identified in a factorial ANOVA. It is important to remember that the independent variables in factorial ANOVA are both between-group variables, which means that each participant belongs to only one level of each independent variable. Since there is no nonparametric equivalent of factorial ANOVA, researchers may want to ensure that their data are appropriate for factorial ANOVA by including a large sample size and using instruments that elicit truly continuous interval data. However, if a study involves repeated measures of a dependent variable, then repeated measures ANOVA, described in the following section, is more appropriate.

Repeated Measures ANOVA

Unlike simple ANOVA and factorial ANOVA, repeated measures ANOVA analyzes multiple measures of the dependent variable from each participant. As described previously, it is used with repeated measures or within-groups research designs. While all three ANOVA tests are based on the same assumptions and involve a single, numeric dependent variable, repeated measures ANOVA requires at least two measurements of the dependent variable for each participant. Repeated measures ANOVA can be used when the research design does not include an independent variable or when it has an independent variable with two or more levels. For example, a researcher could ask a group of L2 speakers from the same L1 background and the same proficiency level to carry out a series of auditory priming activities, such as one activity per day for three days. In this design, there would be one repeated dependent variable—the number of completed or identified words for each of the three days—but no independent variable since the participants had similar backgrounds and followed the same procedure. However, if the researcher divided the participants into three groups and assigned each group to complete a different auditory priming task (either word stem completion, identification, or repetition tasks) then the design would include the independent variable of priming task. Although the dependent variable is repeated, the independent variable separates the participants into groups and each participant belongs to only one group.

Sample data for this hypothetical example are provided in table 5.7. The mean scores indicate that the learners ability to complete, identify, or produce repeated words increased over time. Repeated measures ANOVA can be used to determine whether (a) the change in mean scores over time is significant within groups, (b) the scores for the task groups significantly differ, and (c) there is an interaction between the scores over time and task group.

Table 5.7 Score for repeated words by task and day

Task	Day 1	Day 2	Day 3
Word stem completion	.33	.35	.43
Identification	.32	.36	.41
Repetition	.34	.38	.46

To calculate repeated measures ANOVA, the spreadsheet can be set up with five columns: participant, task group (the independent variable), day 1 score, day 2 score, and day 3 score (which are the repeated measures of the dependent variable). Similar to the previous ANOVA tests, each participant's information is entered into one row. To obtain the test statistic, click on *Analyze* → *General Linear Model* → *Repeated Measures*. The *Repeated Measures Define Factor(s)* dialogue box appears (shown in figure 5.12). In the *Within-Subject Factor Name* box, create and enter a name for the repeated variable, which in the current example might be labeled *time* or *score*. Next, enter the number of levels, which in this example would be 3 because a score was recorded three times (day 1, day 2, and day 3).

Once the repeated variable has been named and its number of levels has been entered, click on *Add* and *Define* and the *Repeated Measures* dialog box appears. The three measures of the repeated variable are entered in the *Within-Subject Variables* box (day 1, day 2, and day 3) and the independent variable *task* is entered in the *Between-Subjects Factor* box. The repeated measures dialog box is similar to the simple ANOVA and the factorial ANOVA dialog boxes, and includes options such as descriptive statistics, estimates of effect size, and post hoc tests, which are necessary since the independent variable *task* has at least three levels.

In order to carry out pairwise post hoc comparisons for the three levels of the independent between-subjects variable *task* (i.e. word stem completion vs. identification, word stem completion vs. repetition, identification vs. repetition), click the *Post Hoc* button at the bottom of the repeated measures analysis window and select the checkboxes next to

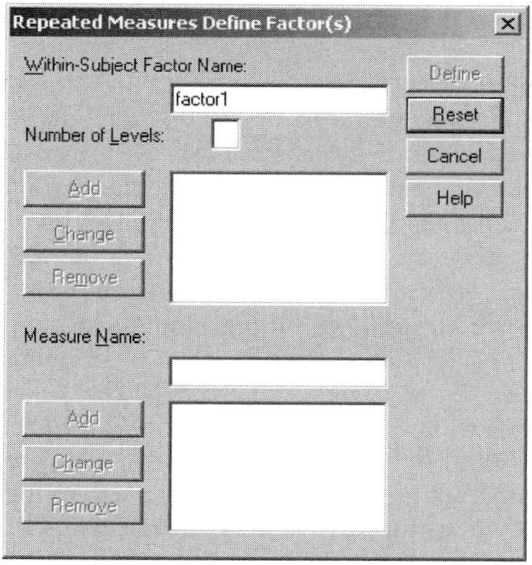

Figure 5.12 Repeated measures define factors dialogue box.

the appropriate post hoc tests (e.g. Bonferroni). In order to compute pair-wise comparisons for the repeated measures variable *time* (day 1 vs. day 2, day 1 vs. day 3, day 2 vs. day 3), click on *Options* and send the repeated measures variable *time* across to the *Display Means for* box and put a tick in the *Compare Main Effects* box. Then, change the *Confidence Interval Adjustment* from *LSD (none)* to *Bonferroni* and click *Continue*.

The output of repeated measures ANOVA is largely similar to that of one-way ANOVA (see figure 5.9) and factorial ANOVA. The sum of squares, degrees of freedom, mean square, F statistic and related prob-ability value is given for the dependent variable (*Tests of Within-Subjects Effects*), the independent variable (*Tests of Between-Subjects Effects*), and the interaction between them. Similar to one-way and factorial ANOVA, the results of repeated measures ANOVA are reported by giving the F statistic, the degrees of freedom, and the *p* value, but this information is reported for both the repeated dependent variable and the between-subjects independent variable.

In addition to being interested in overall main effects of between-subjects and repeated measures (within-subjects) factors, researchers are often interested in simple main effects. Simple main effects refer to the effects of one variable (e.g. *task*) at each level of another variable (e.g. *time*). For example, researchers might be interested in comparing the scores among the three priming tasks separately on day 1, day 2, and day 3. Thus far, however, our examples have shown only how to compute overall main effects (e.g. comparing three levels of the *task* variable, or three levels of the *time* variable). Unfortunately the current version of SPSS does not allow for an easy menu-driven way of computing pairwise comparisons of simple main effects. This procedure is possible only using the syntax function of SPSS.

In order to compute pairwise comparisons of simple main effects in SPSS, a repeated measures analysis needs to be set up from the begin-ning, following the procedures outlined above. However, instead of clicking the OK button to run the analysis, click on *Paste*. This button will display the syntax screen, displayed in figure 5.13.

Each line of syntax represents some of the choices made earlier through menus. For example, the main effects of the two factors will be compared using Bonferroni tests. For pairwise tests of simple main effects, the syn-tax needs to be changed to indicate that a Bonferroni test is conducted on the interaction at /EMMEANS = TABLES(task*time). The following code needs to be added immediately after /EMMEANS = TABLES(task-*time): COMPARE(task) ADJ(BONFERRONI). This code will allow you to compare participants' scores among the three tasks for each testing day. If researchers wish to do the opposite (i.e. to compare participants' scores for each task across the three testing days), then the following code needs to be added immediately after /EMMEANS = TABLES(task*time):

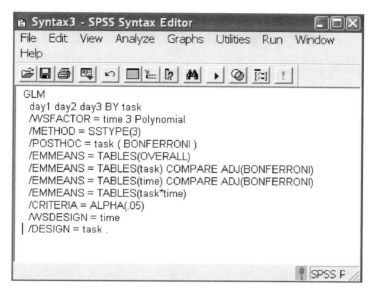

Figure 5.13 SPSS syntax screen for a repeated measures ANOVA.

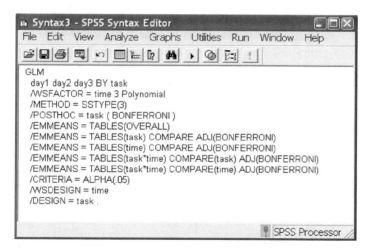

Figure 5.14 SPSS syntax screen for tests of simple main effects in a repeated measures ANOVA.

COMPARE(time) ADJ(BONFERRONI). Figure 5.14 presents a screenshot of the syntax window with both of the above commands entered. To run the entire analysis, go to the *Run* drop down menu at the top of the syntax window and choose *To End*.

If the data do not meet the assumptions of repeated measures ANOVA, the nonparametric Friedman test may be used instead. As a nonparametric test, Friedman does not have any assumptions so it may be more appropriate if the data are not normally distributed, the variance is not equal, or the dependent variable is not truly continuous. To calculate the Friedman test, click *Analyze → Nonparametric Tests → K Related Samples*. The three measures of the dependent variable, day 1, day 2, and day 3, are entered in the *Test Variables* box (see figure 5.15) and descriptive statistics can be obtained by clicking on *Statistics* and ticking the *Descriptive* box.

However, notice that the Friedman test does not allow an independent variable to be entered into the analysis. As a result, individual Friedman tests have to be calculated for each level of the independent variable separately, using the *Split File* option (click *Data → Split File → Organize Output by Groups* and enter the independent variable into the *Groups Based on* box). In addition, Friedman does not have the post hoc test option that is available in repeated measures ANOVA. If a significant difference in the scores is found, individual Wilcoxon signed ranks tests (*Analyze → Nonparametric Tests → 2 Related Samples*) can be carried out to compare each set of scores with the other two sets of scores, adjusting alpha to account for multiple comparisons.

The advantage of repeated measures ANOVA is the inclusion of multiple measures of the same dependent variable. In L2 priming studies, researchers are often interested in language development as indicated by increased production or accuracy, or decreased reaction time or error rate. By including multiple measures over time, a repeated measures ANOVA can identify whether changes in the dependent variable are significant and can locate significance with specific scores through post hoc tests. In addition to within-groups analysis, a repeated measures ANOVA allows researchers to consider between-group factors. This can be useful for L2 researchers who are investigating how priming data change over time with groups from different proficiency levels or L1 backgrounds. However, a

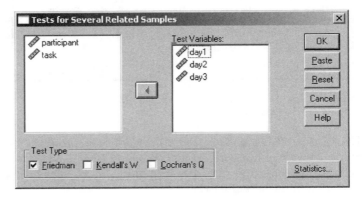

Figure 5.15 Test for several related samples dialog box.

repeated measures ANOVA has a number of disadvantages. Next we discuss an alternative statistical procedure (linear mixed model) that overcomes a number of these disadvantages, offering a powerful tool for analyzing priming data.

Linear Mixed Model

Like the other ANOVA tests (or, technically speaking, General Linear Model, or GLM, procedures) described so far, linear mixed model (LMM) is based on the same assumptions and involves a numeric dependent variable. However, carrying out repeated measures using LMM offers a number of advantages that make this procedure an attractive way of analyzing priming data. One advantage of LMM is that it allows for missing data points. It sometimes happens that researchers do not have a complete dataset for each participant, especially for each sublevel of a repeated factor. Using an example given earlier (see p. 168), some participants may have missing data from day 1, day 2, or day 3 of testing. A repeated measures ANOVA using GLM removes an entire participant's data if one of this participant's data points is missing, thus reducing the sample size and ultimately making the test less powerful. In contrast, for example, a repeated measures LMM allows researchers to analyze the whole dataset without losing an entire participant's data due to missing data at a single time point.

Another advantage of LMM is that it allows researchers to use *both* fixed and random factors in their statistical analyses, whereas repeated measures ANOVA does not. The difference between fixed and random factors is a conceptual one. Fixed factors refer to variables for which possible category values (levels) represent the *only* levels of these factors a researcher is interested in. For example, if researchers are interested in age as a between-subjects factor, they could designate (in their priming experiment) age as a fixed factor with two levels: younger learners (aged 15 and younger) and older learners (aged 16 and older). By designating age as a fixed factor, researchers thus assume that they are interested only in these two levels of the age variable (i.e. younger and older than 15) and do not wish to generalize their findings beyond these two levels.

Random factors, in contrast, refer to variables that represent only a random selection of all possible measurable category values (levels). Take, for instance, the design illustrating a repeated measures ANOVA above. In that study, researchers might consider *task* as a random, not fixed (as was done in the repeated measures ANOVA), factor. By doing so, researchers assume that the three priming tasks used to form the three sublevels of this factor (word stem completion, identification, repetition) are only a random selection of all possible auditory priming tasks. Researchers thus wish to generalize their findings beyond these three tasks, strengthening their claims about implicit processing typical of auditory priming tasks. It is important to note that within-subjects (repeated) factors are almost always random factors. Repeated measurements are almost never entirely independent from one another, which suggests that such measurements are only random selections from all other possible measurements. For instance, in the example above, participants' responses on day 1, day 2, and day 3 of testing are always correlated in some way by virtue of the same people being re-tested at different times. These three testing days also represent only a sample of all possible days on which participants could have been tested.

To summarize, LMM allows researchers to model data, especially data from repeated measures designs, in a powerful way. First, unlike repeated measures ANOVA, LMM allows researchers to include datasets with some missing data. Second, LMM allows researchers to use both fixed and random factors in analyzing their data. It is, in fact, this mix of fixed and random effects that gives this procedure its name (i.e. mixed model). LMM is a relatively new and complicated procedure (see West, Welch, & Galecki, 2007, for a comprehensive introduction). Although a complete coverage of this procedure is beyond the scope of this chapter, we now illustrate a basic mixed model analysis for repeated measures designs.

Consider, for example, the hypothetical syntactic priming data in table 5.8. Suppose that the researcher was interested in whether the modality of the sentence completion task (oral or written) affected the magnitude of syntactic priming for transitives.

Table 5.8 Proportion scores by task, prime, and target

Participant	Priming task	Prime	Target	Score
1	Oral sentence completion	Active	Active	.80
		Active	Passive	.15
		Passive	Active	.46
		Passive	Passive	.52
2	Written sentence completion	Active	Active	.85
		Active	Passive	.05
		Passive	Active	.23
		Passive	Passive	.57
3	Written sentence completion	Active	Active	.67
		Active	Passive	.19
		Passive	Active	.26
		Passive	Passive	.63
4	Oral sentence completion	Active	Active	.75
		Active	Passive	.20
		Passive	Active	.32
		Passive	Passive	.57

To test these relationships, 50 participants were randomly assigned to either the oral sentence completion group or the written sentence completion group. In this scenario, the task (oral or written) is a between-groups factor with two levels, which divides the participants into separate, independent groups. The researcher can, of course, designate this factor as a fixed factor, being interested in the participants' performance only in these two priming tasks. Alternatively, however, the researcher can designate this between-groups factor as a random factor because the researcher might wish to generalize the participants' performance beyond the two priming tasks used in this study. This is precisely where LMM is useful, as repeated measures ANOVA would not allow the researcher to designate a between-groups factor as a random factor and analyze the data accordingly.

During the priming task, each participant was exposed to both active and passive primes and produced both active and passive targets. Both prime and target are two-level repeated factors since every participant was exposed to both primes and produced both targets. These two repeated factors could also be designated as either fixed or random. If these factors are treated as fixed, then the assumption is that the researcher is interested only in the particular active and passive primes and targets used in the experiment, seeing these prime-target types as discrete, fixed categories. On the other hand, if these two repeated factors are treated as random, then the researcher wishes to generalize the participants' performance beyond the particular primes and targets used. The reasoning here is that the researcher chose only several representative active and passive primes and targets for the experiment, out of a total sample of all possible active and passive primes and targets. Again, this is exactly where LMM (unlike repeated measures ANOVA) is helpful in allowing researchers to designate certain variables as fixed or random. Using LMM, researchers can thus model their data in a manner consistent with their hypotheses, ultimately improving the generalizability of their findings.

In this particular example of a research design, LMM can determine whether there are any main or interaction effects for the three factors (task, prime, target) on the proportion score. To set up the spreadsheet for LMM, the categorical variables can be entered as string variables. Since there are two repeated variables (prime and target), the information for each participant is entered into four rows. The data in table 5.8 can be entered into SPSS as shown in figure 5.16

Once all the data are entered into the spreadsheet, to obtain LMM, click *Analyze → Mixed Models → Linear*. The dialogue box shown in figure 5.17 is used to identify which variables are repeated—in this example, prime and target—and which variable is the subject variable. After the three variables have been moved to the appropriate boxes, click *Continue*.

	subject	task	prime	target	proportion
1	1	oral	active	active	.80
2	1	oral	active	passive	.15
3	1	oral	passive	active	.46
4	1	oral	passive	passive	.52
5	2	written	active	active	.85
6	2	written	active	passive	.05
7	2	written	passive	active	.23
8	2	written	passive	passive	.57
9	3	written	active	active	.67
10	3	written	active	passive	.19
11	3	written	passive	active	.26
12	3	written	passive	passive	.63
13	4	oral	active	active	.75
14	4	oral	active	passive	.20
15	4	oral	passive	active	.32
16	4	oral	passive	passive	.57

Figure 5.16 Entering data from table 5.8 into SPSS.

The LMM dialogue box appears and the dependent variable (score) is entered in the *Dependent Variable* box and the three factors (task, prime and target) are entered in the *Factors* box. If you decide, for this particular analysis, to treat all factors (both between-groups and repeated) as random, then this choice needs to be made in a special dialogue box. To designate factors as random, click on *Random Effects* and include all factors and their interactions in the model. Alternatively, if you decide to treat one (or more) factors as fixed, then this choice also needs to be indicated. To designate factors as fixed, click on *Fixed Effects* and include all relevant factors and their interactions in the model. Descriptive statistics are available by clicking on *Statistics* and the comparisons of main effects are available by clicking on *EM Means*.

The output of LMM is similar to the previous ANOVA tests. It provides the F statistic and p value for each factor separately, which are the main effects, and for every possible combination of the three factors, which are the interaction effects. If comparison of main effects was selected, the output also provides the pairwise comparisons for all factors. In this example, a significant interaction between prime and target would be expected as there should be a relationship between the syntactic form of

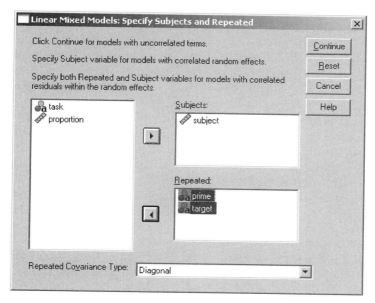

Figure 5.17 Linear Mixed Models specify box.

the prime and the syntactic form of the participants' targets. For more information on mixed model data analysis, interested readers are referred to Norušis (2007) and West et al. (2007).

Having provided a brief overview of the analysis of priming data and use of SPSS to calculate statistical tests, we now turn to issues in the reporting of priming research in psycholinguistics and applied linguistics journals.

Publishing Priming Research

Purpose of the Study

When considering publishing priming research, an important preliminary issue that can help guide subsequent decision-making is the purpose of the study. As the previous chapters have illustrated, auditory, semantic and syntactic priming methods are used in a variety of psycholinguistic and applied linguistics research studies. Although they are similar in that they all use priming methods, their purpose can be quite varied, which makes consideration of the purpose of the study important. For example, in some studies, particularly in psychology literature, the researcher is investigating priming itself. Here, the purpose is to define or refine the phenomenon of priming by exploring the mechanisms responsible for priming. In this case, priming is the object of inquiry and the goal is to contribute to our understanding of what priming is and what mechanisms are implicated in its occurrence. Other topics typically explored in this type of priming research include the linguistic or contextual factors that facilitate (or hinder) its occurrence and persistence, the linguistic structures and features amenable to priming, and the languages in which priming has occurred (both within-language and cross-language priming). Because a great deal of priming research has been carried out in English, several studies have explored whether it also occurs in other languages, particularly languages that allow for different alternating syntactic forms, different phonologies, and different semantic relationships.

However, in other studies priming itself is not the object of inquiry, but is used as a tool to investigate other topics. For example, as described in chapter 4, syntactic priming has been used as a research method for exploring the shared versus separate syntax accounts in bilingual speech processing, linear versus hierarchical models of speech production, the nature of syntactic representations in child L1 acquisition, and the relationship between interaction and L2 development. In this type of priming research, priming methods have been adopted because of their ability to provide insight into these issues. The researchers are generally not interested in contributing to debates about the phenomenon of priming or exploring the mechanisms responsible for it. Instead they adopt priming methods because of their potential to address other issues related to language processing and acquisition. In sum, a researcher's use of priming, as an object of inquiry or as a tool for investigating other topics, has implications for the audience and journal to be targeted.

Target Audience

Closely related to the purpose of the study is the target audience, which is also an important issue to consider when publishing priming research. As was pointed out in the preface to this text, L2 researchers may not be familiar with the psychology journals where much of the priming research described in this book has been reported. Many psychology journals publish empirical studies involving L2 speakers and are an appropriate venue for publishing priming research. However, depending on the purpose of the study and the target audience, L2 researchers may prefer to submit priming research to journals in applied linguistics in order to reach a larger audience of researchers interested in L2 speech processing, production, and acquisition.

When writing for an applied linguistics/second language acquisition audience, researchers may need to include more introductory information about priming and the previous L1 priming research, as this literature may be less familiar to linguists. In addition, explicit information about how priming and the L1 research can contribute to debates in L2 processing and acquisition might be useful. It may also be helpful to frame the study in terms of current debates, theories, or hypotheses in applied linguistics and then explain how priming research provides further insight into these issues. When writing for a psycholinguistics audience, however, less detailed background information about priming and previous priming research findings may be necessary. Instead, more information about theories of second language processing or acquisition might be useful, since these topics may be less familiar to psychologists. In addition, information about linguistic forms may be useful, especially if those structures have been explained from various theoretical frameworks or have an established developmental sequence that may be unfamiliar to psychologists. Finally, when writing for L2 practitioners, researchers may have to provide additional background information about priming and its applicability to L2 learning in classroom contexts and/or to L2 teaching practises. Since priming research of this type is likely to involve classroom-based studies, additional discussion of the pedagogical implications of the findings may be useful when writing for practitioners.

Applied Linguistics and Psychology Journals

Journals that have published priming studies recently (since 2000) are listed below, with a short description of the aims and purpose of the journals as reported on their websites. Each entry on the list includes the publisher and the URL for the publisher's website where more detailed information can be found about the journal, such as the submission guidelines, conventions, and the types of submissions accepted.

- *Applied Psycholinguistics* (Cambridge: www.cambridge.org). *Applied Psycholinguistics* publishes original research about the psychological processes involved in language development, language use, and language disorders in adults and children with a particular emphasis on cross-language studies. A cross-disciplinary journal, it includes studies based in linguistics, psychology, reading, education, language learning, speech and hearing, and neurology.
- *Cognition* (Elsevier: www.elsevier.com) *Cognition* publishes theoretical and experimental papers on the study of the mind, including language-oriented research. It accepts contributions from the fields of psychology, neuroscience, linguistics, computer science, mathematics, and philosophy provided that the studies explore the function of the mind.
- *Developmental Sciences* (Blackwell: www.blackwellpublishing.com) *Developmental Sciences* reports contemporary research in developmental psychology and cognitive neuroscience. It publishes research that

attempts to explain the mechanisms involved in developmental change, including language development.

- *Journal of Memory and Language* (Elsevier: www.elsevier.com) The *Journal of Memory and Language* accepts articles that contribute to theories in the areas of memory, language comprehension and production, and cognitive processes. While theoretical papers are also accepted, emphasis is given to research articles that provide new theoretical insights.

- *Journal of Psycholinguistic Research* (Springer: www.springer.com) *Journal of Psycholinguistic Research* publishes papers situated in linguistics, psychology, biology, and sociology that present psycholinguistic research. A broad range of studies is covered, including the development of speech and language and the psychopathology of language and cognition.

- *Language Learning* (Blackwell: www.blackwellpublishing.com) *Language Learning* publishes research articles from a wide-range of disciplines including psychology, linguistics, cognitive science, educational inquiry, neuroscience, sociolinguistics, and sociology. Studies explore theoretical issues in language learning such as child, second, and foreign language acquisition, language pedagogy, and language representation in mind and brain.

- *Language Learning and Development* (Taylor & Francis: www.tandf.co.uk) *Language Learning and Development*, the journal of the Society for Language Development, encourages interaction among researchers in language learning and publishes studies about language in typical and atypical populations and in native- and second-language learning. It welcomes diverse approaches to understanding language acquisition that employ a variety of research methods.

- *Psychological Science* (Association for Psychological Science: www.psychologicalscience.org) *Psychological Science* publishes articles of interest in the behavioral, clinical, cognitive, neural, and social sciences branches of psychology. It accepts full-length articles and summaries of new research developments.

- *Studies in Second Language Acquisition* (Cambridge: www.cambridge.org). *Studies in Second Language Acquisition* is devoted to second and foreign language acquisition of any language. Articles are based on theoretical topics in the area of second/foreign language learning and may have pedagogical implications. In addition to full-length articles, it also accepts replication studies.

When selecting the appropriate journal, researchers may also consider what type of report is most appropriate for their study. While many of the journals on the previous list publish only full-length manuscripts, a few offer additional options. For example, *Psychological Science* accepts three submission types: research articles, research reports, and short reports. Research articles (up to 4,000 words) emphasize papers with broad theoretical significance and interdisciplinary interest, but generally do not include manuscripts that report complete empirical studies. However, research reports (up to 2,500 words) present new research findings that offer innovations in an approach or method, while short reports (up to 1,000 words) report short experiments of broad interest.

Similarly, *Developmental Sciences* has three submission categories: reports, fast-track reports, and papers. Reports and fast-track reports present empirical studies up to 4,000 words, with fast-track reports receiving rapid review (within one month) and more prompt publication. However, fast-track submissions receive an accept/reject decision only without any feedback, and will only be accepted if no major revisions are necessary. They are also expected to have significant and broad implications for the field. Papers (up to 12,000 words) are devoted to more extensive empirical studies, often consisting of studies with multiple experiments. In addition to full experimental papers, *Cognition* also accepts brief articles that report original research findings, which may consist of a single experiment rather than the series of experiments typically reported in a full experimental paper. Finally, *Studies in Second Language Acquisition* accepts submissions in the category of replication studies, which may be particularly relevant for L2 researchers who are replicating L1 priming studies with L2 speakers.

When preparing a manuscript for submission to journals in psychology and applied linguistics, researchers may find it useful to follow the guidelines in the *Publication Manual of the American Psychological Association*, 5th edition (2001) since many of the journals listed previously follow these conventions. However, each journal may have unique requirements that diverge from the APA guidelines so it may be useful to consult the submission guidelines or information for authors that is available at each journal's website. More detailed information about the organization of information in primary research reports can be found in the APA publication manual as well as in research methods textbooks in applied linguistics, such as Mackey and Gass (2005), Dörnyei (2007), and Huck (2007, chapter 1).

Summary

In this chapter, we have pointed out several issues to consider when analyzing priming data, such as variable types, hypotheses, and between- and within-group designs. We have explained the statistical tests commonly used in priming research and have illustrated how to calculate them using SPSS. We concluded the chapter with some factors to consider when reporting priming research for journals in applied linguistics and psychology.

Follow up Questions and Activities

1. Locate an article that reports the findings of priming research and consider the following questions:

   a) What were the research hypotheses? Even if the researchers did not explicitly state them, can you infer what the null and research hypotheses were?

   b) What types of statistical tests were used to analyze the data?

   c) How were the descriptive and inferential statistics reported in the results section?

   d) If parametric statistics were used, was any information reported about whether the data met the assumptions?

   e) What population do you think the sample was selected to represent?

   f) What factors might limit the generalizability of the findings from the sample to that population?

2. Using the syntactic priming data in table 5.9 (adapted from McDonough, 2006), create a spreadsheet and calculate a repeated measures ANOVA. The relationship under investigation is the impact of syntactic priming on ESL learners' production of double-object datives. The scripted interaction task was used, and the picture description activity was divided into three phases: baseline, priming, post-priming. The baseline and post-priming phases presented the participants with 5 dative verbs in the absence of primes. The priming phase provided them with 12 dative verbs to produce following the scripted interlocutor's 12 double-object dative primes. Their picture descriptions were classified as prepositional dative, double-object dative, or *other*. Table 5.9 shows the number of double-object datives produced by each participant in the baseline phase (n = 5), the priming phase (n = 12), and the post-priming phase (n = 5). Since the number of target sentences was not the same in all phases, you should convert the raw scores to proportions.

   Once you have created the spreadsheet and carried out the repeated measures ANOVA, make a table with the descriptive statistics and write a short description of the results in which you report the appropriate information.

3. Using the hypothetical semantic priming data in table 5.10 (inspired by Phillips et al., 2004), create a spreadsheet and calculate a factorial ANOVA. The relationship under investigation is the impact of proficiency and L1 background on semantic priming in L2 semantic processing. The semantic categorization

Table 5.9 Production of double-object datives by phase

Participant	Baseline phase	Priming phase	Post-priming phase
45	2	5	3
46	2	2	2
48	3	4	3
49	2	2	2
50	2	1	2
51	3	3	2
60	1	3	2
61	2	5	2
63	2	2	1
64	1	5	3
65	2	2	1
69	1	2	2
70	2	1	3
71	1	2	2
72	2	6	2
73	1	1	1
74	1	7	4
75	3	7	4
76	1	3	3
77	3	5	4
78	1	2	2
79	0	1	1
80	1	4	3
81	0	1	1
82	1	4	2
83	1	3	3
84	0	3	1
85	1	4	2
86	1	8	4
87	2	2	2
88	0	4	2
89	1	1	0
90	2	4	2
91	0	2	2
92	1	2	2
93	2	6	3
94	2	8	5
96	3	3	2
97	3	3	4
98	2	1	3
99	0	4	2
100	2	4	3
101	3	6	4
103	2	2	2
104	0	3	2

Table 5.10 Difference in reaction times by proficiency level and L1 background

Participant	Proficiency level	L1 background	Difference score (in ms)
1	Beginner	Chinese	35
2	Advanced	Chinese	55
4	Beginner	Chinese	35
6	Beginner	Spanish	38
7	Beginner	Spanish	48
8	Beginner	Chinese	61
9	Intermediate	Spanish	56
10	Beginner	Spanish	55
12	Beginner	Chinese	37
14	Beginner	Chinese	36
15	Advanced	Chinese	80
17	Beginner	Spanish	35
18	Beginner	Spanish	39
19	Beginner	Chinese	58
21	Intermediate	Spanish	50
22	Beginner	Chinese	59
24	Beginner	Spanish	36
25	Beginner	Chinese	56
26	Beginner	Spanish	60
27	Advanced	Chinese	56
28	Beginner	Spanish	54
31	Beginner	Chinese	48
32	Intermediate	Spanish	60
33	Beginner	Chinese	37
34	Beginner	Spanish	59
35	Advanced	Chinese	68
37	Beginner	Spanish	40
39	Advanced	Chinese	79
40	Intermediate	Spanish	51
41	Advanced	Chinese	57
42	Intermediate	Chinese	63
44	Intermediate	Spanish	52
46	Intermediate	Spanish	59
47	Intermediate	Chinese	50
48	Advanced	Spanish	62
49	Advanced	Chinese	78
51	Advanced	Chinese	55
52	Intermediate	Spanish	58
56	Advanced	Spanish	73
57	Advanced	Spanish	67
58	Intermediate	Chinese	62
59	Intermediate	Spanish	53
60	Advanced	Chinese	67
61	Advanced	Chinese	58
62	Advanced	Spanish	63
63	Advanced	Spanish	55
64	Intermediate	Chinese	49

65	Intermediate	Chinese	47
66	Intermediate	Spanish	57
67	Advanced	Spanish	54
69	Intermediate	Chinese	65
70	Intermediate	Chinese	48
72	Intermediate	Chinese	61
73	Advanced	Spanish	71
75	Intermediate	Chinese	64
77	Advanced	Spanish	64
79	Intermediate	Chinese	49
81	Intermediate	Spanish	54
83	Advanced	Spanish	60
85	Advanced	Spanish	70

task was used in which participants made judgments about whether a noun referred to something living or non-living. The target nouns were either preceded by a semantically-related noun or an unrelated noun. The participants' reaction time was measured in milliseconds, and a difference score was obtained by subtracting their mean reaction time for words preceded by related words from their mean reaction time for words preceded by unrelated words.

Once you have created the spreadsheet and carried out the factorial ANOVA, make a table with the descriptive statistics and write a short description of the results in which you report the appropriate information.

4. Analyze the hypothetical auditory priming data in table 5.11 (modeled after Trofimovich, 2008) first using a repeated measures ANOVA, then using the LMM procedure. Do these two analyses yield similar results? Which factors would you designate as fixed and which as random in an LMM procedure? Do the results of the two analyses depend on which factors are designated as fixed and which are designated as random? The relationship under investigation is the impact of learners' length of residence in an English-speaking country and attentional orientation on auditory priming in L2 auditory processing. An auditory repetition task was used in which participants produced words that they had heard previously in the study phase of the task (repeated words) and those that they had not heard previously (unrepeated words). The participants (L1 Japanese learners of English) were divided into two equal groups based on their length of residence in an English speaking country (short = less than 5 years, long = more than 5 years). Half of the participants in each length of residence group were assigned to a focus-on-meaning condition in which the learners' attention

Table 5.11 Response latency (in milliseconds) for repeated and unrepeated words as a function of learner length of residence and processing orientation

Participant	Length of residence	Processing Orientation	Unrepeated words	Repeated words
1	Long	Control	302	241
2	Long	Meaning	310	262
3	Short	Meaning	342	362
4	Long	Meaning	351	302
5	Short	Control	383	357
6	Short	Control	436	382
7	Long	Control	448	415
8	Short	Meaning	474	461
9	Short	Meaning	478	473
10	Short	Control	495	354
11	Short	Meaning	523	513
12	Long	Meaning	530	486
13	Short	Meaning	533	527
14	Long	Control	538	522
15	Short	Control	553	500
16	Short	Control	568	549
17	Short	Control	569	537
18	Short	Control	587	493
19	Short	Meaning	589	579
20	Long	Control	621	577
21	Long	Meaning	659	613
22	Short	Control	663	599
23	Long	Control	679	608
24	Short	Control	680	637
25	Long	Meaning	685	634
26	Long	Control	734	658
27	Short	Meaning	761	749
28	Long	Meaning	782	741
29	Short	Control	786	762
30	Long	Meaning	809	716
31	Long	Control	846	783
32	Short	Meaning	847	837
33	Long	Meaning	874	827
34	Long	Control	876	803
35	Long	Control	877	803
36	Short	Meaning	901	904
37	Long	Meaning	915	801
38	Long	Meaning	935	888
39	Long	Control	947	895
40	Short	Meaning	959	971

was directed to the meanings of words in the study phase of the task. The other half of the participants was assigned to a control condition in which no attentional orientation was imposed (i.e. learners simply listened to spoken words). The values in table 5.11 represent the response latencies for repeated and unrepeated words as a function of learner length of residence (short, long) and processing orientation (meaning, control).

Once you have created the spreadsheet and carried out both the repeated measures ANOVA and the LMM procedure, make a table with the descriptive statistics and write a short description of the results in which you report the appropriate information.

5. To which journals in applied linguistics or psychology would you submit the following priming studies? Explain what journal(s) would be appropriate in terms of (i) the researcher's use of priming, (ii) an appropriate target audience, (iii) report type.

a) Syntactic priming during learner-learner interaction (McDonough, 2007)

Abstract: Previous classroom-based studies have demonstrated that L2 learners benefit from carrying out collaborative activities by providing each other with interactional feedback, producing modified output, and reflecting on language form (e.g. García Mayo, 2002; Leeser, 2004; McDonough, 2004; Swain & Lapkin, 1998). Recently researchers have questioned whether learners also benefit from interaction because it generates opportunities for syntactic priming, which is the tendency to produce previously heard or spoken structures (McDonough & Mackey, 2006). Although syntactic priming has been shown to occur in L2 speech production, those studies involved interaction between learners and trained interlocutors. No studies to date have explored the occurrence of syntactic priming in less-controlled contexts, such as during collaborative activities in L2 classrooms.

The purpose of the current study was to investigate whether syntactic priming occurs when Thai EFL (N = 30) learners carry out collaborative activities as part of their regular English classes. The activities complemented the course objectives and materials, and involved tasks such as picture description and information exchange. The interaction between the learners was audio-recorded, and the transcripts were examined for evidence of syntactic priming. Preliminary results suggest that syntactic priming occurs during learner-learner interaction, and that its occurrence may be affected by the target structure as well as the learners' proficiency level. The implications are discussed in terms of on-going efforts to understand which features of learner-learner interaction are associated with L2 learning.

b) Lexical and syntactic priming: EFL students' production of passives (Kim, 2006).

Abstract: Syntactic priming refers to a speaker's tendency to repeat syntactic structures across subsequent utterances (Bock, 1986). L1 research has found that syntactic priming is greater when the participant is prompted to produce the target structure with the same verb that occurred in the prime. Although L2 researchers have shown that syntactic priming occurs in L2 speech production, they have not explored the impact of lexical items on its occurrence. The purpose of the current study was to examine whether the occurrence of syntactic priming in L2 speech production was affected by lexical items.

Korean university students ($N = 76$) carried out a picture description activity with the researcher. The pictures illustrated a transitive action in which a person undertook an action involving an animal or inanimate object. Whereas the researcher's pictures were labeled with a complete sentence, either passives or active fillers, the learner's pictures were labeled with a verb only. The picture sets were manipulated so that half of the learner's pictures that followed the researcher's passive sentences were labeled with the same verb produced by the researcher, while the other half were labeled with a different verb. The findings indicate that the learners produced more passives when the prompt repeated the verb that had occurred in the researcher's preceding passive sentence. Implications are discussed in terms of the role of lexical items in learners' production of developmentally-advanced structures and the relationship between interaction-driven L2 learning and syntactic priming.

c) Second language processing: Task effects on listeners' sensitivity to spoken words (Trofimovich & Halter, 2007)

Abstract: Previous research has demonstrated that the outcomes of second language (L2) processing crucially depend on the nature of a processing task. Two types of tasks have often been investigated: those that draw L2 learners' attention to conceptual (meaning-related) aspects of language and those focusing their attention on its perceptual (form-related) aspects. Findings thus far indicate that the conceptual processing inherent in some tasks (asking a general-knowledge question or reading a text to understand its gist) may in fact have a detrimental effect on the processing and learning of L2 linguistic forms—that is, specific aspects of L2 lexicon, morphology, and syntax. However, it is still unknown whether conceptual processing has a similar negative effect on the processing (and ultimately learning) of form-related aspects of learners' L2 phonology. This study investigated this issue.

For this study, 52 native Chinese learners of English varying in amount of L2 experience participated in a psycholinguistic priming experiment. The learners first studied 36 relatively well-known English words (e.g. *ready, people*) under two conditions. In one condition, they focused on word meaning (by means of a secondary task of rating word pleasantness); in the other, no attentional focus was imposed. The learners were later tested in a word-production task on a set of 72 words, of which half were previously studied and half were "new". In addition, half of the studied words were spoken in a familiar voice (by the same speaker) and half were spoken in an unfamiliar voice (by a "new" speaker). The measure of primary interest was the priming effect—the degree of processing facilitation for previously studied versus "new" words, and for words spoken in a familiar versus unfamiliar voice. The presence of a priming effect has previously been shown to be indicative of learners' sensitivity to fine-grained, form-related (phonological) detail in speech (sensitivity to word and voice identity).

Results revealed two findings. The studied words (regardless of voice familiarity) were processed faster than the "new" words as a function of learners' L2 experience, revealing a significant priming effect (64 ms). This finding suggested that, with more L2 experience, learners demonstrate more sensitivity to form-related

189

(phonological) detail in L2 words. However, the priming effect, especially for words spoken in an unfamiliar voice, was drastically reduced for all learners under the instructions to focus on word meaning (15 ms). This finding indicated that a conceptual processing task may reduce learners' sensitivity to form-related (phonological) detail in L2 words, preventing them from generalizing across non-identical instances of L2 words and (ultimately) from establishing their abstract phonological representations. Overall, findings offer insights into L2 phonological processing and learning.

6. Choose two of the journals mentioned in this chapter as having recently published priming studies. Search the current and past issues (for the last five years) to identify how many priming studies were published. How does the amount and type of priming research published in the two journals compare?

7. If you have carried out a priming study recently, how do you intend to report it? Explain what journals would be appropriate for your manuscript in terms of your use of priming methods (as an object of inquiry or as a tool for addressing another issue), target audience, and report type.

APPENDIX

Software Programs Used in Priming Research

Many priming methods involve the use of computer software programs to deliver visual and auditory stimuli, record reaction times, and track participants' responses to decision making tasks. Two software programs commonly used in priming research are *PsyScope* (Cohen, MacWhinney, Flatt, & Provost, 1993) and *E-Prime*, which both allow researchers to design and run psychology experiments through a graphic interface that does not require knowledge of programming languages.

PsyScope was originally created for use with Mac operating systems. The older version of *PsyScope* (version 1.2.5) is available free and unsupported at the following website (http://psyscope.psy.cmu.edu). The website provides a complete user's manual, along with sample scripts and utilities such as plug-ins for sound files and extensions for controlling eye-tracking software. Although *PsyScope 1.2.5* does not work with current Apple systems, it has been ported to the more recent Mac operating system (OSX) by the SISSA Language, Cognition and Development Lab with the assistance of other labs and researchers. Complete information about *PsyScope version X* is available at the website maintained by Luca Bonatti (http://psy.ck.sissa.it/).

E-Prime is a Windows-based software package also used in priming research, distributed by Psychology Software Tools (PST). *E-Prime* consists of several applications that allow researchers to design, generate, and run experiments, and to collect, edit, and analyze the data using a graphic interface. The most recent version (version 2) is available, and a complimentary evaluation and demo version is available by request (for more information see the PST website at http://www.pstnet.com/products/e-prime/). The evaluation and demo version includes a step-by-step illustrated guide to creating a new experiment using *E-Studio* (the getting-started guide), a reference guide and a user's guide (Schneider, Eschman, & Zuccolotto, 2002).

REFERENCES

Altarriba, J. (1992). The representation of translation equivalents in bilingual memory. In R. J. Harris (Ed.), *Cognitive processing in bilinguals* (pp. 157–174). North Holland: Elsevier.

Altarriba, J., & Basnight-Brown, D. M. (2007). Methodological considerations in performing semantic- and translation-priming experiments across languages. *Behavior Research Methods, 39,* 1–18.

Altarriba, J., & Canary, T. M. (2004). The influence of emotional arousal on affective priming in monolingual and bilingual speakers. *Journal of Multilingual and Multicultural Development, 25,* 248–265.

Altarriba, J., Bauer, L. M., & Benvenuto, C. (1999). Concreteness, context-availability, and imageability ratings and word associations for abstract, concrete, and emotion words. *Behavior Research Methods, Instruments, and Computers, 31,* 578–602.

Alvarez, R. P., Holcomb, P. J., & Grainger, J. (2003). Accessing word meaning in two languages: An event-related brain potential study of beginning bilinguals. *Brain and Language, 87,* 290–304.

Publication manual of the American Psychological Association (5th edition) (2001). Washington, D.C.: APA.

Arai, M., van Gompel, R., & Scheepers, C. (2007). Priming ditransitive structures in comprehension. *Cognitive Psychology, 54,* 218–250.

Balota, D. A., & Chumbley, J. I. (1984). Are lexical decisions a good measure of lexical access? The role of word frequency in the neglected decision stage. *Journal of Experimental Psychology: Human Perception and Performance, 10,* 340–357.

Balota, D. A., Black, S. R., & Cheney, M. (1992). Automatic and attentional priming in young and older adults: Reevaluation of the two-process model. *Journal of Experimental Psychology: Human Perception and Performance, 18,* 485–502.

Barcroft, J. (2003). Effects of questions about word meaning during L2 Spanish lexical learning. *The Modern Language Journal, 87,* 546–561.

Barcroft, J., & Sommers, M. S. (2005). Effects of acoustic variability on second language vocabulary learning. *Studies in Second Language Acquisition, 27,* 387–414.

Basnight-Brown, D. M., & Altarriba, J. (2007). Differences in semantic and translation priming across languages: The role of language direction and language dominance. *Memory & Cognition, 35,* 953–965.

Bassili, J. N., Smith, M. C., & MacLeod, C. M. (1989). Auditory and visual word-stem completion: Separating data-driven and conceptually driven processes. *The Quarterly Journal of Experimental Psychology, 41A*, 439–453.

Bates, E., & Liu, H. (1996). Cued shadowing. *Language and Cognitive Processes, 11*, 577–581.

Battig, W. S., & Montague, W. I. (1969). Category norms for verbal items in 56 categories. *Journal of Verbal Learning and Verbal Behavior, 22*, 261–295.

Bernolet, S., Hartsuiker, R., & Pickering, M. (2007). Shared syntactic representations in bilinguals: Evidence for the role of word-order repetition. *Journal of Experimental Psychology: Learning, Memory, and Cognition, 33*, 931–949.

Biber, D., Johansson, S., Leech, G., Conrad, S., & Finegan, E. (1999). *Longman grammar of spoken and written English*. Harlow, Essex: Longman.

Bird, S., & Williams, J. (2002). The effect of bimodal input on implicit and explicit memory: An investigation into the benefits of within-language subtitling. *Applied Psycholinguistics, 23*, 509–533.

Blaxton, T. A. (1989). Investigating dissociations among memory measures: Support for a transfer-appropriate processing framework. *Journal of Experimental Psychology: Learning, Memory and Cognition, 15*, 657–668.

Bock, K. (1986). Syntactic persistence in language production. *Cognitive Psychology, 18*, 355–387.

Bock, K. (1989). Closed-class immanence in sentence production. *Cognition, 31*, 163–186.

Bock, K. (1990). Structure in language: Creating form in talk. *American Psychologist, 45*, 1221–1236.

Bock, K. (1995). Sentence production: From mind to mouth. In J. Miller & P. Eimas (Eds.), *Speech, Language & Communication* (pp. 181–216). San Diego, CA: Academic Press.

Bock, K., & Griffin, Z. (2000). The persistence of structural priming: Transient activation or implicit learning? *Journal of Experimental Psychology: General, 129*, 177–192.

Bock, K., & Loebell, H. (1990). Framing sentences. *Cognition, 35*, 1–39.

Bock, K., Loebell, H., & Morey, R. (1992). From conceptual roles to structural relations: Bridging the syntactic cleft. *Psychological Review, 99*, 150–171.

Bock, K., Dell, G., Chang, F., & Onishi, K. (2007). Persistent structural priming from language comprehension to language production. *Cognition, 104*, 437–458.

Boyland, J., & Anderson, J. (1998). Evidence that syntactic priming is long-lasting. In M. Gernsbacher (Ed.), *Proceedings of the 20th annual meeting of the Cognitive Science Society* (p. 1205). Mahwah, NJ: Erlbaum.

Bradlow, A. R., & Pisoni, D. B. (1999). Recognition of spoken words by native and non-native listeners: Talker-, listener-, and item-related factors. *Journal of the Acoustical Society of America, 106*, 2074–2085.

Bradlow, A. R., Pisoni, D. B., Akahane-Yamada, R., & Tohkura, Y. (1997). Training Japanese listeners to identify English /r/ and /l/: IV. Some effects of perceptual learning on speech production. *Journal of the Acoustical Society of America, 101*, 2299–2310.

Branigan, H., Pickering, M., & Cleland, A. (1999). Syntactic priming in written production: Evidence for rapid decay. *Psychonomic Bulletin & Review, 6*, 635–640.

Branigan, H., Pickering, M., & Cleland, A. (2000). Syntactic co-ordination in dialogue. *Cognition, 75*, B13–25.

Branigan, H., Pickering, M., Stewart, A., & McLean, J. (2000). Syntactic priming in spoken production: Linguistic and temporal interference. *Memory & Cognition, 28*, 1297–1302.

Branigan, H., Pickering, M., McLean, J., & Stewart, A. (2006). The role of local and global syntactic structure in language production: Evidence from syntactic priming. *Language and Cognitive Processes, 21*, 974–1010.

Branigan, H., Pickering, M., Liversedge, S., Stewart, A., & Urbach, T. (1995). Syntactic priming: Investigating the mental representation of language. *Journal of Psycholinguistic Research, 24*, 489–506.

Brown, A. S., & Mitchell, D. B. (1994). A reevaluation of semantic versus non-semantic processing in implicit memory. *Memory and Cognition, 22*, 533–541.

Bueno, S., & Frenck-Mestre, C. (2002). Rapid activation of the lexicon: A further investigation with behavioral and computational results. *Brain and Language, 81*, 120–130.

Cameli, L., & Phillips, N. A. (2000). Age-related differences in semantic priming: Evidence from event-related brain potentials. *Brain and Cognition, 43*, 69–73.

Carlesimo, G., Vicari, S., Albertoni, A., Turriziani, P., & Caltagirone, C. (2000). Developmental dissociation between visual and auditory repetition priming: The role of input lexicons. *Cortex, 36*, 181–193.

Challis, B. H., Velichkovsky, B. M., & Craik, F. I. M. (1996). Levels-of-processing effects on a variety of memory tasks: New findings and theoretical implications. *Consciousness and Cognition, 5*, 142–164.

Chang, F., Bock, K., Goldberg, A. (2003). Can thematic roles leaves traces of their places? *Cognition, 90*, 29–49.

Chapman, L. J., Chapman, J. P., Curran, T. E., & Miller, M. B. (1994). Do children and the elderly show heightened semantic priming? How to answer the question. *Developmental Review, 14*, 159–185.

Chen., H., & Ng, M. (1989). Semantic facilitation and translation priming effects in Chinese-English bilinguals. *Memory and Cognition, 17*, 454–462.

Chincotta, D., & Underwood, G. (1998). Non-temporal determinants of bilingual memory capacity: The role of long-term representations and fluency. *Bilingualism: Language and Cognition, 1*, 117–130.

Church, B., & Fisher, C. (1998). Long-term auditory word priming in preschoolers: Implicit memory support for language acquisition. *Journal of Memory and Language, 39*, 523–542.

Church, B., & Schacter, D. L. (1994). Perceptual specificity of auditory priming: Implicit memory for voice intention and fundamental frequency. *Journal of Experimental Psychology: Learning, Memory, and Cognition, 20*, 521–533.

Clark, H. H. (1973). The language-as-fixed-effect fallacy: A critique of language statistics in psychological research. *Journal of Verbal Learning and Verbal Behavior, 12*, 335–359.

Cleland, A., & Pickering, M. (2003). The use of lexical and syntactic information in language production: Evidence from the priming of noun-phrase structure. *Journal of Memory and Language, 49*, 214–230.

Cleland, A., & Pickering, M. (2006). Do writing and speaking employ the same syntactic representations? *Journal of Memory and Language, 54*, 185–198.

Cohen J., MacWhinney, B., Flatt M., & Provost J. (1993). *PsyScope*: A new graphic interactive environment for designing psychology experiments. *Behavioral Research Methods, Instruments, and Computers, 25,* 257–271.

Cole, R. A., Coltheart, M., & Allard, F. (1974). Memory of a speaker's voice: Reaction time to same- or different-voiced letters. *Quarterly Journal of Experimental Psychology, 26,* 1–7.

Collins, A. M., & Loftus, E. F. (1975). A spreading-activation theory of semantic processing. *Psychological Review, 82,* 407–428.

Craik, F. I. M., & Kirsner, K. (1974). The effect of speaker's voice on word recognition. *The Quarterly Journal of Experimental Psychology, 26,* 274–284.

Craik, F. I. M., Moscovitch, M., & McDowd, J. M. (1994). Contributions of surface and conceptual information to performance on implicit and explicit memory tasks. *Journal of Experimental Psychology: Learning, Memory and Cognition, 20,* 864–875.

Crain, S., & Thornton, R. (1998). *Investigations in universal grammar: A guide to experiments on the acquisition of syntax and semantics.* Cambridge, MA: MIT.

Creswell, J. (2003). *Research design: Qualitative, quantitative, and mixed methods approaches.* Thousand Oaks, CA: Sage.

Dagenbach, D., Carr, T. H., & Wilhelmsen, A. (1989). Task-induced strategies and near-threshold priming: Conscious influences on unconscious perception. *Journal of Memory and Language, 28,* 412–443.

de Bot, K., Cox, A., Ralston, S., Schaufeli, A., & Weltens, B. (1995). Lexical processing in bilinguals. *Second Language Research, 11,* 1–19.

de Bruijn, E. R. A., Dijkstra, T., Chwilla, D. J., & Schriefers, H. (2001). Language context effects on interlingual homograph recognition: Evidence from event-related potentials and response times in semantic priming. *Bilingualism: Language and Cognition, 4,* 155–168.

de Groot, A. M. B. (1984). Primed lexical decision: Combined effects of the proportion of related prime-target pairs and the stimulus-onset asynchrony of prime and target. *Quarterly Journal of Experimental Psychology, 36A,* 253–280.

de Groot, A. M. B., & Nas, G. L. J. (1991). Lexical representation of cognates and noncognates in compound bilinguals. *Journal of Memory and Language, 30,* 90–123.

DeKeyser, R. (2007). Skill acquisition theory. In B. VanPatten & J. Williams (Eds.), *Theories in second language acquisition* (pp. 97–114). Mahwah, NJ: Lawrence Erlbaum.

Dell, G. (1986). A spreading activation theory of retrieval in sentence production. *Psychological Review, 93,* 283–321.

Desmet, T., & Declercq, M. (2006). Cross-linguistic priming of syntactic hierarchical configuration information. *Journal of Memory and Language, 54,* 610–632.

Devitto, Z., & Burgess, C. (2004). Theoretical and methodological implications of language experience and vocabulary skill: Priming of strongly and weakly associated words. *Brain and Cognition, 55,* 295–299.

Dong, Y., Gui, S., & MacWhinney, B. (2005). Shared and separate meanings in the bilingual mental lexicon. *Bilingualism: Language and Cognition, 8,* 221–238.

Dörnyei, Z. (2007) *Research in applied linguistics.* Oxford: Oxford University Press.

Duyck, W. (2005). Translation and associative priming with cross-lingual pseudohomophones: Evidence for nonselective phonological activation in bilinguals. *Journal of Experimental Psychology: Learning, Memory, & Cognition, 31,* 1340–1359.

Duyck, W., Desmet, T., Verbeke, L., & Brysbaert, M. (2004). WordGen: A tool for word selection and non-word generation in Dutch, German, English, and French. *Behavior Research Methods, Instruments, & Computers, 36,* 488–499.

Ellis, A. W. (1982). Modality-specific repetition priming of auditory word recognition. *Current Psychological Research, 2,* 123–128.

Ellis, H., & Ellis, A. (1998). Why we study . . . repetition priming. *The Psychologist, 11,* 492–493.

Ellis, N. (2005). At the interface: Dynamic interactions of explicit and implicit language knowledge. *Studies in Second Language Acquisition, 27,* 305–352.

Ellis, N. (2007). The associative-cognitive CREED. In B. VanPatten & J. Williams (Eds.), *Theories in second language acquisition* (pp. 77–96). Mahwah, NJ: Lawrence Erlbaum.

Elston-Güttler, K. E., & Friederici, A. (2005). Native and L2 processing of homonyms in sentential context. *Journal of Memory and Language, 52,* 256–283.

Elston-Güttler, K. E., Gunter, T. C., & Kotz, S. A. (2005). Zooming into L2: Global language context and adjustment affect processing of interlingual homographs in sentences. *Cognitive Brain Research, 25,* 57–70.

Favreau, M., & Segalowitz, N. S. (1983). Automatic and controlled processes in first- and second-language reading of fluent bilinguals. *Memory and Cognition, 11,* 565–574.

Fellbaum, C. (1998). WordNet: An electronic lexical database. MIT Press.

Field, A. (2005). *Discovering statistics using SPSS.* Thousand Oaks, CA: Sage.

Finkbeiner, M., Forster, K., Nicol, J., & Nakamura, K. (2004). The role of polysemy in masked semantic and translation priming. *Journal of Memory and Language, 51,* 1–22.

Fischler, I. (1977). Associative facilitation without expectancy in a lexical decision task. *Journal of Experimental Psychology: Human Perception & Performance, 3,* 18–26.

Fischler, I., & Goodman, G. O. (1978). Latency of associative activation in memory. *Journal of Experimental Psychology: Human Perception & Performance, 4,* 455–470.

Fisher, C., Hall, G. D., Rakowitz, S., & Gleitman, L. R. (1994). When is it better to receive than to give: Syntactic and conceptual constraints on vocabulary growth. *Lingua, 92,* 333–375.

Fisher, C., Hunt, C., Chambers, K., & Church, B. (2001). Abstraction and specificity in preschoolers' representations of novel spoken words. *Journal of Memory and Language, 45,* 665–687.

Flege, J. E., Yeni-Komshian, G. H., & Liu, S. (1999). Age constraints on second-language acquisition. *Journal of Memory and Language, 41,* 78–104.

Foot, M. (1999). Relaxing in pairs. *ELT Journal, 53,* 36–41.

Forster K. I., & Hector J. (2002). Cascaded versus noncascaded models of lexical and semantic processing: The turple effect. *Memory & Cognition, 30,* 1106–1117.

Fox Tree, J., & Meijer, P. (1999). Building syntactic structure in speaking. *Journal of Psycholinguistic Research, 28,* 71–92.

Fox, E. (1996). Cross-language priming from ignored words: Evidence for a common representational system in bilinguals. *Journal of Memory and Language*, 35, 353–370.

Franks, J. J., Bilbrey, C. W., Lien, K. G., & McNamara, T. P. (2000). Transfer-appropriate processing (TAP) and repetition priming. *Memory and Cognition*, 28, 1140–1151.

Franks, J. J., Plybon, C. J., & Auble, C. J. (1982). Units of episodic memory in perceptual recognition. *Memory and Cognition*, 10, 62–68.

Frenck, C., & Pynte, J. (1987). Semantic representation and surface forms: A look at cross-language priming bilinguals. *Journal of Psycholinguistic Research*, 16, 383–396.

Frenck-Mestre, C., & Bueno, S. (1999). Semantic features and semantic categories: Differences in rapid activation of the lexicon. *Brain and Language*, 68, 199–204.

Frenck-Mestre, C., & Prince, P. (1997). Second language autonomy. *Journal of Memory and Language*, 37, 487–501.

Friedrich, M., & Friederici, A. (2004). N400-like semantic incongruity effect in 19-month-olds: Processing known words in picture contexts. *Journal of Cognitive Neuroscience*, 16, 1465–1477.

Friedrich, M., & Friederici, A. (2005). Processing in one-year-olds: Brain responses to words and nonsense words in picture contexts. *Journal of Cognitive Neuroscience*, 17, 1785–1802.

Fuentes, L. J., & Tudela, P. (1992). Semantic processing of foveally and parafoveally presented words in a lexical decision task. *Quarterly Journal of Experimental Psychology*, 45A, 299–322.

Gahl, S., Jurafsky, D., & Roland, D. (2004). Verb subcategorization frequencies: American English corpus data, methodological studies, and cross-corpus comparisons. *Behavior Research Methods, Instruments, & Computers*, 36, 432–443.

García Mayo, M. (2002). Interaction in advanced EFL pedagogy: A comparison of form-focused activities. *International Journal of Educational Research*, 37, 323–341.

Garrod, S., & Anderson, A. (1987). Saying what you mean in dialogue: A study in conceptual and semantic co-ordination. *Cognition*, 27, 181–218.

Garrod, S., & Doherty, A. (1994). Conversation, co-ordination and convention: an empirical investigation of how groups establish linguistic conventions. *Cognition*, 53, 181–215.

Gass, S. (2003). Input and interaction. In C. Doughty, & M. H. Long (Eds.), *Handbook of second language acquisition* (pp. 224–255). Malden, MA: Blackwell.

Gass, S., & Mackey, A. (2007). Input, interaction and output in second language acquisition. In B. VanPatten, & J. Williams (Eds.), *Theories in second language acquisition* (pp. 175–199). Mahwah, NJ: Erlbaum.

Gass, S., Mackey, A., AlvarezTorres, M. J., & FernándezGarcía, M. (1999). The effects of task repetition on linguistic output. *Language Learning*, 49, 549–581.

Gatbonton, E., & Segalowitz, N. (1988). Creative automatization: Principles for promoting fluency within a communicative framework. *TESOL Quarterly*, 22, 473–492.

Gatbonton, E., & Segalowitz, N. (2005). Rethinking communicative language teaching: A focus on access to fluency. *Canadian Modern Language Review*, 61, 325–353.

Gladwell, M. (2005). *Blink: The power of thinking without thinking*. New York: Little, Brown.

Glass, G. V., Peckham, P. D., & Sanders, J. R. (1972). Consequences of failure to meet assumptions underlying the fixed-effects analysis of variance and covariance. *Review of Educational Research, 42*, 237–288.

Goldberg, A. (1995). *Constructions: A construction grammar approach to argument structure*. Chicago: University of Chicago Press.

Goldinger, S. (1996a). Words and voices: Episodic traces in spoken word identification and recognition memory. *Journal of Experimental Psychology: Learning, Memory, and Cognition, 22*, 1166–1183.

Goldinger, S. (1996b). Auditory lexical decision. *Language and Cognitive Processes, 11*, 559–567.

Goldinger, S. (1998). Echoes of echoes? An episodic theory of lexical access. *Psychological Review, 105*, 251–279.

Gollan, T. H., Forster, K. I., & Frost, R. (1997). Translation priming with different scripts: Masked priming with cognates and noncognates in Hebrew-English bilinguals. *Journal of Experimental Psychology: Learning, Memory, & Cognition, 23*, 1122–1139.

Grainger, J., & Beauvillain, C. (1988). Associative priming in bilinguals: Some limits of interlingual facilitation effects. *Canadian Journal of Psychology, 42*, 261–273.

Grainger, J., & Frenck-Mestre, C. (1998). Masked priming by translation equivalents in proficient bilinguals. *Language and Cognitive Processes, 13*, 601–623.

Greenwald, A. G., Klinger, M. R., & Schuh, E. S. (1995). Activation of marginally perceptible ("subliminal") stimuli: Dissociation of unconscious from conscious cognition. *Journal of Experimental Psychology: General, 124*, 22–42.

Gries, S. (2005). Syntactic priming: A corpus-based approach. *Journal of Psycholinguistic Research, 34*, 365–399.

Gries, S., & Wulff, S. (2005). Do foreign language learners also have constructions? Evidence from priming, sorting and corpora. *Annual Review of Cognitive Linguistics, 3*, 182–200.

Griffin, Z., & Weinstein-Tull, J. (2003). Conceptual structure modulates structural priming in the production of complex sentences. *Journal of Memory and Language, 49*, 537–555.

Habib, R., & Nyberg, L. (1997). Incidental retrieval processes influence explicit test performance with data-limited cues. *Psychonomic Bulletin and Review, 4*, 130–133.

Hare, M., & Goldberg, A. (1999). Structural priming: Purely syntactic? In M. Hahn & S. Stones (Eds.), *Proceedings of the 21st annual meeting of the Cognitive Science Society* (pp. 208–211). Mahwah, NJ: Erlbaum.

Harley, T. (2001). *The psychology of language* (2nd ed.). New York: Psychology Press.

Hartsuiker, R., & Kolk, H. (1998a). Syntactic persistence in Dutch. *Language and Speech, 41*, 143–184.

Hartsuiker, R., & Kolk, H. (1998b). Syntactic facilitation in agrammatic sentence production. *Brain and Language, 62*, 221–254.

Hartsuiker, R., & Westenberg, C. (2000). Word order priming in written and spoken sentence production. *Cognition, 75*, B27–B39.

Hartsuiker, R., Kolk, H., & Huiskamp, P. (1999). Priming word order in sentence production. *Quarterly Journal of Experimental Psychology, 52A*, 129–147.

Hartsuiker, R., Pickering, M., & Veltkamp, E. (2004). Is syntax separate or shared between languages? *Psychological Science, 15,* 409–414.

Hatch, E., & Lazaraton, A. (1991). *The research manual: Design and statistics for applied linguistics.* New York: Newbury House.

Havranek, G. (2002). When is corrective feedback most likely to succeed? *International Journal of Educational Research, 37,* 255–270.

Haywood, S., Pickering, M., & Branigan, H. (2005). Do speakers avoid ambiguities during dialogue? *Psychological Science, 16,* 362–366.

Henson, R. N. A. (2003). Neuroimaging studies of priming. *Progress in Neurobiology, 70,* 53–81.

Heredia, R., & McLaughlin, B. (1992). Bilingual memory revisited. In R. J. Harris (Ed.), *Cognitive processing in bilinguals* (pp. 91–103). North Holland: Elsevier.

Hirshman, E., & Durante, R. (1992). Prime identification and semantic priming. *Journal of Experimental Psychology: Learning, Memory, & Cognition, 18,* 255–265.

Holender, D. (1986). Semantic activation without conscious identification in dichotic listening, parafoveal vision, and visual masking: A survey and appraisal. *Behavior and Brain Sciences, 9,* 1–66.

Horst, M., & Meara, P. (1999). Test of a model for predicting second language lexical growth through reading. *The Canadian Modern Language Review, 56,* 308–330.

Huck, S. W. (2007). *Readings statistics and research* (5th edition) Boston: Pearson.

Huttenlocher, J., Vasilyeva, M., & Shimpi, P. (2004). Syntactic priming in young children. *Journal of Memory and Language, 50,* 182–195.

Ibrahim, R., & Aharon-Peretz, J. (2005). Is literary Arabic a second language for native Arab speakers?: Evidence from semantic priming study. *Journal of Psycholinguistic Research, 34,* 51–70.

Israel, M., Johnson, C., & Brooks, P. (2000). From states to events: The acquisition of English passive participles. *Cognitive Linguistics, 11,* 103–129.

Jackson, A., & Morton, J. (1984). Facilitation of auditory word recognition. *Memory and Cognition, 12,* 568–574.

Jarvis, S. (2000). Methodological rigor in the study of transfer: Identifying L1 influence in the interlanguage lexicon. *Language Learning, 50,* 245–309.

Jensen, E. D., & Vinther, T. (2003). Exact repetition as input enhancement in second language acquisition. *Language Learning, 53,* 373–428.

Jiang, N. (1999). Testing processing explanations for the asymmetry in masked cross-language priming. *Bilingualism: Language and Cognition, 2,* 59–75.

Jiang, N., & Forster, K. I. (2001). Cross-language priming asymmetries in lexical decision and episodic recognition. *Journal of Memory and Language, 44,* 32–51.

Jin, Y. (1990). Effects of concreteness on cross-language priming in lexical decisions. *Perceptual & Motor Skills, 70,* 1139–1154.

Joordens, S., & Becker, S. (1997). The long and short of semantic priming effects in lexical decision. *Journal of Experimental Psychology: Learning, Memory, & Cognition, 23,* 1083–1105.

Joordens, S., & Besner, D. (1992). Priming effects that span an intervening unrelated word: Implications for models of memory representation and retrieval. *Journal of Experimental Psychology: Learning, Memory, & Cognition, 18,* 483–491.

Ju, M., & Church, B. A. (2001, November). *Voice specificity effects in second-language acquisition: Episodic vs. dualist.* Paper presented at the 42nd Annual Meeting of the Psychonomic Society, Orlando, FL.

Ju, M., & Luce, P. A. (2006). Representational specificity of within-category phonetic variation in the long-term mental lexicon. *Journal of Experimental Psychology: Human Perception and Performance, 32,* 120–138.

Juffs, A. (2001). Psycholinguistically oriented second language research. *Annual Review of Applied Linguistics, 21,* 207–220.

Juffs, A., & Harrington, M. (1995). Parsing effects in second language sentence processing: Subject and object asymmetries in wh-extraction. *Studies in Second Language Acquisition, 17,* 483–516.

Jusczyk, P. W. (1997). *The discovery of spoken language.* Cambridge, MA: MIT Press.

Kaschak, M., Loney, R., & Borreggine, K. (2006). Recent experience affects the strength of structural priming. *Cognition, 99,* B73–B82.

Keatley, C. W., Spinks, J. A., & de Gelder, B. (1994). Asymmetrical cross-language priming effects. *Memory and Cognition, 22,* 70–84.

Keatley, C., & de Gelder, B. (1992). The bilingual primed lexical decision task: Cross-language priming disappears with speeded responses. *European Journal of Cognitive Psychology, 4,* 273–292.

Keefe, D. E., & Neely, J. H. (1990). Semantic priming in the pronunciation task: The role of prospective prime generated expectancies. *Memory & Cognition, 18,* 289–298.

Keppel, G. (1982). *Design and analysis: A researcher's handbook.* Englewood Cliffs, NJ: Prentice Hall.

Kerkhofs, R., Dijkstra, T., Chwilla, D. J., & de Bruijn, E. R. (2006). Testing a model for bilingual semantic priming with interlingual homographs: RT and N400 effects. *Brain Research, 1068,* 170–183.

Kim, Y. (2006, October). *Lexical and syntactic priming: EFL students' production of passives.* Paper presented at the annual Second Language Research Forum, Seattle, WA.

Kim, Y., & McDonough, K. (2008). Learners' production of passives during syntactic priming activities. *Applied Linguistics, 29,* 149–154.

Kiran, S., & Tuchtenhagen, J. (2005). Imageability effects in normal Spanish-English bilingual adults and in aphasia: Evidence from naming to definition and semantic priming tasks. *Aphasiology, 19,* 315–327.

Kirsner, K. (1998). Implicit memory. In K. Kirsner, C. Speelman, et al. (Eds.), *Implicit and explicit mental processes* (pp. 13–36). Mahwah, NJ: Lawrence Erlbaum.

Kirsner, K., & Dunn, J. C. (1985). The perceptual record: A common factor in repetition priming and attribute retention? In M. I. Posner & O. S. M. Marin (Eds.), *Mechanisms of attention: Attention and performance XI* (pp. 547–565). Hillsdale, NJ: Erlbaum.

Kirsner, K., Smith, M. C., Lockhart, R. S., King, M. L., & Jain, M. (1984). The bilingual lexicon: Language-specific units in an integrated network. *Journal of Verbal Learning and Verbal Behavior, 23,* 519–539.

Kolers, P. A. (1976). Reading a year later. *Journal of Experimental Psychology: Human Learning and Memory, 2,* 554–565.

Kolers, P. A., & Ostry, D. J. (1974). Time course of loss of information regarding pattern analyzing operations. *Journal of Verbal Learning and Verbal Behavior, 13,* 599–612.

Kormos, J. (2006). *Speech production and second language acquisition*. Mahwah, NJ: Lawrence Erlbaum.

Kotz, S. (2001). Neurolinguistic evidence for bilingual language representation: a comparison of reaction times and event-related brain potentials. *Bilingualism: Language and Cognition, 4*, 143–154.

Kotz, S., & Elston-Güttler, K. E. (2004). The role of proficiency on processing categorical and associative information in the L2 as revealed by reaction times and event-related brain potentials. *Journal of Neurolinguistics, 17*, 215–235.

Kucera, H., & Francis, W. N. (1967). Computational analysis of present-day American English. Brown University Press, Providence.

Lachter, J., Forster, K. I., & Ruthruff, E. (2004). Forty-five years after Broadbent (1958): Still no identification without attention. *Psychological Review, 111*, 880–913.

Larsen, J. D., Fritsch, T., & Grava, S. (1994). A semantic priming test of bilingual language storage and the compound vs. coordinate bilingual distinction with Latvian-English bilinguals. *Perceptual and Motor Skills, 79*, 459–466.

Ledoux, K., Traxler, M., & Swaab, T. (2007). Syntactic priming in comprehension. *Psychological Science, 18*, 135–143.

Leeser, M. (2004). Learner proficiency and focus on form during collaborative dialog. *Language Teaching Research, 8*, 55–81.

Levelt, W., & Kelter, S. (1982). Surface form and memory in question answering. *Cognitive Psychology, 14*, 78–106.

Levelt, W., Roelofs, A., & Meyer, A. (1999). A theory of lexical access in speech production. *Behavioral and Brian Science, 22*, 1–38.

Libben, G., & Jarema, G. (2002). Mental lexicon research in the new millennium. *Brain and Language, 81*, 2–11.

Libben, G., & Jarema, G. (2004). Conceptions and questions concerning morphological processing. *Brain and Language, 90*, 2–8.

Lieven, E., Behrens, H., Speares, J., & Tomasello, M. (2003). Early syntactic creativity: A usage-based approach. *Journal of Child Language, 30*, 333–370.

Lightbown, P. M. (1998). The importance of timing in focus on form. In C. Doughty & J. Williams (Eds.), *Focus on form in classroom second language acquisition* (pp. 177–196). Cambridge: Cambridge University Press.

Liu, H., Bates, E., Powell, T., & Wulfeck, B. (1997). Single-word shadowing and the study of lexical access. *Applied Psycholinguistics, 18*, 157–180.

Lively, S. E., Pisoni, D. B., Yamada, R. A., Tohkura, Y., & Yamada, T. (1994). Training Japanese listeners to identify English /r/ and /l/. III. Long-term retention of new phonetic categories. *Journal of the Acoustical Society of America, 96*, 2076–2087.

Loebell, H., & Bock, K. (2003). Structural priming across languages. *Linguistics, 41*, 791–824.

Lombardi, L., & Potter, M. (1992). The regeneration of syntax in short term memory. *Journal of Memory and Language, 31*, 713–733.

Long, M. (1996). The role of the linguistic environment in second language acquisition. In W. Ritchie & T. K. Bhatia (Eds.), *Handbook of language acquisition: Vol. 2. Second language acquisition* (pp. 413–468). San Diego, CA: Academic Press.

Love, T., Maas, E., & Swinney, D. (2003). The influence of language exposure on lexical and syntactic language processing. *Experimental Psychology, 50*, 204–216.

Lucas, M. (2000). Semantic priming without association: A meta-analytic review. *Psychonomic Bulletin & Review, 7,* 618–630.

Luce, P. A., & Pisoni, D. B. (1998). Recognizing spoken words: The neighborhood activation model. *Ear & Hearing, 19,* 1–36.

Luce, P. A., Goldinger, S. D., Auer, E. T., & Vitevitch, M. S. (2000). Phonetic priming, neighborhood activation, and PARSYN. *Perception and Psychophysics, 62,* 615–625.

Lupiker, S. J. (1984). Semantic priming without association: A second look. *Journal of Verbal Learning and Verbal Behavior, 23,* 709–733.

Lyster, R., & Ranta, L. (1997). Corrective feedback and learner uptake. *Studies in Second Language Acquisition, 19,* 37–66.

Mack, M. (1986). A study of semantic and syntactic processing in monolinguals and fluent early bilinguals. *Journal of Psycholinguistic Research, 15,* 463–488.

Mackey, A., & Gass, S. (2005). *Second language research.* Mahwah, NJ: Lawrence Erlbaum.

Mackey, A. (2007). Interaction as practice. In R. DeKeyser (Ed.), *Practice in a second language* (pp. 85–110). Cambridge: Cambridge University Press.

Marcel, A. J. (1983). Conscious and unconscious perception: Experiments on visual masking and word recognition. *Cognitive Psychology, 15,* 197–237.

Marinelle, S. (2006). Assessing and facilitating complex sentence formulation in picture description tasks. *Advances in Speech-Language Pathology, 8,* 69–78.

Marinis, T. (2003). Psycholinguistic techniques in second language acquisition research. *Second Language Research, 19,* 144–161.

Masson, M. E. J. (1995). A distributed memory model of semantic priming. *Journal of Experimental Psychology: Learning, Memory, & Cognition, 21,* 3–23.

Matthews, D., Lieven, E., Theakston, A., & Tomasello, M. (2005). The role of frequency in the acquisition of English word order. *Cognitive Development, 20,* 121–136.

McDonough, K. (2004). Learner-learner interaction during pair and small group activities in a Thai EFL context. *System, 32,* 207–224.

McDonough, K. (2006). Interaction and syntactic priming: English L2 speakers' production of dative constructions. *Studies in Second Language Acquisition, 28,* 179–207

McDonough, K. (2007, June). *Syntactic priming during learner-learner interaction.* Paper presented at the annual conference of the Canadian Association of Applied Linguistics, Saskatoon, Saskatchewan, Canada.

McDonough, K., & Mackey, A. (2006). Responses to recasts: Repetitions, primed production and linguistic development. *Language Learning, 54,* 693–720.

McDonough, K., & Mackey, A. (2008). Syntactic priming and ESL question development. *Studies in Second Language Acquisition, 30,* 31–47.

McLennan, C. T., Luce, P. A., & Charles-Luce, J. (2003). Representation of lexical form. *Journal of Experimental Psychology: Learning, Memory, and Cognition, 29,* 539–553.

McNamara, T. (1996). *Measuring second language performance.* London: Longman.

McNamara, T. P. (2005). *Semantic priming: Perspectives from memory and word recognition.* New York: Psychology Press.

McNamara, T. P., & Altarriba, J. (1988). Depth of spreading activation revisited:

Semantic mediate priming occurs in lexical decisions. *Journal of Memory and Language, 27*, 545–559.

Meijer, P., & Fox Tree, J. (2003). Building syntactic structures in speaking: A bilingual exploration. *Experimental Psychology, 50*, 184–195.

Melinger, A., & Dobel, C. (2005). Lexically-driven syntactic priming. *Cognition, 98*, B11–B20.

Meyer, D. E., & Schvaneveldt, R. (1971). Facilitation in recognizing pairs of words: Evidence of a dependence between retrieval operations. *Journal of Experimental Psychology, 90*, 227–234.

Meyer, D. E., & Schvaneveldt, R. (1976). Meaning, memory structure, and mental processes. *Science, 192*, 27–33.

Montrul, S. (2004). Psycholinguistic evidence for split intransitivity in Spanish second language acquisition. *Applied Psycholinguistics, 25*, 239–267.

Morris, C. D., Bransford, J. D., & Franks, J. J. (1977). Levels of processing versus transfer appropriate processing. *Journal of Verbal Learning and Verbal Behavior, 16*, 519–533.

Mullenix, J. W., Pisoni, D. B., & Martin, C. S. (1989). Some effects of talker variability on spoken word recognition. *Journal of the Acoustical Society of America, 85*, 365–378.

Mulligan, N. W., Duke, M., & Cooper, A. W. (2007). The effects of divided attention on auditory priming. *Memory & Cognition, 35*, 1245–1254.

Munro, M. J. (1995). Nonsegmental factors in foreign accent: Ratings of filtered speech. *Studies in Second Language Acquisition, 17*, 17–34.

Murphy, V. (1997). The effect of modality on a grammaticality judgment task. *Second Language Research, 13*, 34–65.

Naccahe, L., Blandin, E., & Dehaene, S. (2002). Unconscious masked priming depends on temporal attention. *Psychological Science, 13*, 416–424.

Nakamura, E., Ohta, K., Okita, Y., Ozaki, J., & Matsushima, E. (2006). Increased inhibition and decreased facilitation effect during a lexical decision task in children. *Psychiatry and Clinical Neurosciences, 60*, 232–239.

Nation, K., & Snowling, M. J. (1999). Developmental differences in sensitivity to semantic relations among good and poor comprehenders: Evidence from semantic priming. *Cognition, 70*, B1–B13.

Neely, J. H. (1976). Semantic priming and retrieval from lexical memory: Evidence for facilitation and inhibitory processes. *Memory and Cognition, 4*, 648–654.

Neely, J. H. (1977). Semantic priming and retrieval from lexical memory: Roles of inhibitionless spreading activation and limited-capacity attention. *Journal of Experimental Psychology: General, 106*, 226–254.

Neely, J. H. (1991). Semantic priming effects in visual word recognition: A selective review of current findings and theories. In D. Besner & G. W. Humphreys (Eds.), *Basic processes in reading: Visual word recognition* (pp. 264–336). Hillsdale, NJ: Erlbaum.

Neely, J. H., & Keefe, D. E. (1989). Semantic context effects on visual word processing: A hybrid prospective/retrospective processing theory. In G. H. Bower (Ed.), *The psychology of learning and motivation: Advances in research and theory, vol 24* (pp. 207–248). New York: Academic Press.

Neely, J. H., Keefe, D. E., & Ross, K. L. (1989). Semantic priming n the lexical decision task: Roles of prospective prime-generated expectancies and retrospective semantic matching. *Journal of Experimental Psychology: Learning, Memory, & Cognition, 15,* 1003–1019.

Nelson, D. L., McEvoy, C. L., & Schreiber, T. A. (1998). *The University of South Florida word associations, rhyme, and word fragment norms.* Available online at: http://w3.usf.edu/FreeAssociation/.

Nicol, J. (1996). Syntactic priming. *Language and Cognitive Processes, 11,* 675–679.

Nicol, J., & Pickering, M. (1993). Processing syntactically ambiguous sentences: Evidence from semantic priming. Special Issue: Sentence processing III. *Journal of Psycholinguistic Research, 22,* 207–237.

Nicol., J. & Swinney, D. (1989). The role of structure in coreference assignment during sentence comprehension. *Journal of Psycholinguistic Research: Special Issue on Sentence Processing, 18,* 5–24.

Norton, J. (2005). The paired format in the Cambridge Speaking Test. *ELT Journal, 59,* 287–297.

Norušis, M. J. (2007). *SPSS 15.0 advanced statistical procedures companion.* Upper Saddle River, NJ: Prentice Hall.

Nusbaum, H. C., Pisoni, D. B., & Davis, C. K. (1984). Sizing up the Hoosier mental lexicon: Measuring the familiarity of 20,000 words. *Research on Speech Perception Progress Report No. 10.* Bloomington: Indiana University, Psychology Department, Speech Research Laboratory.

O'Sullivan, B. (2002). Learner acquaintanceship and oral proficiency test pair-task performance. *Language Testing, 19,* 277–295.

Odlin, T. (2003). Cross-linguistic influence. In C. Doughty & M. Long (Eds.), *The handbook of second language acquisition* (pp. 436–486). Malden, MA: Blackwell.

Oldfield, R. C. (1966). Things, words, and the brain. *Quarterly Journal of Experimental Psychology, 18,* 340–353.

Onishi, K. H., Chambers, K. E., & Fisher, C. (2002). Learning phonotactic constraints from brief auditory experience. *Cognition, 83,* B13–B23.

Pallier, C., Colomé, A., & Sebastián-Gallés, N. (2001). The influence of native-language phonology on lexical access: Exemplar-based vs. abstract lexical entries. *Psychological Science, 12,* 445–449.

Panova, I., & Lyster, R. (2002). Patterns of corrective feedback and uptake in an adult ESL classroom. *TESOL Quarterly, 36,* 573–595.

Phillips, N., Segalowitz, N., O'Brien, I., & Yamasaki, N. (2004). Semantic priming in a first and second language: Evidence from reaction time variability and event-related brain potentials. *Journal of Neurolinguistics, 17,* 237–262.

Pickering, M., & Branigan, H. (1998). The representation of verbs: Evidence from syntactic priming in language production. *Journal of Memory and Language, 39,* 633–651.

Pickering, M., & Branigan, H. (1999). Syntactic priming in language production. *Trends in Cognitive Sciences, 3,* 136–141.

Pickering, M., & Garrod, S. (2004). Toward a mechanistic psychology of dialogue. *Behavioral and Brain Sciences, 27,* 169–190.

Pickering, M., Branigan, H., & McLean, J. (2002). Constituent structure is formed in one stage. *Journal of Memory and Language, 46,* 586–605.

Pickering, M., Branigan, H., Cleland, A., & Stewart, A. (2000). Activation of syntactic information during language production. *Journal of Psycholinguistic Research, 29,* 205–216.

Pienemann, M., & Johnston, M. (1987). Factors influencing the development of language proficiency. In D. Nunan (Ed.), *Applying second language acquisition research* (pp. 45–141). Adelaide: National Curriculum Resource Centre, AMEP.

Pilotti, M., & Beyer, T. (2002). Perceptual and lexical components of auditory repetition priming in young and older adults. *Memory and Cognition, 30,* 226–236.

Pilotti, M., Bergman, E. T., Gallo, D. A., Sommers, M., & Roediger, H. L. III (2000). Direct comparison of auditory implicit memory tests. *Psychonomic Bulletin and Review, 7,* 347–353.

Pinker, S. (1984). *Language learnability and language development.* Cambridge, MA: Harvard University Press.

Pisoni, D. B. (1997). Some thoughts on "normalization" in speech perception. In K. Johnson & J. W. Mullennix (Eds.), *Talker variability in speech processing* (pp. 9–32). San Diego: Academic Press.

Plaut, D. C., & Booth, J. R. (2000). Individual and developmental differences in semantic priming: Empirical and computational support for a single-mechanism account of lexical processing. *Psychological Review, 107,* 786–823.

Potter, M., & Lombardi, L. (1990). Regeneration in the short-term recall of sentences. *Journal of Memory and Language, 29,* 633–654.

Potter, M., & Lombardi, L. (1998). Syntactic priming in the immediate recall of sentences. *Journal of Memory and Language, 38,* 265–282.

Pulvermüller, F. (2003). *The Neuroscience of language: On brain circuits of words and serial order.* Cambridge: Cambridge University Press.

Raaijmakers, J. G. W., Schrijnemakers, J. M. C., & Gremmen, F. (1999). How to deal with "The language-as-fixed-effect fallacy": Common misconceptions and alternative solutions. *Journal of Memory and Language, 41,* 416–426.

Radeau, M. (1983). Semantic priming between spoken words in adults and children. *Canadian Journal of Psychology, 4,* 547–556.

Ratcliff, R., & McKoon, G. (1988). A retrieval theory of priming in memory. *Psychological Review, 95,* 385–408.

Robinson, P. (Ed.) (2002). *Individual differences and instructed language learning.* Amsterdam: John Benjamins.

Roediger, H. L. III., Weldon, M. S., & Challis, B. H. (1989). Explaining dissociations between implicit and explicit measures of retention: A processing account. In H. L. Roediger & F. I. M. Craik (Eds.), *Varieties of memory and consciousness: Essays in honor of Endel Tulving* (pp. 3–41). Hillsdale, NJ: Lawrence Erlbaum.

Ryalls, B. O., & Pisoni, D. B. (1997). The effect of talker variability on word recognition in preschool children. *Developmental Psychology, 33,* 441–452.

Saffran, J. R., Aslin, R. N., & Newport, E. L. (1996). Statistical learning by 8-month-old infants. *Science, 274,* 1926–1928.

Salamoura, A., & Williams, J. (2006). Lexical activation of cross-language syntactic priming. *Bilingualism: Language and Cognition, 9,* 299–307.

Salamoura, A., & Williams, J. (2007). Processing verb argument structure across languages: Evidence for shared representations in the bilingual lexicon. *Applied Psycholinguistics, 28,* 627–660.

Salkind, N. (2008). *Statistics for people (who think) they hate statistics* (3rd edition). Thousand Oaks, CA: Sage.

Sanchez-Casas, R. M., Davis, C. W., & Garcia-Albea, J. E. (1992). Bilingual lexical processing : Exploring the cognate/noncognate distinction. *European Journal of Cognitive Psychology*, 4, 293–310.

Savage, C., Lieven, E., Theakston, A., & Tomasello, M. (2003). Testing the abstractness of children's linguistic representations: Lexical and structural priming of syntactic constructions in young children. *Developmental Sciences*, 6, 557–567.

Savage, C., Lieven, E., Theakston, A., & Tomasello, M. (2006). Structural priming as implicit learning: The persistence of lexical and structural priming in 4-year-olds. *Language Learning and Development*, 2, 27–49.

Saville, N., & Hargreaves, P. (1999). Assessing speaking in the revised FCE. *ELT Journal*, 53, 42–51.

Schacter, D. L., & Church, B. A. (1992). Auditory priming: Implicit and explicit memory for words and voices. *Journal of Experimental Psychology: Learning, Memory, and Cognition*, 18, 915–930.

Schacter, D. L., Church, B. A., & Treadwell, J. (1994). Implicit memory in amnesic patients: Evidence for spared auditory priming. *Psychological Science*, 5, 20–25.

Scheepers, C. (2003). Syntactic priming of relative clause attachments: Persistence of structural configuration in sentence production. *Cognition*, 89, 179–205.

Scherlag, A., Demuth, L., Rösler, F., Neville, H. J., & Röder, B. (2004). The effects of late acquisition of L2 and the consequences of immigration on L1 for semantic and morpho-syntactic language aspects. *Cognition*, 93, B97–B108.

Schneider, W., & Chein, J. M. (2003). Controlled and automatic processing: Behavior, theory, and biological mechanisms. *Cognitive Science*, 27, 525–559.

Schneider, W., Eschman, A., & Zuccolotto, A. (2002). *E-Prime user's guide*. Pittsburgh: Psychology Software Tools, Inc.

Schoonbaert, S., Hartsuiker, R., & Pickering, M. (2007). The representation of lexical and syntactic information in bilinguals: Evidence from syntactic priming. *Journal of Memory and Language*, 56, 153–171.

Schwanenflugel, P. J., & Rey, M. (1986). Interlingual semantic facilitation: Evidence for a common representation system in the bilingual lexicon. *Journal of Memory and Language*, 25, 605–618.

Segalowitz, N. (1997). Individual differences in second language acquisition. In A. M. B. de Groot & J. Kroll (Eds.), *Tutorials in bilingualism: Psycholinguistic perspectives*. Hillsdale, NJ: Erlbaum.

Segalowitz, N., & Hulstijn, J. (2005). Automaticity in bilingualism and second language learning. In J. F. Kroll & A. M. B. de Groot, (Eds.), *Handbook of bilingualism: Psycholinguistic approaches* (pp. 371–388). Oxford: Oxford University Press.

Sheen, Y. (2004). Corrective feedback and learner uptake in communicative classrooms across instructional settings. *Language Teaching Research*, 8, 263–300.

Sheffert, S. M. (1998). Voice-specificity effects on auditory word priming. *Memory and Cognition*, 26, 591–598.

Shimpi, P., Gámez, P., Huttenlocher, J., & Vasilyeva, M. (2007). Syntactic priming in 3- and 4-year-old children: Evidence for abstract representations of transitive and dative forms. *Developmental Psychology*, 43, 1334–1346.

Silverberg, S., & Samuel, A. G. (2004). The effect of age of second language acquisition on the representation and processing of second language words. *Journal of Memory and Language*, 51, 381–398.

Slowiaczek, L. M. (1994). Semantic priming in a single-word shadowing task. *American Journal of Psychology, 107*, 245–260.

Smith, M. C. (1991). On the recruitment of semantic information for word fragment completion: Evidence from bilingual priming. *Journal of Experimental Psychology: Learning, Memory, and Cognition, 17*, 234–244.

Sommers, M. S., & Barcroft, J. (2007). An integrated account of the effects of acoustic variability in first language and second language: Evidence from amplitude, fundamental frequency, and speaking rate variability. *Applied Psycholinguistics, 28*, 231–249.

Sternberg, S. (1966). High-speed scanning in human memory. *Science, 153*, 652–654.

Sternberg, S. (1969). Memory-scanning: Memory processes revealed by reaction-time experiments. *American Scientist, 57*, 421–457.

Swain, M. (1998). Focus on form through conscious reflection. In C. Doughty & J. Williams (Eds.), *Focus on form in classroom second language acquisition* (pp. 64–81). Cambridge: Cambridge University Press.

Swain, M., & Lapkin, S. (1998). Interaction and second language learning: Two adolescent French immersion students working together. *Modern Language Journal, 82*, 320–338.

Swick, D., Miller, K. M., & Larsen, J. (2004). Auditory repetition priming is impaired in pure alexic patients. *Brain and Language, 89*, 543–553.

Szmrecsanyi, B. (2005). Language users as creatures of habit: A corpus-based analysis of persistence in spoken English. *Corpus Linguistics and Linguistic Theory, 1*, 113–150.

Taube-Schiff, M., & Segalowitz, N. (2005). Within-language attention control in second language processing. *Bilingualism: Language and Cognition, 8*, 195–206.

Tenpenny, P. L. (1995). Abstractionist versus episodic theories of repetition priming and word identification. *Psychonomic Bulletin and Review, 2*, 339–363.

Tomasello, M., & Brooks, P. (1998). Young children's earliest transitive and intransitive constructions. *Cognitive Linguistics, 9*, 379–395.

Trofimovich, P. (2005). Spoken-word processing in native and second languages: An investigation of auditory word priming. *Applied Psycholinguistics, 26*, 479–504.

Trofimovich, P. (2008). What do second language listeners know about spoken words? Effects of experience and attention in spoken word processing. *Journal of Psycholinguistic Research, 37*, 309–329.

Trofimovich, P., & Baker, W. (2006). Learning second-language suprasegmentals: Effect of L2 experience on prosody and fluency characteristics of L2 speech. *Studies in Second Language Acquisition, 28*, 1–30.

Trofimovich, P., & Baker, W. (2007). Learning prosody and fluency characteristics of second-language speech: Child learners' acquisition of five suprasegmentals. *Applied Psycholinguistics, 28*, 251–276.

Trofimovich, P., & Gatbonton, E. (2006). Repetition and focus on form in L2 Spanish word processing: Implications for pronunciation instruction. *The Modern Language Journal, 90*, 519–535.

Trofimovich, P., & Halter, R. (2007, June). *Second language processing: Task effects on listeners' sensitivity to spoken words.* Paper presented at the 6th International Symposium on Bilingualism, Hamburg, Germany.

Trofimovich, P., Ammar, A., & Gatbonton, E. (2007). How effective are recasts? The role of attention, memory, and analytical ability. In A. Mackey (Ed.),

Conversational interaction in second language acquisition: A series of empirical studies (pp. 171–195). Oxford: Oxford University Press.

Tulving, E., & Schacter, D. L. (1990). Priming and human memory systems. *Science, 247,* 301–306.

Tulving, E., Schacter, D. L., & Stark, H. A. (1982). Priming effects in word-fragment completion are independent of recognition memory. *Journal of Experimental Psychology: Learning, Memory, and Cognition, 8,* 336–342.

Turnbull, M., Lapkin, S., Hart, D., & Swain, M. (1998). Time on task and immersion graduates' French proficiency. In S. Lapkin (Ed.), *French as a second language education in Canada: Recent empirical studies.* Toronto: University of Toronto Press.

Tzelgov, J., & Eben-Ezra, S. (1992). Components of the between-language semantic priming effect. *European Journal of Cognitive Psychology, 4,* 253–272.

Ueda, C., & Mandler, G. (1980). Prototypicality norms for 28 semantic categories. *Behavior Research Methods, Instruments, and Computers, 12,* 587–595.

VanPatten, B. (1990). Attending to content and form in the input: An experiment in consciousness. *Studies in Second Language Acquisition, 12,* 287–301.

VanPatten, B. (1996). *Input processing and grammar instruction: Theory and research.* Norwood, NJ: Ablex.

VanPatten, B., & Williams, J. (Eds.). (2007). *Theories in second language acquisition: An introduction.* Mahwah, NJ: Lawrence Erlbaum Associates.

Vigliocco, G., & Nicol, J. (1998). Separating hierarchical relations and word order in language production: Is proximity concord syntactic or linear? *Cognition, 68,* B13–B29.

Vitevitch, M. S. (2002). Naturalistic and experimental analyses of word frequency and neighborhood density effects in slips of the ear. *Language and Speech, 45,* 407–434.

Watanabe, Y., & Swain, M. (2007). Effects of proficiency differences and patterns of pair interaction on second language learning: Collaborative dialogue between adult ESL learners. *Language Teaching Research, 11,* 121–142.

Waxman, S. R., & Markow, D. B. (1995). Words as invitations to form categories: Evidence from 12- to 13-month-old infants. *Cognitive Psychology, 29,* 257–302.

Weber-Fox, C. M., & Neville, H. J. (1996). Maturational constraints on functional specializations for language processing: ERP and behavioral evidence in bilingual speakers. *Journal of Cognitive Neuroscience, 8,* 231–256.

West, B. T., Welch, K. B., & Galecki, A. T. (2007). *Linear mixed models: A practical guide using statistical software.* Boca Raton, FL: Chapman & Hall/CRC.

West, R. F., & Stanovich, K. E. (1978). Automatic contextual facilitation in readers of three ages. *Child Development, 49,* 717–727.

Wilcox, R. R. (2005). Outlier detection. In B. S. Everitt & D. C. Howell (Eds.), *Encyclopedia of statistics in behavioral science, vol. 3* (pp. 1494–1497). Chichester, UK: John Wiley & Sons.

Woutersen, M., Cox, A., Weltens, A., & de Bot, K. (1994). Lexical aspects of standard dialect bilingualism. *Applied Psycholinguistics, 4,* 447–473.

Woutersen, M., de Bot, K., & Weltens, A., (1995). The bilingual lexicon: Modality effects in processing. *Journal of Psycholinguistic Research, 24,* 289–298.

Zeelenberg, R., & Pecher, D. (2002). False memories and lexical decision: Even twelve primes do not cause long-term semantic priming. *Acta Psychologica*, *109*, 269–284.

Zeelenberg, R., Pecher, D., & Raaijmakers, J. G. W. (2003). Associative repetition priming: A selective review and theoretical implications. In J. S. Bowers & C. J. Marsolek (Eds.), *Rethinking implicit memory* (pp. 262–283). Oxford: Oxford University Press.

Zwitserlood, P. (1996). Form priming. *Language and Cognitive Processes*, *11*, 589–596.

SUBJECT INDEX

AUTHOR INDEX